Trauma
and
Rebirth

TRAUMA
AND
REBIRTH

Intergenerational Effects of the Holocaust

JOHN J. SIGAL
and
MORTON WEINFELD

New York
Westport, Connecticut
London

Library of Congress Cataloging-in-Publication Data

Sigal, John J.
    Trauma and rebirth : intergenerational effects of the
Holocaust / John J. Sigal and Morton Weinfeld.
        p.   cm.
    Bibliography: p.
    Includes index.
    ISBN 0–275–92906–X (alk. paper)
    1. Holocaust survivors—Québec (Province)—Montréal—Cross-sectional
studies.   2. Children of Holocaust survivors—Québec (Province)—
Montréal—Cross-sectional studies.   3. Jews—Québec (Province)—
Montréal—Cross-sectional studies.   4. Holocaust survivors—Research—
Québec (Province)—Montréal.   5. Social surveys—Québec (Province)—
Montréal.   6. Intergenerational relations—Québec (Province)—
Montréal.   7. Montréal (Québec)—Ethnic relations.   I. Weinfeld,
M. (Morton)   II. Title.
F1054.5.M89J57   1989
971.4′27004924—dc19   88–34027

Library of Congress Catalog Card Number: 88–34027
ISBN: 0–275–92906–X

First published in 1989

Praeger Publishers, One Madison Avenue, New York, NY 10010
A division of Greenwood Press, Inc.

Printed in the United States of America

The paper used in this book complies with the
Permanent Paper Standard issued by the National
Information Standards Organization (Z39.48–1984).

10 9 8 7 6 5 4 3 2 1

Copyright Acknowledgments

To those who perished

and those who survived

Contents

Tables

Preface

This book is about the long-term consequences of the Holocaust on survivors and their children. Studies of Holocaust survivors are important not only in themselves but also for their value in assessing the long-term and intergenerational effects of severe victimization and of other forms of exposure to excessive, prolonged stress.

Our main argument is implicit in the title. There is no doubt that many of these consequences have been harmful, particularly for the aging survivors themselves. Yet we are struck more by the variability in the survivors' experiences and in the general degree to which they, and certainly their children, have overcome the traumas of the past. In this observation we present a counterpoint to most of the clinical and academic literature on Holocaust survivors, which has emphasized impairment or dysfunction.

Our work represents the culmination of nine years of collaborative effort. It consists primarily of findings drawn from two sample surveys of Jewish residents of Montreal. One survey focused on Holocaust survivors; the other, on children of survivors. Both included control groups, and both were drawn from unbiased, nonclinical, and nonself-selected populations.

Many of the findings we discuss have appeared elsewhere; nine of them are based directly on our own research. These publications span the disciplines of psychology, psychiatry, sociology, and ethnic studies, and are spread over four countries: the United States, Canada, Sweden, and Israel. This disparate pattern reflects the many disciplinary and geographical constituencies interested in Holocaust survivor research. One value of this study is that it assembles these findings together, since it is doubtful that readers would be familiar with the full corpus of the research.

A good deal of material is presented here that was not included in any of those published articles. This includes a detailed description of the Montreal context and its relevance, a discussion of the various methodological approaches and difficulties that affected the data collection process, and an attempt to identify unifying themes and implications. Moreover, some findings are also presented here for the first time. We report a descriptive statistical analysis of the range of Holocaust effects reported by children of survivors, for themselves and for their parents. We also present original data bearing on possible third generation effects, taken from responses by children of survivors about their own children. And we use our data to discover the possible sources of some discrepancies between clinical reports and the results of empirical investigations.

Many organizations and individuals helped us over the years. We would like to thank the Nathan Steinberg Foundation of Montreal; the Maxwell Cummings Foundation; the Quebec Ministry of Education; the Multiculturalism Directorate of the Secretary of State, Canada; the Social Sciences and Humanities Research Council of Canada; McGill University; and the Jewish Community Research Institute. These provided financial assistance that supported data collection, subsequent analyses and publications, and preparation of this manuscript.

Henry Kravitz, then Psychiatrist-in-Chief, Department of Psychiatry, Sir Mortimer B. Davis–Jewish General Hospital in Montreal, approved our use of the staff and facilities of the Department for the conduct of most of the studies that form the basis of this book, and for the preparation of most of the manuscripts based on them, including the present one. We are grateful for his material and moral support.

Dr. William W. Eaton, formerly of the Institute for Community and Family Psychiatry (a unit of the Department of Psychiatry, Sir Mortimer B. Davis–Jewish General Hospital), and the McGill University Department of Sociology, now at the Department of Mental Hygiene, Johns Hopkins University, was a collaborator on the first survey and related set of studies. Rebecca Augenfeld, Judy Csillag, Harry Finkelstein, Sharon Friedman, Myra Gibarovitch, Lillian Shaffer, and particularly Irit Sterner and Jonathan Levy contributed greatly to the formulation of many of the questions for earlier drafts of the questionnaire used in the second survey. Irit Sterner also had primary responsibility for selecting the respondents from the lists used to construct the second sample. Data collection for the first survey was coordinated by Melvin Niederhoffer; for the second survey, by Yitty Gutner, Nettie Harris, and Irit Sterner; and for the survey of the clinic population of grandchildren by Vincenzo DiNicola and Michael Buonvino, with the assistance of Annette Woolf, David Grauer, and Emily Sigal. Barbara Hill and Melina Rich voluntarily contributed much time and effort to reliability studies, most of which were conducted by Deborah Mizener. Deborah Mizener and Michael Buonvino assisted in the voluminous and sometimes complex data analysis. Jim Robbins offered constructive statistical advice, and Ruth Stilman and Judy Grossman provided important bibliographic assistance.

Many people commented on our work, and provided methodological and substantive advice. We wish to thank several anonymous reviewers for their helpful comments. Others who helped either through commenting on manuscripts or through discussion were Yael Danieli, Leo Eitinger, William Helmreich, Harold Himmelfarb, Henry Kravitz, Roger Krohn, Gloria Leon, Ruth Nabi, Jim Robbins, and Laura Rose-Friedman.

Laura Rose-Friedman, with the collaboration of Alice Dind and Louise Veilleux, had primary responsibility for the onerous task of shepherding the book through its various drafts and coordinating the secretarial work associated with it. Laura Rose-Friedman, Goldie Sigal, and Peggy Lehrer assisted with proofreading.

Many people helped in the typing process, both of earlier articles and of this book: Lynda Bastien, Luvana di Francesco, Geraldine Harris, Zelda Naimer, Laura Rose-Friedman, Eva Sandor, Anne Woolgar, and, most particularly, Madeleine Lissade and Pia Sevilla, who bore the main brunt of the work with patience and forbearance.

We also would like to express our sincere thanks to our wives, Goldie Sigal and Phyllis Zelkowitz, who read and discussed with us much of this material, and who offered steadfast encouragement over the years.

We thank all these people, and those whom we may have inadvertently omitted, for their assistance. They are not responsible for errors in fact or interpretation in the final product. That responsibility rests solely with us.

We found our collaboration in this work invigorating. John Sigal is a psychologist and psychoanalyst, at home equally in clinical work and in large-scale survey research. Morton Weinfeld is a sociologist specializing in ethnic relations. We each reflected in our contributions the specific features of our training and disciplines. There was plenty of good-natured interdisciplinary ribbing and one-upmanship.

But one lesson that emerged is that disciplinary boundaries are best seen as points of contact, as doorways to cooperation rather than as rigid barriers that foster parochialism. These boundaries must yield—and in our case they did—to the prior demand of the study and understanding of the human condition in its variegated complexity. This task is ultimately enriched, not hindered, through competing disciplinary perspectives.

Trauma
and
Rebirth

1

Historical Context

THE HOLOCAUST

This book is a scientific study of survivors of the Holocaust and their families, some three and a half decades after the end of the war. We shall report on findings from three sets of studies, focusing on Holocaust survivors, adult children of survivors, and grandchildren of survivors. (Throughout the course of this monograph, we shall use the term "survivor" to refer to a person who was subjected to, but survived, the Holocaust; in other words, as a generic term to refer to persons who were in concentration camps, in labor camps, in hiding, in the ghettos, in partisans groups, and so on.)

Before we turn to our discussion of the survivors and their postwar adjustments, it is fitting that we remind ourselves just what it was they survived. This reminder is not important only for its intrinsic tie to the research at hand. It is also important for an evaluation of the generalizability of our findings to other situations.

Our adherence to the canons of scientific inquiry in the chapters that follow should never let us lose sight of the human dimensions of unimaginable tragedy that underlie our quantitative data. The Holocaust is perhaps the most dramatic example we have of the extreme victimization of a specific group. There have been—and alas, there continue to be—many other instances of group victimization. Yet one might argue that if long-term and second-generation consequences of severe victimization are ever to be observed, they will be observed among survivors of the Holocaust and their children.

"Holocaust," a term derived from Greek meaning "burnt whole," refers to the savage persecution of all Jews who found themselves in Nazi-occupied Europe before and during World War II. An estimated 6 million Jews perished. Others escaped in advance of the Nazi onslaught, and still others somehow survived while spending all or some of the war years in Nazi-occupied Europe.

To be sure, Jews were not the only victims of the Nazi death machine. At least 10 million other noncombatants were murdered by the Nazis, including several million Soviet prisoners of war, scores of thousands of defenseless Poles, Ukrainians, Greeks, Russians, Yugoslavs, and others—men, women, and children. Among them were perhaps a quarter of a million Gypsies, and thousands of homosexuals and mental defectives (Gilbert 1987, p. 824).

Yet, as Elie Wiesel and others have noted, if not all the victims were Jews, all Jews were victims. The relentless psychological pressure that was the lot of every Jew trapped in Europe was an element of victimization possibly as devastating as the physical degradation they suffered. In the Nazi blueprint, all Jews were marked for extermination, regardless of their nationality, religiosity, or politics. In macrosociological terms, the Nazi death machine was horribly efficient. Dawidowicz (1976, p. 544) has estimated that the final toll comprised 67% of the prewar Jewish population in Europe. In many countries—notably Poland, the Baltic states, Germany/Austria, and Norway—the proportions reached 90%.

But these numbers shed no light on the specific fates that befell individual Jews. The word "genocide" has become overused, and abused. The horrors of the Nazi concentration camps and extermination camps have been diluted by the profusion of other camps in which victims have been grouped: Communist prison or reeducation camps; internment camps such as those for Japanese Canadians relocated during the war; and refugee camps that dot the international landscape from the Middle East to Pakistan to Hong Kong. These other camps are all intolerable affronts to human dignity. And yet there is a difference.

The survivors whom we have studied lived through a hell that the most perverse writer of fiction could not have imagined. There is a large memoir literature that has captured the record of those horrors. Conditions in the camps and the ghettos have been preserved in powerful compilations of this material.

The work of historians, the written memoirs of survivors, and related anthologies form only one avenue by which the Holocaust trauma has entered world consciousness. Literary works, intermingling fact and fiction, have likewise captured various dimensions of the nightmare. André Schwarz-Bart's *The Last of the Just,* Elie Wiesel's *Night,* Romain Gary's *The Dance of Genghis Cohn,* and William Styron's *Sophie's Choice* are but a few examples. It is only more recently that social scientists have joined with historians and writers to provide one more avenue of exploration into the world of the survivors, the world of the Holocaust.

We cannot hope to convey to the reader the full range of horrors, both physical and psychological, experienced by those who survived. One passage, cited by Des Prés in his study of the anatomy of the death camps, refers to the "excremental assault" that began during the boxcar rides to the camps.

The temperature started to rise, as the freight car was enclosed and body heat had no outlet. . . . The only place to urinate was through a slot in the skylight, though whoever tried this usually missed, spilling urine on the floor. . . . When dawn finally rose . . . we were all quite ill and shattered, crushed not only by the weight of fatigue but by the stifling, moist atmosphere and the foul odor of excrement. . . . There was no latrine, no provision. . . . On top of everything else, a lot of people had vomited on the floor. We were to live for days on end breathing these foul smells, and soon we lived in the foulness itself. (Kessel 1972, pp. 50–51, cited in Des Prés 1977, p. 53)

Perhaps the definitive single-volume account of the Holocaust in all its manifestations, drawing from a vast array of personal recollections and archival material, is Martin Gilbert's monumental *The Holocaust* (1987). Gilbert intermingles accounts from the camps, the ghettos, Jews in hiding passing as Gentiles, and members of partisan groups, to provide a full panorama of the range of suffering that Europe's Jews experienced.

The following accounts, taken from Gilbert's work, are examples of life in the camps. They are by no means unusual or extraordinary.

Here is the story of a dying Jewish girl in Birkenau, as recorded by Salmen Leventhal, a survivor.

She was left the only one of a numerous family. All the time she had been working hard, was undernourished, suffered the cold. Still, she was in good health and was well. She thought she would survive. Eight days ago no Jewish child was allowed to go to work. The order came. "Juden, antreten!" "Jews, leave the ranks!" Then the blocks were filled with Jewish girls. During the selection nobody paid attention whether they looked well or not, whether they were sick or well.

They were lined outside the block and later they were led to Block 25, where they were ordered to strip naked; [allegedly] they were to be examined as to their health. When they had stripped, all were driven to three blocks; one thousand persons in a block and there they were shut for three days and three nights, without getting a drop of water or a crumb of bread, even.

So they had lived for three awful days and it was only the third night that bread was brought; one loaf of bread weighing 1,40 kilogrammes for sixteen persons. . . .

"If they had shot us then, gassed us, it would have been better. Many [women] lost consciousness and others were only semi-conscious. They lay crowded on bunks, motionless, helpless. Death would not have impressed us at all then." (Gilbert 1987, pp. 650–651)

Fania Fenelon recalls the conditions in the Belsen concentration camps, weeks before the liberation:

Hastily built to last a few months, our temporary barracks were half-collapsing; the planks were coming apart. Looking at the damage, a scornful SS man said, speaking of us, the Jews: "They rot everything, even wood. . . . "

A few days later, I too had typhus. My last vision as a healthy person was of the women of the camp, like everyone else, outside naked, lining up to wash our dresses and underclothes in the thin trickle of water from the pierced pipe. On the other side of the barbed wire, the men were doing the same; we were like two troops of cattle at the half-empty trough of an abattoir.

Now the illness took me over entirely; my head was bursting, my body trembling, my intestines and stomach were agony, and I had the most abominable dysentery. I was just a sick animal lying in its own excrement.

From April 8 everything around me became nightmarish. I existed merely as a bursting head, an intestine, a perpetually active anus. One tier above, there was a French girl I didn't know; in my moments of lucidity, I heard her saying in a clear, calm, even pleasant voice: "I must shit, but I must shit on your head, it's more hygienic!" She had gone mad; others equally unhinged guffawed interminably or fought. (Gilbert 1987, pp. 790–791)

Life in the ghettos was also traumatic. Here is an account of life in the Jewish community of Jaworow, in eastern Galicia, Poland.

During the Passover holidays of 1942, there came to Jaworow a high-ranking Nazi, a fellow by the name of Steuer. His ferocious deeds will never be erased from the memory of Jaworow Jews, and those of Grodek, Krakowice and Janow. Each time this Hitler satrap visited a town or village, he left a trail of tears, torture and sorrow. His appetite for loot was insatiable, and the Jewish Council had no choice but to supply him with whatever they could. . . .

Steuer made surprise visits to the Council and lashed out at those present. Unexpectedly he forced his way into Jewish homes, swept the dishes from the table to the floor, smashed the furniture and obscenely humiliated the women. He flogged Ida Lipshitz. He grabbed Polka Cipper who was married to the Jew, Dolek Guttman, ordered her to undress, ground her bare toes with his boots, and whipped her unmercifully. He delighted in striking blows at women with bare fists until their blood flowed, and chasing them nude into the cold outdoors. (Gilbert 1987, p. 315)

Even those Jews who managed to hide or to pass as Gentiles endured frequent crises of major psychological impact. Here is Gilbert's description of a traumatic episode that befell Helena Manaster.

Among the Jews in hiding in Poland was Helena Manaster. A survivor of several ghettos and "actions," including the Petlura Day massacre in Lvov, she had found refuge in the Capuchin monastery in Cracow. There, posing as a Catholic, and as the wife of a Polish army officer, she was safe. At the same time, she was expecting a baby. On October 6, at two in the morning as labour pains began, Helena Manaster was driven to the hospital. There, in the delivery room, as she later recalled:

. . . all of a sudden a nurse rushed in frightened, and told me, "Get up quick! The Gestapo are waiting for you."

Forty years have passed and I am still not able to describe the shock I was in. Helped by two nurses, one on each side, shaking all over, probably more from fear than labour pains, I walked out to the lobby to face the Gestapo agents. They were young, very tall and strong-looking, and when I noticed their insignia, the skull with two crossed bones, insignia of death, I knew that this was my end.

I don't remember what thoughts went through my mind then, I only remember apologizing to my unborn child for having created him, when I would not be able to bring him up to see the light, to let him live.

At the moment a miracle happened: the two butchers looked at me—I kept calm—told me to go back to bed and turned away.

A few hours later, my oldest son, Arthur, was born. I learned later that the Gestapo were not exactly checking on me, but on the midwife who had been out after curfew on her way to assist me in labour. They just wanted to see her patient and didn't suspect that the patient was Jewish. (Gilbert 1987, pp. 623–624)

Our study will make no effort to address the question of how they survived. Indeed, their survival must rank as one of the rare triumphs of the human spirit, which defies neat analysis. Each survivor's experience is unique. To say that some managed to survive in ghettos, some in labor or concentration camps, some with forged documents, some hiding in closets or on farms, some as partisans, and some in combinations of these conditions is to miss the tremendous variability of the drama. Human qualities of endurance and courage often intersected with luck. A softhearted prison guard, a train missed or not taken, a cry not uttered, a friend abandoned, a suspicious neighbor, a dead camp inmate's jacket, a bribe offered or not offered were the stuff of survival as surely as were well-crafted plans.

One estimate is that between 400,000 and 500,000 Jews survived the German occupation during 1939–1945. Of these, an estimated 75,000 were survivors of concentration or extermination camps. The largest group of survivors found their way to Israel, many from displaced persons (DP) camps. An estimated 92,000 European Jews emigrated to the United States during the years 1945–1951 (Rabinowitz 1976, p. 3) and 20,000–30,000 to Canada (Kage 1962, p. 36).

REBUILDING IN CANADA

Our study focuses on Jewish survivors in Montreal. In Canada, the immediate postwar years saw little change in the tight immigration policy that had barred the doors to Jewish refugees in the 1930s (Abella & Troper 1982). At first it seemed that postwar Jewish DPs would fare no better than prewar Jewish refugees. But slowly, by 1947–1948, Canadian immigration policy loosened up. Between 1947 and 1950, Canada allowed 98,000 DPs to immigrate, of whom 11,000 were Jews, the third ethnic group behind Poles and Ukrainians (Kage 1962, p. 129). Among the Jews who came to Canada in the years 1945–1951 many may have been from the United States, England, or Palestine/Israel, but the vast majority were survivors, either from DP camps or through other routes (Kage 1962, p. 260).

The relative impact of the survivor migration was far greater in Canada than in the United States. The Jewish population in Canada in 1951 numbered 204,000; thus recently arrived survivors may have comprised 12–15 percent of the total. In the United States, if we assume a Jewish population of about 5 million in the early 1950s (Goldstein 1974, p. 103), survivors would represent only 2 percent of the total. This means that the relative impact of survivors within Jewish communal life, and the legacy of the Holocaust itself, has been stronger in Canada than in the United States. Indeed, as we shall see, our 1978 survey of Jewish household heads in Montreal found a full 20% identified as survivors of the Holocaust.

Survivors in both Canada and the United States continued to arrive even after the early 1950s. Some came after trying unsuccessfully to reintegrate into their European countries of origin. The Hungarian uprising of 1956 triggered a renewed wave of Jewish immigrants, many of whom were also Holocaust survivors. Similarly, many survivors were among Jews fleeing to Canada or the United States from Czechoslovakia and Poland in 1968, or emigrating from the Soviet Union beginning in the 1970s.

Holocaust survivors, both in Canada and in the United States, clustered in their own subcommunities. Like all ethnic or immigrant groups, they tended to seek each other out. This was certainly the case in the large Canadian centers of Toronto and Montreal, where circles of survivors—for whom other survivors were often surrogate family members—would congregate.

Most arrived in North America impoverished, not knowing much English, still traumatized by the horrors they had experienced and by the loss of immediate and extended family members. On top of all the trials and tribulations facing any immigrant, they brought with them their own unique set of baggage, the legacy of the Holocaust. Like earlier Jewish immigrants, they spoke either Yiddish or, for a minority, the language of their country of origin, such as Polish, German, French, Hungarian, Romanian, Russian, or Ukrainian. The survivors slowly became established and began to put down roots in the community. Many survivors joined or formed *Landsmanschaften,* Jewish fraternal or mutual aid organizations of members from specific locations in Eastern Europe.

But the experience of the Holocaust was never far from mind. They formed associations of survivors of specific concentration camps, as well as general organizations of Holocaust survivors. Apart from the Holocaust Committee of the Canadian Jewish Congress there are organizations such as the Association of Survivors of Nazi Oppression and the Canadian Holocaust Remembrance Association, as well as the Toronto branch of the Los Angeles-based Simon Wiesenthal Institute. Indeed, the Congress Holocaust Committee, Quebec Region, lists 31 organizations as comprising the complete list of organizations of survivors in Montreal. More recently, at least in Montreal and Toronto, associations of children of survivors, dedicated to perpetuating the memory of the Holocaust, have been organized.

Survivors and survivor organizations have been seen, and have seen themselves, as a kind of conscience of the Jewish community on matters relating to the Holocaust and anti-Semitism. It was not always this way. When they arrived, they were labeled DPs and were dependent on the existing Jewish community. With the passage of time and the new importance accorded the Holocaust in Jewish self-understanding, the survivors emerged from the shadows of the Jewish community. Now not as DPs but as survivors, they speak with moral force in the community.

In the early 1970s, for example, the Saidye Bronfman Centre in Montreal, a community center of the arts sponsored by the Jewish community, wished to mount a production of *The Man in the Glass Booth,* by Robert Shaw. The play deals with the theme of the guilt of the survivor, and blurs the distinction between victim and persecutor. The survivor associations found the play offensive, and launched a campaign of protest. A heated debate divided the community. But in the end the survivors won the day. The play was canceled by the Centre, and the Centre's artistic director subsequently resigned.

Survivors, as individuals, and through their representative organizations, play an important watchdog role in relation to the issue of alleged Nazi war criminals. Indeed, there is a strong militant subgroup among the survivors that sees itself as being in perpetual tension with, if not in opposition to, the Jewish establishment organizations. Thus, Toronto's Sabina Citron, a feisty survivor and antiestablishment rebel, decided to launch criminal proceedings against Canadian philo-Nazi publisher Ernst Zundel. She did so over the hesitations of the organized leadership, whom she accused of timidity. Using the long-neglected section 177 of the Canadian Criminal Code, a provision prohibiting the spreading of false news, she was able to secure a conviction on one of the two counts.

Survivors did not just fill the role of community critic or conscience. They also played important roles in organized Jewish life. Many assumed high positions in community organizations. Others became educators. Yet others were integrated into Yiddish cultural institutions.

Our research, however, does not focus on the collective or organizational role of survivors, but on their behavior as individuals and within families. At the time of our research, many of the survivors had been in Montreal for over three decades; their European experiences had begun to blend into the particular environment of Montreal and of the Montreal Jewish community. It is because of the nature of the position of Jews in the province of Quebec that a study of survivors and their families in Montreal may yield results different from one of survivors in New York or Los Angeles. If there are long-term or second-generation consequences of the Holocaust, it is likely that these special political conditions would be most likely to elicit their emergence and observation.

The two community-based surveys reported in this volume were conducted in 1978 and 1981. The dominant backdrop to Montreal Jewish communal life in these years was the reemergence of a nationalistic, pro-independence movement epitomized by the electoral victories in 1976, and again in 1981, of the pro-independence Parti Québecois (a name signifying that the party is uniquely Quebec-oriented in its origins, interests, and commitments). The feeling of anxiety arising from these election results was heightened among those who did not support the Parti Québecois in the campaign preceding a provincial referendum on the independence issue in 1980.

THE MONTREAL SETTING

To speak of the roughly 100,000 Jews in Quebec is really to speak of the Jews of Montreal. Quebec Jews, in general, tend to reside in geographically limited areas—usually in west-end sections of Montreal with significant Jewish populations—and are not scattered throughout the province as a whole, or even through the many sections of Montreal that are predominantly French speaking. What has captivated Montreal Jewry is the city's cosmopolitan, as well as its intensely Jewish, character. The Jewish neighborhoods—with their bakeries and butcher shops, parks, playgrounds, delicatessens, cinemas, synagogues, Jewish schools, and other communal institutions—combine with the appeal of the downtown core, old Montreal, and the Laurentian Mountains and other selected spots to cement the tie of Montreal Jews to their city. It is this unique ambience that is captured historically in some of the fictional reconstructions of Mordecai Richler's St. Urbain Street. This ambience can be found today in the streets and shopping centers of Jewish neighborhoods several miles further west. Thus, to the extent that the true historic character of Quebec lies outside the Montreal metropolis—in smaller cities, towns, and villages—Montreal Jews have had little contact with it.

Within Montreal, Jewish residential segregation continues to be very high, as it is for most other minority groups in the city. In 1978, nearly one-third of Montreal Jews were concentrated in one neighborhood (the Snowdon–Côte des Neiges area of Montreal), with a further 18% in another (the Côte St. Luc area). Virtually no Jews live east of the north-south street Boulevard St. Laurent.

Like all minority groups in Quebec, the Jewish community includes a large proportion of foreign-born members. Only about half of Jewish household heads we sampled were born in North America. (The comparable figure in the United States would be about 80%.) This high proportion of immigrants reflects migration processes of the prewar and postwar periods (including Holocaust survivors), as well as more recent waves of immigrants from the Soviet Union, Israel, and North Africa.

From the beginning of the nineteenth century, the Jewish community of Quebec was integrated into the language, culture, and institutions of the English minority in the province. Jewish immigrants to Quebec found an ethnically stratified society, with a rural and urban working class, largely English. With English perceived as the language of economic opportunity in Quebec and throughout North America, Jews and most other immigrants to Quebec opted into the English-speaking community. In addition, the Catholicism of the French Canadians, typified by a confessional public school system permeated by Catholic doctrine (permitted under Canadian law), predisposed Jewish immigrants to educate their children in the more flexible English-language Protestant school system.

The Jewish response to life in Quebec is a paradox. On the one hand, Jews prosper economically and enjoy full religious freedom and state support for Jewish schools and other institutions. They are among the bilingual of Quebec's English-speaking groups. On the other hand, except for the French-speaking Moroccan Jews, Quebec Jews have lived for decades in nearly total isolation from French Canadians, the majority in the province, with few social or political contacts. This Jewish residential and social isolation approximates conditions existing in Europe prior to World War II.

Fear of anti-Semitism has contributed to this isolation. Of course, anti-Semitism was, and is, no stranger to anglophone Quebec, yet it differed from the French variety. The former represented the snobbish elitism of the economically powerful; it was for the most part polite anti-Semitism. The latter was more populist in nature, reflecting the resentment of the economically disadvantaged, and with a potential for physical violence—the anti-Semitism of the mob. In many ways, the Jewish economic position in Quebec was that of a classic middleman minority, often occupying roles as small shopkeepers, traders, businessmen, or professionals. Jews would often be visible to the francophone working-class person, and thus might be the target of some of the rage felt against the dominant, yet inaccessible or invisible, Anglo corporate elite. In this way, French Canadian anti-Semitism resembled that directed by blacks against Jews in the United States, or by Ukrainian peasants against Jews in the seventeenth century, when Jews often managed the estates of absentee Polish landlords and, thus, had most direct contact with the Ukrainian masses.

To understand Jewish fear of anti-semitism, one must take into account not only the historical record of Quebec society but also supranational events such as the Holocaust. Many survivors of the Holocaust cannot help but remain forever alert to possible dangers; many other Ashkenazi Jewish adults lost family either during the tragedy or while they were fighting the Nazis with the Allied armies. The memories of the Holocaust linger on and, inevitably, they color perceptions of current local events. Moreover, for many Jews, to survive the Holocaust and to emigrate to North America was to escape Europe, the Old World, and come to a different New World, where the nationalism, ideologies, and class conflicts from which Jews had suffered supposedly would not exist.

The European legacy shared by so many of the foreign-born is complemented by the historical anti-Semitism of Quebec before, during, and after World War II, internalized by many of the older Montreal-born members of the community. Beginning in the 1930s, Premier Maurice Duplessis and his conservative Union Nationale government ruled the province with the cooperation of the powerful Catholic Church, and did little to discourage the anti-Semitism that flourished in the province, stimulated by the hardships of the Depression. While fascist anti-Semitism never appealed to more than a small minority of the French population, the nationalistic French Canadian anticonscription movement enjoyed the support of a broad segment of the population, including many Quebecers destined for prominence in later years, such as the recent mayor of Montreal, Jean Drapeau. Typified by the slogan *á bas les Juifs* (down with the Jews), anti-Semitism was a motivating ideology for many of these young nationalists. Another indicator of governmental involvement in anti-Semitic practices is that in 1943 and 1944 Premier Duplessis circulated a letter—quickly revealed to be a forgery—describing a secret plot by the "International Zionist Fraternity" to settle thousands of Jews in Quebec.

The demise of the Union Nationale government was followed by a period of communal quiescence that lasted some years. The interethnic tensions rose again. In the 1960s, Quebec experienced both rapid modernization and the rise of a new French nationalism. This crystallized in the formation of the Parti Québécois, a political party dedicated to the independence of Quebec. One effect of the Parti Québécois victory in 1976 was increased psychological pressure on minority group members, both individually and collectively. This phenomenon was felt widely in the Jewish community, which, with its sense of history, is wary about the way in which nationalist movements can accentuate minority status.

Particularly sensitive to such developments were those Jews who came to Montreal to escape the horrors of persecution in Europe. For many other older members of the community, Quebec's own history heightened fears that they might suffer in an increasingly nationalistic French Canadian environment. The fact that the province saw open displays of anti-Semitism during the 1930s contributed to the belief that it could surface again.

Let it be said clearly that the Parti Québécois gave no evidence whatsoever of overt anti-Semitic tendencies or influences. On the contrary, many of its leaders had distinguished records as civil libertarians to whom anti-

All appeared to be well with the world. Emaciated bodies filled out. Wounds healed. The anticipation was that with adequate nutrition, housing, and medical care, the ravages of the camps would be undone.

Shortly after the war, researchers began to conduct systematic studies of camp survivors and other victims. Reserchers in Denmark were the first to establish the persistence of physical and psychological damage resulting from interment in the camps. In a study of some 1,300 repatriated Danish, non-Jewish concentration camp survivors in 1947–1948 (all residing in Copenhagen), they noted a constellation of aftereffects. Optimistically, they first termed these effects "repatriation neurosis" and "hunger reconvalescence" (Helweg-Larsen et al. 1952). Their choice of these labels clearly reflected their anticipation that the syndrome was a transitory one.

By 1954, as a result of an intensive study of 120 survivors, it was found that the effects were not disappearing (Hermann & Thygesen 1954). The label was changed to "concentration camp syndrome," the first use of this term. Among the physical manifestations noted were pathological fatigue, persistent failure to gain weight, diarrhea, dizziness, headaches, nightly sweating, sleep disturbances, reduced sexual potency, and premature aging. Among the psychological manifestations they noted were depression and moodiness, psychosomatic symptoms (nightly sweating, palpitations, frequent urination), nightmares and other manifestations of anxiety, reduction in memory and/or the ability to concentrate, crying spells, and psychotic reactions.

Shortly after the Danish studies appeared, Eitinger and Strøm (1973), in a retrospective study, examined mortality rates in a population of almost 5,000 non-Jewish Norwegians who survived Nazi concentration camps, prisons, or penitentiaries. They found much higher mortality rates in the ex-prisoners, primarily due to tuberculosis, other infectious diseases, coronary heart disease, lung cancer, and violent death (accident and homicide).

Eitinger and Strøm also reported the morbidity rates of a randomly selected subsample and a well-matched control sample. In these studies they found much evidence for impaired biopsychosocial functioning. Survivors had more frequent changes of job and decline in occupational status, had more frequent and longer sick leaves, and were hospitalized more often and for longer periods of time. Their physical disorders occurred with frequencies ranging from about 70% to about 500% higher than in the control group, and affected all organ systems—heart, lungs, stomach, genito-urinary, and skeletal.

Similar mortality and morbidity rates were reported in large-scale follow-up studies of American ex-prisoners of war (POWs) interned in the Japanese camps during World War II and the North Korean camps during the Korean war (Nefzger 1970; Bebe 1975; Keehn 1980). The fact that such effects were not noted among Allied military personnel who

Semitism was as revolting a concept as it was to fair-minded individuals anywhere in the world. Moreover, most Jews appreciated the personal honesty and respect for democracy that characterized the public career of René Lévesque, the first Parti Québécois premier, and earned him the grudging admiration of even the most bitter foes of independence. When the Montreal Jews considered Lévesque, the European analogue they feared was never Hitler or Stalin, but Kerensky. They saw Lévesque as threatened by factions of the left and the right, and elements both within and without his party that were eager to assume control and to shape Quebec's destiny according to their own visions.

This, then, was the sociopolitical context of the surveys of Montreal Jews, who provide the data base for this monograph. Survivor families in Montreal were embedded in a Jewish community that was traditional and cohesive, with a wide foreign-born representation. And Montreal Jewry itself comprised a community socially segregated from the non-Jewish world, and apprehensive about swirling currents of French Canadian nationalism.

These characteristics of the Montreal setting, in short, would seem likely to increase the chance of observing long-term consequences of the Holocaust for survivors and their children. The traditionalism and insularity of the Jewish community were coupled with the nationalist tensions between English and French reminiscent of Old World conflicts. These might exacerbate or trigger dysfunctional attitudinal and behavioral responses that have been demonstrated in the considerable scientific literature on the long-term consequences of exposure to the stressful experiences of World War II and similar situations.

2

Research on Survivors and Their Families: An Overview

In this chapter we shall highlight only the major findings of this scientific literature. Eitinger and Krell (1985) provide a comprehensive bibliography on the medical and psychological affects of concentration camps and related persecutions. Russell (1980) provides a comprehensive review of the effects on the children, and Solkoff (1981) reviews some of this work critically.

LONG-TERM EFFECTS: THE SURVIVORS

General Effects

As the Allied armies in Europe advanced, the first pictures of the skeletal survivors of the concentration camps were released. Gradually the Western world began to accept the stories of the horror of the camps that had been told by escapees during the war. A similar process occurred after the end of the wars in the Pacific with respect to the surviving prisoners held in Japanese and North Korean camps.

Some Jewish concentration camp victims in Europe tried to return to their homes, only to find them demolished or confiscated, and anti-Semitic feelings still rife among the local population. Some did not want to return under any circumstances. Others were unable to return because they were too weak or too ill. Tens of thousands of them congregated in DP camps, waiting to be given the opportunity to reestablish themselves somewhere. Military personnel, and non-Jews in the resistance movements, returned to their homes as soon as transportation was available, generally to be welcomed as heroes.

were in German POW camps makes it clear that the increased mortality and morbidity rates were the immediate consequences of forced labor and malnutrition in the Nazi concentration and labor camps, and the Japanese and Korean POW camps. Similar findings were reported for Canadian and British ex-POWs from the Pacific theater (Kral, Pazder, & Wigdor 1967; Khan 1981).

The preceding studies were primarily based on non-Jews or on samples containing only relatively small percentages of Jews. The experience of Jewish civilians subjected to the Nazi persecution was fundamentally different from that of the above groups. They were of a much wider age range (from young adolescents to the aged), for the most part they were not in as good physical condition because they had not had military training, they were not unified by a common cause, and they were not organized in a unifying administrative structure once they had been deported to the camps from their towns, cities, or ghettos.

As a group, they were not subjected to the beatings, particularly on the head, and other forms of torture to which captured members of the resistance were subjected. They were, however, all slated for extermination if they were found unfit as slave workers or as "field whores" to satisfy the desires of the German armies, or because they faltered in these roles due to exhaustion or illness. The relative mortality rates for non-Jewish and Jewish Norwegians deported to the German camps reflect the consequence of this difference. Only 3% of the Jews survived (Eitinger 1980), whereas 55–92% of the non-Jews did, depending on the camps in which they were imprisoned.

As we have already noted, the social supports offered to Jews after their release from the camps were very different from those of military or paramilitary personnel. They were seldom welcomed as heroes; coldness or outright hostility was common. There were no governmentally sponsored or facilitated housing developments, educational grants, or disability pensions. Despite these differences, the effects of malnutrition, forced labor, and possibly the prolonged, excessive stress experienced by both groups appear to have had an overwhelmingly leveling effect; Jewish survivors were found to experience the same negative consequences as the others.

Working independently with Jewish concentration camp survivors in the United States, Krystal and Niederland (1968) pursued Niederland's (1961) early clinical descriptions of the symptoms that delineated what he called "total reactive personality changes caused by the overwhelming traumatization [experienced by survivors]" (Niederland 1968, p. 14). They reviewed the case records of 149 randomly selected patients who were concentration camp survivors. They found the same depression, anxiety, disturbances of cognition and memory, and some psychosomatic symptoms. In addition, they found that survivors tended to be rigid, withdrawn, or infantile in their social relationships. They coined the term "survivor syndrome" for this constellation of signs and symptoms.

It is noteworthy that Chodoff (1963) found no differences in the signs or symptoms among concentration camp survivors and those who had been in the ghettos, in labor camps, or undercover, using false documents. On the other hand, in a study of patients hospitalized in a psychiatric ward, Klein, Zellermayer, and Shanon (1963) did find differences among these groups. They found the greatest instance of severe disturbance (psychotic syndromes) among those who suffered the severest forms of oppression (those in ghettos, concentration camps, and extermination camps) or for whom isolation and chronic fear were important (those in hiding or passing as non-Jews with the help of illegal documents). Those who had been in labor camps or among the partisans did not show any of these severe disturbances. Differences between the samples and the vagaries of clinical impressions could well explain the discrepancy between the two sets of findings.

In a general sense, two studies of randomly selected community samples in Israel confirmed the clinical observations. In a study of menopausal women aged 45–54, conducted 25 years after the end of World War II, psychiatrists found women who had been in concentration camps to have poorer emotional health than a matched control group. In addition, the concentration camp survivors rated themselves lower on a feeling of well-being scale, on a coping scale, and on a mood scale, and higher on a worry scale than did the comparison group (Antonovsky, Moaz, Dowty, & Wijsenvbeek, 1971). Levav and Abramson (1984) administered an eight-item scale of emotional distress (tapping anxiety, sadness, and hopelessness) to a random sample drawn from the entire Jewish population 25 years or older of a neighborhood in Jerusalem. They found both male and female concentration camp survivors to be more distressed than their counterparts in the comparison group.

Although these two community studies yielded results that were consistent with each other, the former relied exclusively on subjective rating scales, and the latter on a little-known scale developed in a previous study. Furthermore, the differences between the groups in the second study, though statistically significant, were very small. Finally, both studies were conducted in Israel, where the majority was not alien to the survivors, and where there was a common enemy that legitimized the externalization of aggression. As a result, it is difficult to know whether the findings are generalizable to other communities.

Stability of Coping Style and Differences in Personality

With the exception of case studies, most reports, framed within broad categories such as "survivor of the Nazi persecution" or "concentration camp survivors," lump together people who had very different experiences and gloss over personality differences in survival or coping strategies. Furthermore, most studies of the long-term effects of the Nazi persecution document the deterioration in physical or mental capacity (e.g., Matussek 1975; Krystal 1971; Nathan, Eitinger, & Winnik 1964). Only two deal at length with the stability of personality traits over the years following the experience of prolonged stress (Danielli 1981, 1982; Eitinger 1964); a third study, by Matussek (1975), suggests such stability.

Matussek interviewed and tested 245 concentration camp survivors, randomly selected from a list of those seeking reparation payments, who resided in or near Munich, in Israel, or in New York at the time of the study, some 15 years after the end of World War II. In the group of survivors who had been incarcerated for religious or political reasons, the largest group in his study, he found many relationships between their personalities and home environment prior to their incarceration, and their psychosocial functioning 15 years after their release. He noted two subgroups on follow-up. The first subgroup gave evidence of feeling unable to deal actively with the demands of their current lives. They were characterized by resignation and despair, and tended to attribute their survival to luck. The members of the second subgroup were free of feelings of resignation and despair, and tended to attribute their survival to their own efforts to deal actively with the exigencies of the camp situation, including the work stress. Furthermore, he found that these personality traits were present in the two groups before their incarceration; that is, the traits were not changed as the result of a stress experience, as well as could be determined from a retrospective interview.

The many relationships between personality and home environment did not hold for a second group Matussek studied. The subjects, all of whom were Jews, had been incarcerated for ethnic reasons (termed racial reasons by the Nazis). The slave labor, malnutrition, and beatings to which they were subjected had a much greater impact on them 15 years after their release than did their preincarceration personalities or home environments.

Yet, even among them, Matussek identified two subgroups on the basis of their success in coping with their current lives. The successful copers were faring well socially, occupationally, and in their marriages. In addition, memories of events during their incarceration no longer intruded into these areas of their functioning, nor did these survivors block out their experiences. Those who were coping unsuccessfully were impaired socially and occupationally, had poor marriages, and continued to relive the horrors of their wartime experiences in memories by day and in dreams at night. Matussek reports that prior to their incarceration, the first subgroup had taken more initiative in contacting the opposite sex and had left home more frequently than had the second subgroup. Of particular relevance is the fact that even in the camps, the former had a more active approach to coping. They either planned escapes or thought up ways of improving the situation.

The unsuccessful copers adopted a more passive and conformist attitude in the camps, trying to seek safety in anonymity.

Similar evidence is provided by Danieli (1981, 1982), who reported on her contact with 75 survivors and 300 of their children in the course of individual, family, group, and community work of a clinical and semiclinical nature some 25 years after the end of World War II. (She has since expanded her sample considerably.) She found that a number of these people, whom she labeled Victims, predominantly identified themselves with a totally passive and helpless posture in the face of the Holocaust. On follow-up they continued to relate to the world around them as if it were a fearsome, dangerous place from which they attempted to seek refuge. She found that other survivors, the Fighters, some of whom described themselves as being actively driven to resist and survive during the Nazi persecution, manifested the same active tendency to confront and strive for achievement at the time of follow-up.

The consistency of the observations in these two independent studies suggests the validity of the investigator's findings, despite the nonrandom nature of their samples. These studies may be criticized, however, because they were based on interviewers' ratings of the survivors' retrospective reports of remote events. The reports may have contained elements of selectivity determined by the respondents' psychological or physical health at the time of the study. Depressed, despairing, or discouraged people tend to view themselves in negative terms. These affects and attitudes of the respondents may also have colored the interviewers' ratings.

Eitinger (1964) provided somewhat more objective evidence for this stability in the context of an exhaustive follow-up study of concentration camp survivors in Norway and Israel that he completed some 16 years after World War II. He reported that 54.6% of those (N = 66) who chose to live a communal (kibbutz) life, his "work group," attributed their survival to being with friends and relatives in the camps, whereas only 14.1% of the group of nonhospitalized psychiatric patients (N = 92), who were presumably city dwellers, did so. This suggests a lasting difference between the groups in the importance of group affiliation in their lives. But many of the objections raised above apply equally to Eitinger's study. Evidence of a more objective nature would strengthen the argument for the persistence of personality traits over time despite the person's exposure to severe, prolonged stress.

LONG-TERM EFFECTS: CHILDREN OF SURVIVORS

It will now be evident to the reader that the research and clinical literature consistently demonstrates that survivors of extreme, prolonged stresses are susceptible to enduring physical and psychological impairment. It seems reasonable to assume that depression, anxiety, or chronic physical illness in one parent is likely to adversely affect the spouse and children (Sigal, Silver, Rakoff, & Ellin 1973). The spouses have to cope with more than spouses generally have to cope with, and, if the burden is too great for their coping capacities, they are going to be at risk for depression, anxiety, or somatic problems themselves. As a result the children are at risk for having less-than-optimal parenting, and may have less adequate parental figures for identifying with or using as role models. In brief, it seems reasonable to hypothesize that the children of survivors of situations of excessive, prolonged stress are likely to be emotionally at risk.

Evidence for such intergenerational transmission has been found among children of parents with poor physical or psychological health who were not war victims (Langner & Michael 1963; Rutter, Quinton, & Yule 1976; Weissman, Paykel, & Klerman 1972). One might expect to find similar intergenerational effects among children of war victims.

In examining this hypothesis, it is important to separate civilian from military or paramilitary groups, such as members of the resistance move-ments, and to distinguish among subsets within these sets of groups. The effects they transmit may differ markedly, not only because the ways in which they are affected differ but also because of the way they were received by the community on their return. If they suffer visible impairment as a result of their wartime experience, parents seen as victimized foreign aliens by the community provide different role models to their children than do those perceived as heroes.

Children of Ex-POWs

The similarity of the negative long-term effects on survivors of the Nazi Holocaust and ex-POWs of the Japanese and North Korean POW camps would suggest similar intergenerational effects. There have been several studies of children of armed forces personnel. In a clinical, impressionistic study of the families of Canadian Army survivors of the Japanese POW camps who had been identified as having been adversely affected physically and psychologically by their imprisonment, Sigal (1976) found that the oldest child appeared to have been affected, provided that child was a girl. He observed that she was likely to manifest depressive affect and to be described by her parents as either overcontrolled or undercontrolled.

He suggested that the mothers were depressed because their debilitated spouses were unable to fulfil their roles as husbands and fathers but required care and comforting instead. The mothers turned to their eldest daughters for this care and comforting. These daughters were expected to provide the mothers with what might be seen as a transitional relationship (Winnicott 1953), but paid a price for it in their own development. Sigal proposed that sons were spared these developmental difficulties because they could identify with the image of a heroic soldier-father. These observations were made in a nonrandom sample of families in which the fathers were known to be suffering the negative consequences of their incarceration. There were no appropriate control observations.

In a convincing case report, Rosenheck and Nathan (1985) demonstrated a link between a Vietnam veteran's delayed response to his stressful combat experiences and his son's difficulty in the development of his ego boundaries, as well as in the son's high levels of guilt, anxiety, and aggressiveness. Two studies of the children of American ex-POWs from Vietnam, however, yielded contradictory results. Nice (1978) was unable to replicate McCubbin and Dahl's (1976) finding that the children of Vietnam veterans were faring poorly psychologically. Since Nice's findings were based on a comparison with a control group and those of McCubbin and Dahl were based on a comparison with outdated normative data obtained some 20 years before, Nice's findings are probably more reliable. They are also consistent with findings from a five-year controlled follow-up study of the families of American naval officers who had been POWs in the Vietnamese camps (Hunter 1986). Thus, the father's POW trauma may not have had negative psychosocial repercussions.

Children of Jewish Survivors of the Nazi Persecution

Clinical Studies and Anecdotal Reports. Studies of children of civilian Jewish survivors of the Nazi persecution are more numerous, beginning with the pioneering observations by Rakoff (1966), Rakoff, Sigal, and Epstein (1966), and Trossman (1968), and continuing to the present. Russell (1980) provides a comprehensive survey of these studies. Because they stimulated such a wealth of subsequent studies and controversies, the content of these initial reports will be reviewed in some detail.

It is perhaps not surprising that these pioneering reports originated in Montreal, a city containing some 110,000 Jews, of whom about 20% of the household heads were survivors of the Nazi persecution. These first reports came from the Department of Psychiatry of the Jewish General Hospital, which had strong ties to the Jewish community. Vivian Rakoff, then a psychiatric resident (and later chairman, Department of Psychiatry, University of Toronto), noted that an unusually large number of parents consulting the department for help with one or more of their children were European immigrants. It then occurred to him that they were also survivors of the Holocaust. Gradually it dawned on him that despite the heterogeneity of the presenting symptomatology of some of the children, there appeared to be common family dynamics that prevented the children from developing a sense of identity. Rakoff stated, "The love and ambition of whole family members were resurrected in memory and imposed as hopes on the children, who were expected to supply the gratification normally coming from mothers, fathers, brothers, sisters, cousins, uncles and aunts, and to live out in their own lifetimes those truncated lives" (Rakoff 1966, p. 21).

Semitism was as revolting a concept as it was to fair-minded individuals anywhere in the world. Moreover, most Jews appreciated the personal honesty and respect for democracy that characterized the public career of René Lévesque, the first Parti Québécois premier, and earned him the grudging admiration of even the most bitter foes of independence. When the Montreal Jews considered Lévesque, the European analogue they feared was never Hitler or Stalin, but Kerensky. They saw Lévesque as threatened by factions of the left and the right, and elements both within and without his party that were eager to assume control and to shape Quebec's destiny according to their own visions.

This, then, was the sociopolitical context of the surveys of Montreal Jews, who provide the data base for this monograph. Survivor families in Montreal were embedded in a Jewish community that was traditional and cohesive, with a wide foreign-born representation. And Montreal Jewry itself comprised a community socially segregated from the non-Jewish world, and apprehensive about swirling currents of French Canadian nationalism.

These characteristics of the Montreal setting, in short, would seem likely to increase the chance of observing long-term consequences of the Holocaust for survivors and their children. The traditionalism and insularity of the Jewish community were coupled with the nationalist tensions between English and French reminiscent of Old World conflicts. These might exacerbate or trigger dysfunctional attitudinal and behavioral responses that have been demonstrated in the considerable scientific literature on the long-term consequences of exposure to the stressful experiences of World War II and similar situations.

2

Research on Survivors and Their
Familes: An Overview

In this chapter we shall highlight only the major findings of this scientific literature. Eitinger and Krell (1985) provide a comprehensive bibliography on the medical and psychological affects of concentration camps and related persecutions. Russell (1980) provides a comprehensive review of the effects on the children, and Solkoff (1981) reviews some of this work critically.

LONG-TERM EFFECTS: THE SURVIVORS

General Effects

As the Allied armies in Europe advanced, the first pictures of the skeletal survivors of the concentration camps were released. Gradually the Western world began to accept the stories of the horror of the camps that had been told by escapees during the war. A similar process occurred after the end of the wars in the Pacific with respect to the surviving prisoners held in Japanese and North Korean camps.

Some Jewish concentration camp victims in Europe tried to return to their homes, only to find them demolished or confiscated, and anti-Semitic feelings still rife among the local population. Some did not want to return under any circumstances. Others were unable to return because they were too weak or too ill. Tens of thousands of them congregated in DP camps, waiting to be given the opportunity to reestablish themselves somewhere. Militry personnel, and non-Jews in the resistance movements, returned to their homes as soon as transportation was available, generally to be welcomed as heroes.

All appeared to be well with the world. Emaciated bodies filled out. Wounds healed. The anticipation was that with adequate nutrition, housing, and medical care, the ravages of the camps would be undone.

Shortly after the war, researchers began to conduct systematic studies of camp survivors and other victims. Reserchers in Denmark were the first to establish the persistence of physical and psychological damage resulting from interment in the camps. In a study of some 1,300 repatriated Danish, non-Jewish concentration camp survivors in 1947–1948 (all residing in Copenhagen), they noted a constellation of aftereffects. Optimistically, they first termed these effects "repatriation neurosis" and "hunger reconvalescence" (Helweg-Larsen et al. 1952). Their choice of these labels clearly reflected their anticipation that the syndrome was a transitory one.

By 1954, as a result of an intensive study of 120 survivors, it was found that the effects were not disappearing (Hermann & Thygesen 1954). The label was changed to "concentration camp syndrome," the first use of this term. Among the physical manifestations noted were pathological fatigue, persistent failure to gain weight, diarrhea, dizziness, headaches, nightly sweating, sleep disturbances, reduced sexual potency, and premature aging. Among the psychological manifestations they noted were depression and moodiness, psychosomatic symptoms (nightly sweating, palpitations, frequent urination), nightmares and other manifestations of anxiety, reduction in memory and/or the ability to concentrate, crying spells, and psychotic reactions.

Shortly after the Danish studies appeared, Eitinger and Strøm (1973), in a retrospective study, examined mortality rates in a population of almost 5,000 non-Jewish Norwegians who survived Nazi concentration camps, prisons, or penitentiaries. They found much higher mortality rates in the ex-prisoners, primarily due to tuberculosis, other infectious diseases, coronary heart disease, lung cancer, and violent death (accident and homicide).

Eitinger and Strøm also reported the morbidity rates of a randomly selected subsample and a well-matched control sample. In these studies they found much evidence for impaired biopsychosocial functioning. Survivors had more frequent changes of job and decline in occupational status, had more frequent and longer sick leaves, and were hospitalized more often and for longer periods of time. Their physical disorders occurred with frequencies ranging from about 70% to about 500% higher than in the control group, and affected all organ systems—heart, lungs, stomach, genito-urinary, and skeletal.

Similar mortality and morbidity rates were reported in large-scale follow-up studies of American ex-prisoners of war (POWs) interned in the Japanese camps during World War II and the North Korean camps during the Korean war (Nefzger 1970; Bebe 1975; Keehn 1980). The fact that such effects were not noted among Allied military personnel who were in German POW camps makes it clear that the increased mortality and morbidity rates were the immediate consequences of forced labor and malnutrition in the Nazi concentration and labor camps, and the Japanese and Korean POW camps. Similar findings were reported for Canadian and British ex-POWs from the Pacific theater (Kral, Pazder, & Wigdor 1967; Khan 1981).

The preceding studies were primarily based on non-Jews or on samples containing only relatively small percentages of Jews. The experience of Jewish civilians subjected to the Nazi persecution was fundamentally different from that of the above groups. They were of a much wider age range (from young adolescents to the aged), for the most part they were not in as good physical condition because they had not had military training, they were not unified by a common cause, and they were not organized in a unifying administrative structure once they had been deported to the camps from their towns, cities, or ghettos.

As a group, they were not subjected to the beatings, particularly on the head, and other forms of torture to which captured members of the resistance were subjected. They were, however, all slated for extermination if they were found unfit as slave workers or as "field whores" to satisfy the desires of the German armies, or because they faltered in these roles due to exhaustion or illness. The relative mortality rates for non-Jewish and Jewish Norwegians deported to the German camps reflect the consequence of this difference. Only 3% of the Jews survived (Eitinger 1980), whereas 55–92% of the non-Jews did, depending on the camps in which they were imprisoned.

As we have already noted, the social supports offered to Jews after their release from the camps were very different from those of military or paramilitary personnel. They were seldom welcomed as heroes; coldness or outright hostility was common. There were no governmentally sponsored or facilitated housing developments, educational grants, or disability pensions. Despite these differences, the effects of malnutrition, forced labor, and possibly the prolonged, excessive stress experienced by both groups appear to have had an overwhelmingly leveling effect; Jewish survivors were found to experience the same negative consequences as the others.

Working independently with Jewish concentration camp survivors in the United States, Krystal and Niederland (1968) pursued Niederland's (1961) early clinical descriptions of the symptoms that delineated what he called "total reactive personality changes caused by the overwhelming traumatization [experienced by survivors]" (Niederland 1968, p. 14). They reviewed the case records of 149 randomly selected patients who were concentration camp survivors. They found the same depression, anxiety, disturbances of cognition and memory, and some psychosomatic symptoms. In addition, they found that survivors tended to be rigid, withdrawn, or infantile in their social relationships. They coined the term "survivor syndrome" for this constellation of signs and symptoms.

It is noteworthy that Chodoff (1963) found no differences in the signs or symptoms among concentration camp survivors and those who had been in the ghettos, in labor camps, or undercover, using false documents. On the other hand, in a study of patients hospitalized in a psychiatric ward, Klein, Zellermayer, and Shanon (1963) did find differences among these groups. They found the greatest instance of severe disturbance (psychotic syndromes) among those who suffered the severest forms of oppression (those in ghettos, concentration camps, and extermination camps) or for whom isolation and chronic fear were important (those in hiding or passing as non-Jews with the help of illegal documents). Those who had been in labor camps or among the partisans did not show any of these severe disturbances. Differences between the samples and the vagaries of clinical impressions could well explain the discrepancy between the two sets of findings.

In a general sense, two studies of randomly selected community samples in Israel confirmed the clinical observations. In a study of menopausal women aged 45–54, conducted 25 years after the end of World War II, psychiatrists found women who had been in concentration camps to have poorer emotional health than a matched control group. In addition, the concentration camp survivors rated themselves lower on a feeling of well-being scale, on a coping scale, and on a mood scale, and higher on a worry scale than did the comparison group (Antonovsky, Moaz, Dowty, & Wijsenvbeek, 1971). Levav and Abramson (1984) administered an eight-item scale of emotional distress (tapping anxiety, sadness, and hopelessness) to a random sample drawn from the entire Jewish population 25 years or older of a neighborhood in Jerusalem. They found both male and female concentration camp survivors to be more distressed than their counterparts in the comparison group.

Although these two community studies yielded results that were consistent with each other, the former relied exclusively on subjective rating scales, and the latter on a little-known scale developed in a previous study. Furthermore, the differences between the groups in the second study, though statistically significant, were very small. Finally, both studies were conducted in Israel, where the majority was not alien to the survivors, and where there was a common enemy that legitimized the externalization of aggression. As a result, it is difficult to know whether the findings are generalizable to other communities.

Stability of Coping Style and Differences in Personality

With the exception of case studies, most reports, framed within broad categories such as "survivor of the Nazi persecution" or "concentration camp survivors," lump together people who had very different experiences and gloss over personality differences in survival or coping strategies. Furthermore, most studies of the long-term effects of the Nazi persecution document the deterioration in physical or mental capacity (e.g., Matussek 1975; Krystal 1971; Nathan, Eitinger, & Winnik 1964). Only two deal at length with the stability of personality traits over the years following the experience of prolonged stress (Danielli 1981, 1982; Eitinger 1964); a third study, by Matussek (1975), suggests such stability.

Matussek interviewed and tested 245 concentration camp survivors, randomly selected from a list of those seeking reparation payments, who resided in or near Munich, in Israel, or in New York at the time of the study, some 15 years after the end of World War II. In the group of survivors who had been incarcerated for religious or political reasons, the largest group in his study, he found many relationships between their personalities and home environment prior to their incarceration, and their psychosocial functioning 15 years after their release. He noted two subgroups on follow-up. The first subgroup gave evidence of feeling unable to deal actively with the demands of their current lives. They were characterized by resignation and despair, and tended to attribute their survival to luck. The members of the second subgroup were free of feelings of resignation and despair, and tended to attribute their survival to their own efforts to deal actively with the exigencies of the camp situation, including the work stress. Furthermore, he found that these personality traits were present in the two groups before their incarceration; that is, the traits were not changed as the result of a stress experience, as well as could be determined from a retrospective interview.

The many relationships between personality and home environment did not hold for a second group Matussek studied. The subjects, all of whom were Jews, had been incarcerated for ethnic reasons (termed racial reasons by the Nazis). The slave labor, malnutrition, and beatings to which they were subjected had a much greater impact on them 15 years after their release than did their preincarceration personalities or home environments.

Yet, even among them, Matussek identified two subgroups on the basis of their success in coping with their current lives. The successful copers were faring well socially, occupationally, and in their marriages. In addition, memories of events during their incarceration no longer intruded into these areas of their functioning, nor did these survivors block out their experiences. Those who were coping unsuccessfully were impaired socially and occupationally, had poor marriages, and continued to relive the horrors of their wartime experiences in memories by day and in dreams at night. Matussek reports that prior to their incarceration, the first subgroup had taken more initiative in contacting the opposite sex and had left home more frequently than had the second subgroup. Of particular relevance is the fact that even in the camps, the former had a more active approach to coping. They either planned escapes or thought up ways of improving the situation.

The unsuccessful copers adopted a more passive and conformist attitude in the camps, trying to seek safety in anonymity.

Similar evidence is provided by Danieli (1981, 1982), who reported on her contact with 75 survivors and 300 of their children in the course of individual, family, group, and community work of a clinical and semiclinical nature some 25 years after the end of World War II. (She has since expanded her sample considerably.) She found that a number of these people, whom she labeled Victims, predominantly identified themselves with a totally passive and helpless posture in the face of the Holocaust. On follow-up they continued to relate to the world around them as if it were a fearsome, dangerous place from which they attempted to seek refuge. She found that other survivors, the Fighters, some of whom described themselves as being actively driven to resist and survive during the Nazi persecution, manifested the same active tendency to confront and strive for achievement at the time of follow-up.

The consistency of the observations in these two independent studies suggests the validity of the investigator's findings, despite the nonrandom nature of their samples. These studies may be criticized, however, because they were based on interviewers' ratings of the survivors' retrospective reports of remote events. The reports may have contained elements of selectivity determined by the respondents' psychological or physical health at the time of the study. Depressed, despairing, or discouraged people tend to view themselves in negative terms. These affects and attitudes of the respondents may also have colored the interviewers' ratings.

Eitinger (1964) provided somewhat more objective evidence for this stability in the context of an exhaustive follow-up study of concentration camp survivors in Norway and Israel that he completed some 16 years after World War II. He reported that 54.6% of those (N = 66) who chose to live a communal (kibbutz) life, his "work group," attributed their survival to being with friends and relatives in the camps, whereas only 14.1% of the group of nonhospitalized psychiatric patients (N = 92), who were presumably city dwellers, did so. This suggests a lasting difference between the groups in the importance of group affiliation in their lives. But many of the objections raised above apply equally to Eitinger's study. Evidence of a more objective nature would strengthen the argument for the persistence of personality traits over time despite the person's exposure to severe, prolonged stress.

LONG-TERM EFFECTS: CHILDREN OF SURVIVORS

It will now be evident to the reader that the research and clinical literature consistently demonstrates that survivors of extreme, prolonged stresses are susceptible to enduring physical and psychological impairment. It seems reasonable to assume that depression, anxiety, or chronic physical illness in one parent is likely to adversely affect the spouse and children (Sigal, Silver, Rakoff, & Ellin 1973). The spouses have to cope with more than spouses generally have to cope with, and, if the burden is too great for their coping capacities, they are going to be at risk for depression, anxiety, or somatic problems themselves. As a result the children are at risk for having less-than-optimal parenting, and may have less adequate parental figures for identifying with or using as role models. In brief, it seems reasonable to hypothesize that the children of survivors of situations of excessive, prolonged stress are likely to be emotionally at risk.

Evidence for such intergenerational transmission has been found among children of parents with poor physical or psychological health who were not war victims (Langner & Michael 1963; Rutter, Quinton, & Yule 1976; Weissman, Paykel, & Klerman 1972). One might expect to find similar intergenerational effects among children of war victims.

In examining this hypothesis, it is important to separate civilian from military or paramilitary groups, such as members of the resistance movements, and to distinguish among subsets within these sets of groups. The effects they transmit may differ markedly, not only because the ways in which they are affected differ but also because of the way they were received by the community on their return. If they suffer visible impairment as a result of their wartime experience, parents seen as victimized foreign aliens by the community provide different role models to their children than do those perceived as heroes.

Children of Ex-POWs

The similarity of the negative long-term effects on survivors of the Nazi Holocaust and ex-POWs of the Japanese and North Korean POW camps would suggest similar intergenerational effects. There have been several studies of children of armed forces personnel. In a clinical, impressionistic study of the families of Canadian Army survivors of the Japanese POW camps who had been identified as having been adversely affected physically and psychologically by their imprisonment, Sigal (1976) found that the oldest child appeared to have been affected, provided that child was a girl. He observed that she was likely to manifest depressive affect and to be described by her parents as either overcontrolled or undercontrolled.

He suggested that the mothers were depressed because their debilitated spouses were unable to fulfil their roles as husbands and fathers but required care and comforting instead. The mothers turned to their eldest daughters for this care and comforting. These daughters were expected to provide the mothers with what might be seen as a transitional relationship (Winnicott 1953), but paid a price for it in their own development. Sigal proposed that sons were spared these developmental difficulties because they could identify with the image of a heroic soldier-father. These observations were made in a nonrandom sample of families in which the fathers were known to be suffering the negative consequences of their incarceration. There were no appropriate control observations.

In a convincing case report, Rosenheck and Nathan (1985) demonstrated a link between a Vietnam veteran's delayed response to his stressful combat experiences and his son's difficulty in the development of his ego boundaries, as well as in the son's high levels of guilt, anxiety, and aggressiveness. Two studies of the children of American ex-POWs from Vietnam, however, yielded contradictory results. Nice (1978) was unable to replicate McCubbin and Dahl's (1976) finding that the children of Vietnam veterans were faring poorly psychologically. Since Nice's findings were based on a comparison with a control group and those of McCubbin and Dahl were based on a comparison with outdated normative data obtained some 20 years before, Nice's findings are probably more reliable. They are also consistent with findings from a five-year controlled follow-up study of the families of American naval officers who had been POWs in the Vietnamese camps (Hunter 1986). Thus, the father's POW trauma may not have had negative psychosocial repercussions.

Children of Jewish Survivors of the Nazi Persecution

Clinical Studies and Anecdotal Reports. Studies of children of civilian Jewish survivors of the Nazi persecution are more numerous, beginning with the pioneering observations by Rakoff (1966), Rakoff, Sigal, and Epstein (1966), and Trossman (1968), and continuing to the present. Russell (1980) provides a comprehensive survey of these studies. Because they stimulated such a wealth of subsequent studies and controversies, the content of these initial reports will be reviewed in some detail.

It is perhaps not surprising that these pioneering reports originated in Montreal, a city containing some 110,000 Jews, of whom about 20% of the household heads were survivors of the Nazi persecution. These first reports came from the Department of Psychiatry of the Jewish General Hospital, which had strong ties to the Jewish community. Vivian Rakoff, then a psychiatric resident (and later chairman, Department of Psychiatry, University of Toronto), noted that an unusually large number of parents consulting the department for help with one or more of their children were European immigrants. It then occurred to him that they were also survivors of the Holocaust. Gradually it dawned on him that despite the heterogeneity of the presenting symptomatology of some of the children, there appeared to be common family dynamics that prevented the children from developing a sense of identity. Rakoff stated, "The love and ambition of whole family members were resurrected in memory and imposed as hopes on the children, who were expected to supply the gratification normally coming from mothers, fathers, brothers, sisters, cousins, uncles and aunts, and to live out in their own lifetimes those truncated lives" (Rakoff 1966, p. 21).

Shortly thereafter Rakoff and his colleagues (Rakoff, Sigal, & Epstein 1966) expanded on these observations in the following way:

Because of their total pre-occupation with tormenting memories and with an un-ending re-living of their traumatic past, the parents have few emotional resources left over to meet any but the most routine psychological pressures. The [children's] continually changing emotional needs and their requests for attention and care are either ignored or dealt with as unfair demands. They expect the children to help them with their burdens, rather than being able to react to their children's needs. . . . To achieve their wish to have the children compensate for the lost ones, they either hound them with rigid discipline to achieve their idealized version of the strivings and values of the dead or, alternatively, the child who embodies so many of their yearnings is seen as inviolate, a princeling who is allowed to come and go as he pleases and gratify all his desires.

When in the course of their development the children do not fulfil the idealized wishes of their parents, they are reproached, pleaded with and harangued as if the very psychological survival of the parents hinged on their children's conformity. And in turn, the suffering of the parents renders them inviolate for the children. The consequence is impasse, a lack of true emotional engagement. (p. 24f)

One can often observe a deterioration in the organization of the family; limit-setting may be either rigid or chaotically ineffectual, but rarely related to the needs of the child; in the children there is a curious lack of appropriate involvement in the world; often apathy, depression and emptiness appear, while in other cases there may be an agitated hyperactivity reflecting great dissatisfaction with the parents themselves and society at large. (p. 24)

The emptiness, depression and apathy appear in these children because they have never been allowed to assume an individual identity; they have become receptacles for identities which they do not understand, with which they have had no contact, which in time they grow to resent, and which are rarely meaningfully related to what they actually are or can become. In effect they are deprived children because the parents are so involved with their own depressive pre-occupations that there is little left to give to others. (p. 25).

Trossman (1968), working in a university health clinic in Montreal, also linked psychopathology in children of survivors (COS) to excessive involvement with, and oveprotectiveness by, their parents.

Other investigators subsequently described survivors' relationships to their children as detached, numb, and incapable of feeling and relating warmly to them (Aleksandrowicz 1973; Barocas & Barocas 1979; Danieli 1981; Freyberg 1980; Klein 1973; Krystal 1971; Podietz et al. 1984); as suspicious of the world around them and imposing their perceptions of a dangerous world upon their children (Davidson 1980; Danieli 1981; Podietz et al. 1984); as characterologically confronting and not tolerating expressions of need for care (Danieli 1981); or as not fostering autonomy in the children (Aleksandrowicz 1973; Davidson 1980; Podietz et al. 1984). The children were observed to be bound to their parents by unexpressed anger or by guilt that interfered with the task of establishing a sense of identity within themselves, in their relationships with others, and with the broader community (Aleksandrowicz 1973; Danieli 1980a; Davidson 1980; Klein 1973). Unspecified numbers were observed ultimately to fail in this task (Freyberg 1980). Anecdotal reports suggest that such relationships and identity problems are common among children of survivors (Epstein 1979). Similar findings are cited in reports of therapeutic or encounter groups of adult COS (Fogelman & Savran 1979). The other most commonly noted problems are in the control of aggression—COS have been observed to be either overcontrolled or undercontrolled—and the related problems of guilt, anxiety, depression, and low self-esteem.

In brief, within the framework of structural family theory, the clinical and anecdotal literature suggests that survivors' families are enmeshed. Within the framework of psychodynamic concepts, the children are seen to suffer from excessive parental narcissistic investment or defective parental cathexis, with attendant problems in separation-individuation or self-object differentiation, and superego development (Levine 1982).

The extensive contribution of psychoanalysts to the study of survivors' families calls for further elaboration. Their work is best exemplified by the book *Generations of the Holocaust* (Bergmann & Jucovy 1982), which presents the distillation of more than a decade of work on the topic by a group of psychoanalysts in New York. Since their work is an excellent example of a style of investigation different from that used in our study, it deserves careful consideration.

The editors of the book note the difficulty the group experienced in obtaining hard evidence linking the Holocaust experience of the parents and the psychological functioning of their patients, the children of survivors. Sometimes analysts in the group, or those who presented their cases to the group, neglected to obtain any information about the parents' experiences. Others who obtained information ignored the obvious links between the parents' Holocaust experience and the patients' difficulties that become obvious as a result of the group's discussions. Yet others tended to see these links everywhere. Either tendency could be a reflection of the analysts' own problems in coming to terms with the Holocaust (Danieli 1980a, 1984; Fogelman & Savran 1979, 1980).

Some of the case material in the book provides convincing evidence for a link between the parents' Holocaust experience and the children's problems, even when the parents may not have spoken to their children about the experiences. One analyst reports the case of a seven-year-old girl who was brought for a consultation because of amnesia and "absences" (Gampel 1982). She would appear to lose contact with her surroundings, and when she recovered, she would be confused. In a response to a question during the interview, the child said she did not want to be "... an electric fence in the Warsaw ghetto. They put the soldier's children there and if they touch the fence and electrocute themselves, they will die" (p. 120). When, in the next session, the analyst asked the mother to help her understand the significance of this statement, the mother blanched. She informed the analyst that her husband had been in the Warsaw ghetto as a child, and then in a concentration camp, but had never spoken to the child about his experiences. When asked about his origins, he would only volunteer that he had come to Israel as a child. The analyst reports that as a result of working on the link between the girl's symptoms and her father's history, the symptoms disappeared.

Another analyst gives a brief report of a four-year-old boy who had a bus phobia and was a bed wetter (Kestenberg 1982). Only when pressed did his father remember a bus trip to a farm where he sought refuge from the Nazis. After an initial denial, the father also remembered that his father was asked to remove him from their hiding place when he wet himself at the age of eight. The analyst suggests that the father probably also wet himself at the age of four, when the family fled Germany.

In yet another case that is described, a patient revealed, with great shame, that when her son was very small, she would occasionally forget to feed him (Herzog 1982). Her family complained tht she had them all on a diet. In fact, she used her grocery money to make contributions to an international relief fund. In her analysis she remembered sitting in what might have been a high chair. Her mother seemed to be hurriedly forcing food into her mouth. It appears that the patient was continuing to feed starving children, via the relief fund, as her mother had done, and her family was reexperiencing the starvation and the consequences of maternal preoccupation that she had experienced.

The links to the parents' experiences were found in adults, too. An analyst tells of a 30-year-old patient who would become very anxious if he had to become involved in any project that would require his presence over an extended period of time (Herzog 1982). The patient once commented, "It's harder for them to catch you if they don't know where you are." The analyst links these anxieties to the fact that the patient's father had escaped the Nazis and made his way to Russia, where he was interned in Siberia. The same patient's preoccupation with themes of killing and being killed, and images of his mother as a murderess, became linked in his analysis to his mother's wartime activities with the partisans.

There are many more such illustrations in the book. Some are brief vignettes. Others are longer descriptions of the flow of the analysis. Some are detailed reports of the parents' backgrounds, with allusions to how they affected the children. Others emphasize the children, with selected references to relevant aspects of the parents' backgrounds.

Not all the vignettes or more detailed expositions are as convincing as the ones just reported. There are places where one wonders whether the associations are the patient's or the analyst's. For example, one analyst, referring to a patient's constipation, says that the patient had become the mother of all Jews, whom she (symbolically) imprisoned in her intestines (Kestenberg 1982). When she did empty her bowels, she was letting them all escape. Or again, "Her death wishes against her siblings were connected with her ideas about relatives who had died in the Holocust." Another analyst describes a boy who had been sent for a religious education by parents who had turned away from religion (Oliner 1982). The boy began to force his parents to observe Jewish rituals. The analyst suggests that the boy did so because he had assumed the role of the rabbi in the family (he had perished in the Holocaust).

Such interpretations as the ones just mentioned may seem strange, or even bizarre, to those who are not familiar with the symbols and linkages of the unconscious mind. Patients' apparent ramblings (free associations) in the course of psychoanalytic treatment, the associations evoked in dreams, and their emotional discharges in the course of these ramblings and associations offer convincing evidence for the acceptability of such interpretations. But in the absence of the stuff of the analysis that led the analyst to these conclusions, one must consider the possibility that they reflect the analyst's wish to prove a point, and do not necessarily derive from links in the patient's unconscious.

The preceding illustrations serve to highlight the difficulties confronting the research group. They recognize these limitations and others. They are aware that the general formulations derived from the cases studied by the group do not necessarily apply to those who have not sought analysis. They acknowledge that the group had studied too few cases to be able to suggest that their observations encompass all the problems faced by survivors that were transmitted to their children, even among those who do come for analysis (Bergman & Jucovy 1982, p. 287; Kestenberg 1982).

The editors also acknowledge that the group did not succeed in its attempts to define a syndrome for children of survivors. Yet one can find, scattered through various chapters of the book, some attempts to generalize. The most consistently presented view is that the parents, particularly the mothers, are overwhelmed by anxieties deriving from their experiences of persecution by the Nazis. These unresolved anxieties result in a variety of difficulties for the children. Most of these difficulties are reflected in problems they have in establishing their own identity and separateness from the parents. Among these difficulties are the feeling of being the incarnation of one or many dead relatives; acting as a punitive parent or a sexual partner to the parent; a fear of involvement with others or of commitment to careers; problems in the expression of aggression, manifested through rebelliousness and a need to dominate others, passivity and allowing oneself to be victimized, or phobic states; and other manifestations or experiences of anxiety. The list of potential negative consequences is great.

Some of the contributors do mention that some children may achieve constructive, subliminatory solutions. The circumstances in which they are raised give these children the impetus to assume responsibilities maturely, to be active, creative, and socially aware. The editors cite with approval Hillel Klein's observation that survivor's guilt found in survivors and their children is not necessarily pathological. It can provide a link to the past, a sense of continuity with the Jewish people, and a sense of identity.

An overwhelming proportion of *Generations of the Holocaust* is devoted to presentation and discussion of psychopathology in survivors and their children. In this respect the book is rich in clinical insights, and the contributors draw on a number of psychoanalytic theories—drive theory, structural theory, Mahlerian theory, self-psychology—for their formulations. But what about the well-functioning aspects of the same patients' personalities, or those who are psychologically sound? And how applicable are the clinical observations and the theoretical formulations to children of survivors as a group?

When Melanie Klein, a prominent, controversial psychoanalyst, was asked by a student why she never discussed the healthy aspects of the personality of patients in analysis, she replied, "That's not where the trouble is." Clinical psychoanalysis deals with troubles. It should not be surprising, therefore, that psychoanalysts presenting case material emphasize psychopathology rather than health. They do not have the opportunity to observe healthy functioning with the same depth as they observe psychopathology. Nor do they have the nuances in their vocabulary for healthy functioning that they have to describe psychopathology.

The second question is more difficult to answer. It actually consists of two questions. First, how accurate is any given interpretation of the clinical observations that were made? Second, to what proportion of the entire group do these observations apply? There are at least two tests for the correctness of an interpretation. The first is the consistency of the patient's associations with the analyst's formulation. The other is the consistency of the patient's associations and affective reactions following the interpretation, and the degree to which the patient gains new insights as a result of the interpretation. Waelder (1936) pointed out that many aspects of a person's unconscious determine his or her assocations at any given moment. Thus, many interpretations may be correct. The issue is one of salience or relevance to the patient at any given point in an analysis. And it is the analyst's intuition concerning the issues that are most salient for the patient that determines which of many possible meanings will be interpreted. It is at this juncture that the analyst's personal interest rather than the patient's unconscious may determine the course of the patient's associations, and even the course of the analysis. Here is where a great deal of subjectivity enters into the understanding of people by the psychoanalytic method.

Arriving at universally applicable generalizations on the basis of associations obtained from patients in analysis is a notoriously difficult task.

Genius of Freud's caliber is rare. The task is made more difficult by the fact that survivors are such a heterogeneous group. They differ not only in the personalities brought to the camps but also in their experiences there and their responses to them. The different orientations of Elie Wiesel, Viktor Frankl, and Bruno Bettelheim to their Holocaust experiences provide sufficient evidence for this point. The task is further complicated by the fact that clinicians have in-depth access only to those who seek help, a minority in any general population. Nevertheless, the editors concluded their work by asserting, "It is not possible for a child to grow up, without becoming scarred, in a world where the Holocaust is the dominant psychic reality" (Bergmann & Jucovy 1982, p. 312).

This conclusion suggests the possibility that in at least some survivors' families the Holocaust is not the dominant psychic reality. Even in families where it is, its dominance may appear in a variety of ways because of the great variety of experiences to which the parents were subjected. Many of these ways may not be dysfunctional.

De Graaf (1975) explicitly recognized the importance of distinguishing between families in which the parents had been adversely affected by their experiences during the Nazi persecution and those who had not. From the files of all Israeli soldiers who had been referred to him for psychiatric evaluation in a military psychiatric outpatient clinic over a five month period, he was able to find a group of COS, a group of soldiers whose parents had lost one or more close relatives during World War II but had not been directly persecuted by the Nazis, and a group whose parents had neither lost a close relative nor been persecuted by the Nazis. He conducted in-depth psychodynamically oriented clinical interviews with about half of their parents. (They were selected on the basis of availability of his time and the parents' accessibility.) The interviews suggested to him that the survivors and their children were reenacting the SS-prisoner diad. He found that the parents were compelled to repeatedly seduce their children into irresponsible behavior, which they could criticize, and then magnanimously pardon, while complaining of the abuse they suffered from the children. In other words, he suggests that the problems in the children emanated from the parents' unresolved problems with guilt over their stifled hostile reactions to their Nazi persecutors. But he was careful to note that what may be true for the families in a clinical population does not necessarily apply to families in which the parents remain relatively unscathed by the Nazi persecution.

As an aside, it is interesting to note here that, in an empirical study of the data he derived from his interviews with the soldiers, de Graaf found significantly more personality disorders and delinquency traits among the COS. This difference between the COS and the first comparison group disappeared, however, when only those with physically healthy parents were compared. This last finding also argues for caution in making generalizations based on even an apparently homogeneous clinical population.

Danieli's conclusions from her work with more than 600 families of survivors in an essentially nonclinical population also caution against an assumption of homogeneity among survivors, and extend her earlier descriptions of the families of four types of survivors of the Nazi persecution: the Numb Ones, the Victims, the Fighters, and Those Who Made It (Danieli 1980b, 1981, 1982).

The Numb Ones have become affectively depleted by their exposure to stress. They are unable to relate warmly to themselves or to others. Those who are Victims are depressed and anxious, and remain fearful of a recurrence of the traumatic events, even though they may be far removed from the place where these events originally occurred. They are quarrelsome and are guilt-inducing in their relationships with others. The Fighters have adopted a confronting, challenging, defiant stance in their dealings with the world. They are intolerant of any show of weakness in themselves or others, and push themselves and those close to them to achieve. They are determined that neither they nor others will ever again be subjected to what they experienced. Those Who Made It are a less well defined and less heterogeneous group. They are very successful in the socioeconomic sense. Some of them distance themselves from the traumatic events of their past and from the people with whom they experienced them. Others offer financial or personal support, sometimes in substantial amounts, but tend to vaunt their contributions.

This heterogeneity of response by the parents gives rise to a heterogeneity of psychic realities for the children and, hence, a heterogeneity in behavioral or affective intergenerational consequences, which Danieli describes.

Survey-Type Community Studies. Studies based on clinical samples cannot yield firm generalizations about long-term or intergenerational effects. Controlled studies of nonclinical samples, which might do so, have generally failed to demonstrate differences between late adolescent or young adult COS and control groups (Gay & Shulman 1978; Leon, Butcher, Kleinman, Goldberg, & Almagor 1981; Zlotogorski 1983). Two exceptions to this rule are studies by Last and Klein (1981) and by Karr (1973). The former found that COS had a higher need for succor on Stein's Need Hierarchy Scale, and that male COS had a higher need for affiliation and a lower need for dominance. Karr's study bears most directly on the clinical findings. Using scales derived from the Minnesota Multiphasic Personality Inventory that claim to measure the over- or undercontrol of aggression, Karr found that male COS with one parent who was a survivor reported more inhibition of aggression than did control subjects. He found no statistically significant differences between the groups on anxiety or depression, although COS scored higher on these scales than did control subjects.

The vast majority of these controlled studies are based on self-selected or nonrandom samples. Generalizations from them are, therefore, open to question. Only Last and Klein's study (1981) was based on an entire population—all students attending the four secular high schools in Jerusalem. They encountered sampling problems, however, since only about 50% of COS agreed to be interviewed. Furthermore, since the study was conducted in Israel, it may be that the long-term impact of survival of the Nazi persecution, and therefore the impact on the second generation as well, was diminished by the mitigating influence of the political ideals of the country and the sense of community (Aleksandrowicz 1973). The homogenizing effect of constant threat of attacks by an enemy that legitimizes the expression of aggression in Israel may also have contributed to their failure to find more differences.

The majority of these studies also define a COS as one who has at least one survivor parent. In doing so, they introduce another possible source of bias in their results. In those families in which only one parent is a survivor, the spouse who was not subjected to the Nazi persecution may have a mitigating effect of unknown dimensions on any impact, positive or negative, a survivor might have on the child (Sigal 1971, 1973). The clinical relevance of such mitigating effects has been demonstrated in other contexts (Quinton, Rutter, & Liddle 1984).

Experimental Design-Type Community Studies. At least three studies that employed quasi-experimental designs challenge the assumption of homogeneity of intergenerational effects, and that the effects are only negative, inherent in most clinical descriptions. Ofman (1981) found that the degree to which survivors overvalued their children depended on whether the parents were in the resistance, in hiding, in a concentration camp, or in a labor camp. He also found that this overvaluation appeared to result in better boundary differentiation among children of survivors compared with others, contrary to clinical observations, particularly in mother-daughter pairs.

In a similar vein, Kav-Venaki, Nadler, and Gershoni (1985) found more open discussion of Holocaust-related issues among families of ex-partisans than among families of concentration camp survivors. They also found that sons and daughters of the former had more knowledge of Holocaust-related events and more favorable attitudes toward the victims.

Finally, Zlotogorski (1983) found that children of survivors who had a high level of ego development (as measured by the Washington University Sentence Completion Test; Loevinger & Wessler 1970) viewed their families as significantly more structured or rigid than equivalent comparison subjects viewed their own families.

Unfortunately, these studies, too, suffer from a very limited, potentially biased sampling base.

CONCLUSION

It is clear from the above review that because of defects in sampling or other aspects of methodology, we cannot yet make a statement about the intergenerational impact of exposure to extreme, prolonged stress. A controlled study, based on unbiased samples of children of survivors, or of those exposed to combat or other situations of prolonged, excessive stress of defined duration, is required. Such a study would permit clearer statements on this issue than, for example, would studies of populations subjected to other forms of persecution or to prolonged, extreme poverty in an affluent society. The reason is that, unlike the children in the latter populations, the children born after the survivors' liberation or after the soldiers' return from POW camps or the front are not subjected to the same events as their parents; the confounding effect of the children's suffering the same events as the parents is removed.

The remainder of this work details such a study of the long-term and intergenerational effects of the Nazi persecution, including possible effects on the third generation.

3

The Montreal Surveys

In the chapters that follow, we attempt to fill some gaps in information about Jewish survivors of the Holocaust. We then examine the generalizability of the clinical observations and anecdotal reports of psychopathology in the second generation, and investigate the possibility that these negative effects might be found even among grandchildren of survivors.

We derived our information about the survivors from data gathered in a community survey that was conducted for a different purpose, which we shall describe below.

Our information about intergenerational effects was derived from two independent samples; the first was community-based, the second, clinic-based.

In the community-based study, we drew our sample from the entire population of young adult Jews (aged 19–36) in Montreal. The questionnaire used in that study was specifically designed to examine the generalizability of observations made by clinicians on the problems in families of survivors and the negative consequences for the children. The questionnaire also examined social attitudes and knowledge in areas that might be affected by the parents' experiences or attitudes deriving from events during World War II. We used this sample to obtain information about young adults' children as well, that is, about the third generation.

Our second source of information about possible third-generation effects was derived from a sample of patients in a psychiatric outpatient clinic. As in our study of survivors, we relied on information from a questionnaire that was not specifically constructed for the purposes for which we used it.

A description of the three samples and the questionnaires follows.

THE SURVIVOR STUDIES

Our studies of survivors developed more by chance than through a carefully crafted research project. Textbooks on research methods, for better or worse, generally ignore the randomness of real life as a factor in the research process. But we know that in fact, much research takes place where preexisting data sets designed for one purpose are discovered to lend themselves to the investigation of other problems.

Morton Weinfeld had been approached in early 1978 by the Jewish Community Research Institute (JCRI) to carry out a sociodemographic survey of the Montreal Jewish community. The JCRI was an agent of the two major Montreal Jewish organizations, the Allied Jewish Community Services (AJCS) and the Canadian Jewish Congress. The survey was to be used as an aid in planning and providing social services. In addition, the survey had as a focus the investigation of the responses of Montreal Jews to the election of the pro-independence Parti Québécois in the provincial elections of 1976. Weinfeld set out to organize the project in conjunction with William W. Eaton, then working both in the McGill Sociology Department and at the Institute of Community and Family Psychiatry of the Jewish General Hospital.

As the questionnaire was being designed and finalized, John J. Sigal, research director at the Institute and a psychoanalyst and psychologist, phoned Weinfeld. He inquired whether there would be room on the questionnaire for two questions that might ascertain whether respondents were survivors of the Holocaust, and if so, the nature of their primary experience during the war. Sigal and his colleragues at the Jewish General Hospital had done pioneering work in Canada on survivor families, with cases drawn mainly from clinical settings. Here was an opportunity to investigate long-term effects on survivors using a representative nonclinical community sample.

Weinfeld, a sociologist specializing in ethnic relations, recognized that such questions were directly germane to his discipline as well. The social scientific literature on prejudice and discrimination had focused almost exclusively on studies of the bigots and their bigotry, not on their victims. Here was a missing element in the ethnic relations equation, and the Holocaust survivors could be seen as representing the extreme in ethnic or racial victimization. Eaton, Weinfeld's associate on the community survey and Sigal's colleague at the Institute, was a sociologist with a strong interest in mental health and stress, and in relating physiological and psychological symptomatology. Thus was born the three-way collaboration for the first set of studies. Since this survey, and that of the children of survivors, posed interesting methodological and practical problems, we now discuss sampling and fieldwork in some detail.

The survivor questions were piggybacked on the demographic Jewish community survey. Both for the purposes of the survivor studies and for effective communal planning, it was imperative that the survey design yield a reasonably representative sample of the Jewish community. The survey was not conceived as one aimed primarily at the entire population of Jewish origin in Montreal.

The first task was to define precisely who was to be included under the rubric "Jewish community." "Community" implies participation and interaction in the group; therefore, Jewish persons involved in any Jewish groups, functions, or organizations were to be included. The definition of participation and interaction in Jewish groups, functions, or organizations was as broad as possible, so as to include as many people as possible. To measure communal ties, a wide variety of membership lists was used, as described below.

The decision to represent the Jewish community through membership lists might exclude some people included in other definitions of the Jewish community. For example, it might exclude assimilated Jews—that is, those persons of Jewish descent who have no formal contact with the Jewish community though they are of Jewish origin and identify themselves to Canadian census takers as Jews by ethnicity or religion. It could also exclude certain Hasidic (ultra-Orthodox) groups, who are isolated from other segments of the Jewish community. Third, this definition may exclude Jewish persons who may feel very Jewish but have no discoverable connection to the formal organizational life of the community. Finally, it may exclude young persons who have very recently formed their own households, or Jews recently arrived in Montreal.

It is important to stress again that this is a survey of the Jewish "community," not of all Jews—or people of Jewish origin—in Montreal. From a sociological perspective, the latter definition would be more appealing as it is a group such as the assimilated Jews that might be of great scientific interest. Practical considerations, as well as theoretical ones, guided the definition of the universe of the study. It was felt that the great majority of Jews in Montreal could be linked in some way to the formal community. The time, effort, and resources needed to find marginal persons might, therefore, not be warranted in terms of eventual yield. The outcome of our sampling bore this out. Those of our findings that could be compared with those of others proved to be consistent with them. Moreover, it was felt that any important planning decisions to be made regarding community priorities and specific service agencies might best be made with the help of data drawn from a sample of potential supporters or users of those services.

Sample

It was decided to let household heads, not individuals, represent the community in the study. The household is a common unit of analysis in demography, as are individuals. One reason for this decision was that household heads can provide information about themselves as well as about the other members of the household. Also, it is more practical to survey household heads because membership lists often refer to households, not individuals.

The universe was constructed by obtaining lists from various sources and collating them into one master list. Each list was unique and presented special problems in obtaining it, copying it, correcting it, eliminating duplications, and integrating it with the master list. The general procedure was to read a name from a new list, search for that name in the master card file, and insert the new name into the master file if there was no one with that name at the same address. Some of the lists were obtained only under conditions of strictest confidentiality. In several instances the list integration was done by the relevant agency for reasons of confidentiality, and thus survey staff had little or no control over the process. This was true for social service agency lists, whose clientele might include low-income and new immigrant Jewish households. The order of collation of lists was roughly as follows: The Combined Jewish Appeal (CJA) campaign list was used as a base. Other large lists used were those of the YM-YWHA, the Canadian Zionist Federation, divisions within the Allied Jewish Community Services, the Golden Age Association, the Jewish Public Library, and the Communauté Sépharade du Québec (Sephardic Community of Quebec). The lists were integrated in order of expected net yield, so that if the task became too difficult, lengthy, and expensive, the procedure could be stopped. As it turned out, we were able to use almost 100% of most major lists of Jewish agencies and groups. The notable exceptions were the various synagogue membership lists, which would have overwhelmed our staff, and the list of members of Bnai Brith lodges in Montreal, which was unavailable.

Subgroups of the Jewish community were targeted in separate initiatives. A list of Jewish graduates of McGill University was provided by a recent graduate. A list of ex-Israelis was provided by a person affiliated with the Canadian Zionist Federation. A list was obtained from the Lubavitch Hasidic group, though other Hasidic sects refused. A snowball sample attempted to build up the representation of young households. Some people known to the staff were asked to generate names of young Jews who had recently formed households, who in turn were asked for names. Although there was substantial effort put into this snowball approach, the yield was quite low. The list operation required the organized and concerted efforts of one supervisor (half time), four students (full time), one typist (half time), and the co-investigators for three months. The final master list contained 35,739 names. This corresponded roughly to the number of Jewish households subsequently found in Montreal in the 1981 Canadian census (personal communication, J. Torczyner and officials of Allied Jewish Community Services of Montreal).

With the universe complete, the sample was drawn and verified. One thousand random numbers between 1 and 35,739 were selected, and the cards were drawn out of the master file for verification. Thus, the sampling fraction is .0280, or about 3% of the universe, and the sample is a simple random sample of households.

The list of 1,000 for the sample was verified to ensure that the market research firm organizing the interviewing would have a high yield of completed interviews from the list of households provided. The person on the list was telephoned and asked if the name, address, and telephone number were correct. The justification given was that AJCS was verifying its records.

Of the 1,000 cards drawn, 551 had correct names, addresses, and phone numbers; 310 cards had incorrect names, addresses, and/or telephone numbers that were corrected during the verification procedure; 139 cards were unusable for various reasons—of these, 28 (2.8%) claimed not to be Jewish, and 25 (2.5%) had definitely or probably moved away from Montreal. These proportions likely applied to the master list itself. Among the 139 not verified, many had unlisted telephone numbers, while others probably had moved or changed their marital status in a way that affected their address. Yet some of those not traced were felt to be still in Montreal, based on evidence obtained in the search procedures. A smaller group may have been resident in Montreal and had a published telephone number, but simply were not reached during the verification procedure. It is improbable that more than a few of those not traced were deceased or hospitalized.

A second batch of cards from the master list was drawn randomly and verified as they were drawn, to provide a total of 1,000 households. It was necessary to draw 166 new cards to obtain the necessary 139 verified households. Roughly the same percentage of households were not verifiable as in the first draw (27 of 166 or 16%, compared with 139 out of 1,000 or 14%).

In the first draw there were no duplicate households, but in the second draw there were two duplicates: one household listed under a different name but at the same address as a household in the first draw, and where verification revealed they were the same household; and one household with identical name, address, and telephone number as in the first draw. Thus, the best estimate of the proportion of the master file that was duplicated is two out of 1,166 or .0016 (0.16%).

The resulting 1,000 households were placed in order by area to facilitate assignment to interviewers, and were given to the fieldwork company. The master list was destroyed after completion of the survey because of organizational concerns over confidentiality.

Several comments on the subsample of survivors are in order. There is no denying the heterogeneous nature of the survivor sample, in terms of the actual experiences included in the group. We are well aware of the differences among these types of experiences. We shall present tentative findings that focus on within-group differences among survivors.

Yet social scientific analysis consists, in essence, of comparisons using groups that are both homogeneous (relative to other groups) and heterogenous: racial, sexual, or occupational groups come to mind. We feel that the variance in life experiences in our group of Jewish survivors is no greater than that found in most other groups, and does not impede valuable comparisons with our controls.

Moreover, survivors who hid or were hidden, or fought in armies or with guerrillas, suffered from the daily insecurity and fears of discovery, betrayal, capture, or death in combat; they also lived in situations of non-normative stress for prolonged periods of time (Wijsenbeek 1979). There is some evidence that such prolonged life-threatening stress may have negative long-term consequences similar to those experienced by concentration camp survivors (Askevold 1980).

Perhaps those 41 repondents who did not identify their specific experiences in wartime Europe may have somehow biased the sample, and thus the ensuing results. Clinical findings led us to believe that these respondents, reticent about identifying their Holocaust experiences, are likely to have been more severely victimized, possibly concentration camp inmates. This simply magnifies the difference between the survivor group and controls, increasing our expectation of significant between-group differences.

Finally, the setting of this study in Montreal raises the hypothetical possibility of different initial selection and migration patterns of survivors, with Montreal's survivors being in some way unique. Any case study in social sciences must deal with the issue of generalizability. However, familiarity with the migration process of survivors from postwar Europe suggests that the two major factors at work were the presence of family or friends in a specific location, and simple luck—the destination of the first available ship, a random disembarkation, and so on. A systematic, selective migration of survivors to Montreal, as opposed to other North American cities, seems unlikely.

On the other hand, survivors who chose to immigrate to North America might well differ from those who either immigrated to Israel or resettled in postwar Europe. These differences may well include ideological predispositions as well as psychological orientations. They would also reflect prewar migration patterns of family members. Thus more caution is required in generalizing to survivors in Europe or Israel.

Questionnaire

The questionnaire contained three sets of questions, a total of 332. One set dealt with basic sociodemographic background questions for the respondents and their families. A second set concerned the Jewish background of the respondents and their immediate families, ranging over religious, educational, cultural, and organizational experiences. It included the questions on the Holocaust. The third set focused on political attitudes in Quebec, migration propensities over the next five years, and perceived anti-Semitism in Quebec. A 22-item emotional distress scale (Langner 1962) was included as well. Although the particular relevance of this set of questions for survivors is clear, it is important to note that this questionnaire was not originally designed to yield information that would examine the generalizability of clinical observations of impairment in survivors of the Nazi persecution or in ex-POWs.

The questionnaire was translated into French for French-speaking respondents. In addition, a Yiddish lexicon was prepared to help Yiddish-speaking interviewers to conduct interviews in Yiddish. Only three interviews could not be completed because of a language barrier between respondent and interviewer.

Fieldwork

The fieldwork was coordinated and directed by a respected professional survey firm, the Centre de Recherche sur l'Opinion Publique (CROP). During July and August 1978, a list of potential interviewers was compiled for submission to CROP. It was decided that the ideal interviewer would be a middle-aged Jewish female. Because of the sensitive nature of our survey and apprehension in the Jewish community, it was decided to use only Jewish interviewers to increase rapport between interviewer and respondent.

About 40 interviewers were in the original interviewing group; of these, about 20 persisted throughout the entire period of the survey—these included the interviewers found to be most effective.

The interviewers selected by CROP were given thorough instruction in interview procedures designed to prepare them for all usual contingencies (reluctance to respond, for instance).

The fieldwork lasted three months—September, October, and November 1978. Formally, interviews were discouraged on Saturday (the Sabbath), but individual Sabbath appointments between respondents and interviewers were permitted. The fieldwork was drawn out because of the Jewish High Holidays and the onset of colder weather in November, which increased the attrition of interviewers. In addition, the length of the questionnaire exceeded our earlier estimates, further slowing down our completion rate.

On August 30, 1978, letters were sent from the survey sponsors to all the households in the sample, informing them of the impending interview and encouraging them to participate. In the following week, the interviewers took to the field. The objective was to interview the head of the household. When it became apparent that the head of the household would not be available, it was decided to interview the next most knowledgeable/authoritative adult in the household. A minimum of three attempts per respondent were made before designating the respondent as unreachable, but individual interviewers often exceeded this limit. (Of course, respondents who indicated a firm refusal to participate were not approached again.) Following the survey, 10% of the respondents were called by CROP to verify both the fact and the quality of the completed interview.

A final total of 657 completed interviews was obtained, as shown in Table 3.1. Ten of the 1,000 respondents were omitted because they resided outside the Montreal metropolitan area. Sixty-three households were excluded from the sample for the reasons specified in the table. The 23 persons who moved could not be traced. Of the 937 eligible households, 51 (5.4%) never responded to any interview contacts, though the address appeared to be correct for the given respondent; 215 (23%) refused to respond (either themselves or via another household member); 14 (1.5%) declared they were too ill.

The final response rate was 70% (657 out of 937). Reports from the field shed some light on reasons for nonresponse, apart from a general reluctance by North Americans to participate in lengthy interviews. Some respondents feared that the results of the survey might not be truly confidential or that the master list could be used by anti-Semites. A small number expressed resentment toward the establishment communal organizations and reluctance to participate in a survey under their sponsorship.

We identified the survivors with the following questions: "Excluding service in the Allied armed forces, were you in Europe during World War II?" Of our final 657 respondents, 135 answered "Yes" to that question, and it is this group that comprised the sample of survivors. A second question was "What type of situation were you in?" Our 135 survivors included those who specified a concentration camp (N = 39), a labor camp (N = 17), in hiding (N = 25), in armed resistance or a regular army (N = 13), and those who did not specify (N = 41). It was decided to create two control groups. (Non-Ashkenazim were not chosen for the controls, since all survivors were Ashkenazim; in addition, only respondents over 40 were included in both control groups and the survivor group, since most survivors were over 40.) The first control group (N = 120) consisted of foreign-born Jewish respondents who had not experienced the Holocaust; the vast majority had immigrated to Canada before the 1930s. The second control group (N = 196) consisted of Canadian-born respondents. Table 3.2 shows the demographics of the sample used in this study.

Table 3.1
Community Sample of Survivors and Comparison Groups: Results of Fieldwork

	N	% of Sample
Outside Montreal	10	1.0
Moved	23	2.3
Wrong address[1]	3	0.3
Not Jewish	15	1.5
Incapacitated[2]	7	0.7
Other (dead)	2	0.2
Language barrier[3]	3	0.3
Completed contacts	937	93.7
Total sample	1000	100.0

	N	% of Contacts
Completed interviews	657	70.0
No response[4]	27	2.9
Temporary absence[5]	9	1.0
Prolonged absence	15	1.6
Individual refusal[6]	206	22.0
Household refusal[7]	9	1.0
Sick	14	1.5
Completed contacts	937	100.0

[1]Nonexistent, nonresidential.
[2]Physical or mental incapacity.
[3]Arabic, Russian.
[4]No answer at presumed correct address.
[5]Vacation, business trip, etc.
[6]Respondent refuses to be interviewed.
[7]Member of respondent's household refuses to be interviewed.

Table 3.2
Demographic Characteristics of Survivors and Comparison Groups

Variable	Men Survivor	Men Immigrant	Men Native Born	Women Survivor	Women Immigrant	Women Native Born
Age (years)						
M	59.9_x	71.0_y	55.7_z	60.7_x	69.8_y	59.7_x
S.D.	10.5	11.0	9.7	14.5	9.1	13.5
N	99	73	143	36	36	53
Education[a]						
M	1.39_x	0.98_y	2.32_z	2.32_x	1.50_y	1.98_{xy}
S.D.	1.31	0.99	1.29	1.39	1.41	1.13
N	79	56	106	34	32	47
Occupation[b]						
M	4.47_x	45.2_x	5.47_y	4.05_x	4.30_x	4.67_x
S.D.	1.60	1.63	1.16	1.66	1.30	1.04
N	91	67	133	21	20	45
Marital Status						
Married %	97.9	93.3	92.9	84.0	68.8	69.7
Single %	1.1	3.3	4.3	4.0	18.8	9.1
Separated or divorced %	1.1	3.3	2.8	12.0	12.5	21.2
N	94	60	141	25	16	33

Note: t-tests for means with different subscripts (x, y, z) differ significantly at the .01 level.
[a]0 = elementary school not completed; 1 = elementary school; 2 = high school; 3 = post-high school but not bachelor's degree; 4 = bachelor's degree; 5 = master's degree.
[b]Based on Blishen's scale (Blishen & McRoberts, 1976) for occupations. 5 = lower-prestige white collar workers; 6 = upper-prestige white collar workers and lower-prestige professionals.

THE SECOND-GENERATION STUDY

Sample

Our second survey, conducted three years after our study of survivors, focused on the second generation. We wished to generate three comparable, randomly selected community samples of young adult Jews aged 19–36. The first, the index group, was to consist of children of survivors (COS). For sampling purposes, we defined a COS as any respondent with at least one parent who had lived in Nazi-occupied Europe during all or part of World War II, regardless of the nature of the parent's experience.

We elected to have two control groups. The first (COI), to control for the effects of immigration, was to be comprised of respondents with at least one parent who was born in a part of Europe occupied by the Nazis, lived there at least until the age of 16, and had come to Canada or to the United States before the occupation. The second (CON), to control for the effects of ethnicity, consisted of respondents with two native-born parents.

To control for the possible confounding effects of intervening variables such as culture and tradition of the home or the community, all respondents had to have been born in the United States or Canada after World War II or to have immigrated prior to the age of two, and to be Jews of the Ashkenazi tradition.

In order of precedence, when one parent was a survivor, regardless of the category of the other parent, the respondent was placed in the COS group. When one parent was another type of immigrant and the other was native born, the respondent was placed in the COI group.

The task of constructing the sample was greatly simplified by two facts. The first is that Canada uses door-to-door enumeration to construct census lists every ten years, and updates the information every five years. The second is that electoral lists are available to those of voting age in every household in Montreal. These lists also are constructed by door-to-door canvassing and revised at even more frequent intervals. The first enabled us to determine the 16 census tracts in which at least 5% of the population were Jews. The second permitted us to identify the addresses of Jewish households with a reasonable degree of accuracy by selecting those families with Jewish-sounding names. This name recognition technique has been shown to generate samples comparable with those generated by strict random sampling methods (Himmelfarb, Loar, & Mott 1983). Random numbers were used to select names from the lists. When any number resulted in a non-Jewish-sounding name, the first succeeding Jewish-sounding name was selected. This procedure had to be repeated when we found that we did not have a sufficient number of children of survivors following our initial phone calls to determine into which group the potential respondents would fall (see below).

Those selected first received a letter asking them to participate in a study of "people's attitudes and feelings in many areas including family, friends and personal outlook." The letters were followed by a phone call to determine if they were willing to participate and to arrange a time for the interview. To avoid any response set that might have biased responses, respondents were not told about the investigators' concern with the Holocaust per se.

We selected 3,505 names. Of these, 1,104 had unlisted numbers, so we could not phone them. Table 3.3 gives the size of the final samples and the reasons for which persons were excluded or declined to participate. The reader will note that the technique for selecting Jewish names proved to be quite successful. Only 8.7% of those we contacted were not Jewish.

Placement in the respective groups for the analysis of the data was determined on the basis of the respondents' answers to the questions "When was your father (mother) born?" "Where was he (she) raised up to 16 years?" "At what age did he (she) arrive in Canada?" This placement was verified by similar closed-ended questions during the interview.

Of those contacted by phone, 75.9% of the COS, 62.6% of the COI, and 46.3% of the CON agreed to participate. The survey yielded 242 COS, 76 COI, and 209 CON with usable questionnaires. All respondents received a lengthy summary of all the major findings of the study by mail some two years later.

Table 3.4 shows the demographic characteristics of the sample. The data in this table suggest the adequacy of our sampling techniques.

First, we obtained a relatively high rate of participation of the COS (75.9%). This rate stands in marked contrast with those of other community studies of COS, which report obtaining information on about 50% of the potential sample (Gay & Shulman 1978; Leon et al. 1981; Podietz et al. 1984). The low rate among the CON (about 50%) in the present study may reflect a lesser sense of urgency conveyed to them by the telephone recruiters because of the larger number available in the base population, or possibly a more negative predisposition to participation in community activities. Support for the latter argument is suggested by the fact that 51.7% of them reported not having participated in activities of any Jewish organization in the past 12 months, compared with only 36.8% and 32.9% in the other two groups.

Second, the ratio of men to women in our sample closely resembles that of the general population for this age group: 49% men and 51% women (Statistics Canada 1983a). In contrast, in the only other similar community study for which these data are reported, women outnumber men two to one (Leon et al. 1981).

Third, the COS were younger and of lower birth order than the COI. This is as one might expect, since their parents came to North America after World War II, whereas those of the COI came prior to World War

Table 3.3
Community Sample of Adult Children of Survivors and Comparison Groups: Results of Fieldwork

	N	% of Sample
Outside Montreal	155	6.5
Wrong number	275	11.4
Couldn't contact	142	5.9
Completed contacts	1829	76.2
Total sample	2401	100.0

	N	% of Contacts
Completed interviews	530	29.0
Declined	378	20.7
Duplicates	22	1.2
Not included because sample		
complete (CON)	356	19.5
Didn't show	66	3.5
Parents dead/divorced	19	1.0
Parents' immigration		
history disqualifies	109	6.0
R not Jewish	155	8.5
R is Sephardi	53	2.9
R not born in USA or Canada	74	4.0
Wrong age	34	1.9
Mentally/Intellectually		
handicapped	9	0.5
Disqualified interviews	20	1.1
Other	4	0.2
Completed contacts	1829	100.0

Table 3.4
Demographic Characteristics of Adult Children of Survivors and Comparison Groups

	Men			Women		
	COS	COI	CON	COS	COI	CON
Variable	N = 122	N = 39	N = 99	N = 120	N = 37	N = 110
Age (years)						
M	28.7_x	32.6_y	27.5_x	28.5_x	32.4_y	29.1_x
S.D.	4.74	4.08	4.75	4.83	4.47	5.09
Education[a]						
M	4.07_x	4.03_x	3.72_y	3.34_y	2.84_z	3.35_y
S.D.	1.14	1.31	1.03	0.87	1.01	0.98
Occupation[b]						
M	5.82	5.69	5.67	5.18	5.00	5.29
S.D.	1.14	1.21	1.05	0.96	0.86	0.94
Marital status						
Married %	49.2_x	71.8_y	40.4_x	56.3_x	78.4_y	50.0_x
Single %	48.4	25.6	58.6	36.1	16.2	46.4
Separated or divorced %	2.5	2.6	1.0	7.6	5.4	3.6

Note: COS = Children of Jewish survivors of the Nazi persecution; COI = children of other immigrant Jews; CON = children of native-born Jews. t-tests for means with different subscripts (x, y, z) in any row differ significantly at the .01 level.
[a]0 = elementary school not completed; 1 = elementary school; 2 = high school; 3 = post-high school but not bachelor's degree; 4 = bachelor's degree; 5 = master's degree.
[b]Based on Blishen's scale (Blishen & McRoberts, 1976) for occupations 5 = lower-prestige white collar workers; 6 = upper-prestige white collar workers and lower-prestige professionals.

Source: Sigal & Weinfeld 1985b.

II. Consistent with this finding is the fact that fewer of the COS than the COI were married. The fact that the female COS had more education than female COI is likely due to a similar cohort effect. The COI were raised at a time when there was pressure for females to go to work or get married rather than to pursue their education.

Questionnaire

The questionnaire consisted of over 500 questions, divided into a self-administered and an interviewer-administered part. The questions ranged over many subjects, including sociodemographic background variables; questions on Jewish identification; sociopolitical attitudes; knowledge of World War II in general and the Nazi persecution in particular; measures of personality and the mental and physical health of the respondents, their parents, and their children; questions about relationships with parents, siblings, and spouses. The questionnaire was pretested and modified accordingly. Details of the contents will be given in the appropriate sections of Chapter 5.

The comparatively few open-ended questions were coded by three coders who had also been interviewers. Interrater reliabilities were computed twice, using 30 different questionnaires each time. In cases where the text of a response seemed ambiguous, individual coders would consult with other coders, code the item independently again, and then score it on the basis of the majority of the independent ratings.

The coefficients of reliability ranged from .64 to .82, with a median of .76 (Light 1971).

Fieldwork

Interviews were held in group meetings at several Jewish community centers throughout the Montreal area, for the convenience of respondents. The atmosphere was relaxed and informal; coffee and Danish pastry were served. This cost-effective procedure was selected over home visits because we wanted to minimize interference in the interviews (the questionnaire was lengthy, taking an average of 2.5 hours to complete) and to avoid response bias on personal items that might result from the presence of others at home. Approximately 75% of the interviews were conducted in this way. The remainder were conducted in the respondents' homes.

What would lead any young adult aged 19–36 to agree to give up a midweek evening for such a survey, especially out of the home? Several factors may have operated here. Single respondents (a good 50%) may have seen the event as a social occasion. For married respondents with young children, the survey may have offered a legitimate excuse for a night away from home duties. The organizational affiliations of the investigators, as identified in letters and phone calls, were reasonably high status—McGill University and the Sir Mortimer B. Davis-Jewish General Hospital. Respondents who would participate were promised a token but symbolic honorarium of a tree planted in Israel, which they could dedicate to any (living or deceased) family member.

A team of 30 interviewers participated in the survey. All but four were Jewish. Most were either enrolled in or had completed a course in family life education, and were recommended by the director. They attended three training sessions of approximately two hours each and practiced their skills in a pretest of the questionnaire.

During the study, the interviewers administered half of the questionnaire, including the open-ended questions, to half of the group in attendance on a one-to-one basis while the other half of the respondents were completing the self-administered part. This was an efficient use of the interviewers' time. Attention was paid to emphasing the importance of careful recording of these replies and of probing for fuller responses or additional material. In addition, interviewers recorded their perceptions of respondents' affective state where relevant.

THE THIRD-GENERATION STUDY—
CLINIC SAMPLE

By culling the files of the Department of Child Psychiatry in the same hospital in which Rakoff and his colleagues conducted their pioneering studies of the second generation, we were able to obtain a profile of a clinic population of grandchildren of survivors (GCOS). (Questions we asked of the COS in the above study provided us with information about grandchildren in a community sample.) Historically, the hospital had close ties with the Jewish community, so immigrant Jews were likely to go there with their health problems.

Sample

We examined the charts of all patients who attended the child psychiatry clinic over a ten-year period ending in June 1985. From the beginning of that decade, standard questionnaires were introduced to obtain historical data and information about the children's personalities and their behavior and functioning, at home and at school. The questionnaires had to be completed prior to the first clinical interview with the child. Shortly after this procedure was implemented, the immigration history of the parents and grandparents was also systematically recorded at intake.

On the basis of the immigration history we were able to identify two index groups, Index 1 (N = 58) and Index 2 (N = 11), and two comparison groups, GCOI (N = 28) and GCON (N = 30). To qualify for inclusion in the Index 1 group, at least one grandparent must have been in Nazi-occupied Europe during World War II. The other grandparents and both parents had to be born in Canada or the United States. To qualify for inclusion in the Index 2 group, one or more grandparent *and* parent had to have been in Nazi-occupied Europe, and the remainder had to be native born.

In the GCOI group, no grandparent or parent could meet the criteria for inclusion in the GCOS (Index) groups, and at least one grandparent had to have lived, until she/he was at least 16 years old, in a part of Europe that was later occupied by the Nazis, and to have immigrated directly to Canada or the United States prior to World War II. The remaining grandparent(s) and both parents had to be native born. In the GCON group, all grandparents and parents had to be born in Canada or the United States. All parents and grandparents were Jewish, of the Ashkenazi tradition. In addition, all children had to have been born in Canada or the United States and to have lived with their biological parents since birth. Only cases for which three raters agreed that there was clear evidence as to their classification were included in the study.

It is noteworthy that in 10 of the 11 Index 2 families, the father was the survivor; in three of these families the mother was a survivor as well. In the remaining family only the mother was a survivor. Furthermore, of 11 children in this group, 9 were boys. The relevance of this information will emerge when we discuss the findings of this study.

Table 3.5 presents some of the other demographic characteristics of the sample.

Questionnaires

The data base consisted of information routinely obtained from parents and from the school prior to the child's and the parents' first interview in the clinic. This information is reported on a standard form containing closed-ended questions and checklists. The 25 items from the questionnaire completed by the parents that were used for this study included items referring to the child's character and mood, and a behavior problem checklist. Some of the items in the checklist were selected from each of the factors in Peterson and Quay's (1967) checklist and from the flag items in that list. (A flag item is one that is suggestive of psychopathology and requires further investigation for clarification of its nature.) Others were added because professionals working in the clinic had noted their frequent occurrence in the general population of the clinic. Responses were on a six-point scale (never, used to, only recently, sometimes, often, very often). The parents also completed a questionnaire relating to the child's school performance.

A 30-item checklist completed by the school (usually the child's teacher) provided the second source of data. It consisted of most of the items in the

Table 3.5

Demographic Characteristics of Clinic Sample of Grandchildren of Survivors and Their Parents

	GCON N = 30	GCOI N = 28	Index 1 N = 58	Index 2 N = 11
Mother's age at intake				
M	36.23_x	41.32_y	33.62_z	39.55
SD	3.40	6.07	3.33	6.52
Father's age at intake				
M	38.57_x	44.96_y	36.36_z	46.73
SD	4.48	8.09	3.73	4.88
Child's age at intake				
M	9.17	9.57	8.10	10.82
SD	2.61	3.80	2.86	2.60
Father's occupation[a]				
M	4.86	5.04	4.48	6.00
SD	1.46	1.65	1.52	1.20

Note: GCON=grandchildren of native-born grandparents and parents; GCOI=grandchildren whose parents were native born and with at least one grandparent who immigrated to Canada before World War II but was raised in a European country later occupied by the Nazis; Index 1=grandchildren whose parents were native born and with at least one grandparent who was a survivor of the Nazi persecution; Index 2=grandchildren with at least one parent and one grandparent who were survivors of the Nazi persecution, and the remainder native born. t-tests for means with different subscripts (x, y, z) differ significantly at the .01 level except GCON and Index I's fathers' age at intake which differ at the .05 level.
[a]Based on Blishen's scale (Blishen & McRoberts 1976) of occupational prestige: 5 = lower prestige-level white collar workers; 6 = upper prestige-level white collar workers, and lower prestige-level professionals.

Source: Sigal, DiNicola, & Buonvino 1988.

checklist completed by the parents as well as some items tapping potential problem areas that the teacher would likely note (such as reading, writing, memorizing, intellectual curiosity). Responses were on the same six-point scale. The school was also asked for a narrative explanation of whatever problems it reported, and then asked which, if any, of a list of five possible causes might explain the difficulties (emotional difficulties; limited intelligence; learning, language difficulties; physical health, handicap, medications; siblings, friends, family).

Responses to the only open-ended question used in this study (the school's narrative attribution of the cause of the child's problems) were coded and rated by four independent judges. The interrater reliability determined by the method suggested by Light (1971) was .66. Although we did not determine the reliability of the checklist responses, similar checklists have reliabilities of .70 and higher.

We now turn to a consideration of the findings from our three studies, beginning with the survivors.

4

Long-Term Effects on Survivors

From our review of the literature, it will be apparent to the reader that there is a paucity of evidence about the effects on civilians of exposure to prolonged, excessive stress based on well-controlled, representative community samples.

In this chapter we examine the data from our sample of Jewish household heads to determine if the survivors among them suffered the negative psychological and physical effects that have been documented in community studies of military or paramilitary personnel. We also examine some aspects of the quality of life of our respondents, thereby casting our net wider than that of previous studies. For example, we determine whether the prolonged persecution to which they were subjected affected their perception of the political climate in Quebec (see Chapter 2). Finally, we examine the social and economic adaptation of the survivors.

PSYCHOLOGICAL AND PHYSICAL STATUS

The context within which the first of our studies was conducted severely constrained the space we could allot to our measures of psychological impairment or distress of our respondents. Therefore, we elected to use Langner's 22-item index (1962) as a direct measure of this impairment or stress. In addition, we were able to obtain some indirect measures by asking our respondents how threatened they felt by the political unrest at the time of the survey, and their intended reactions to it. We shall discuss these questions later in this chapter.

Table 4.1
**Langner Scores and Visits to the Doctor for Holocaust Survivors and
Controls, by Sex**

	Men				Women			
	Survivors		Controls		Survivors		Controls	
Item	N	%	N	%	N	%	N	%
Langner score[a]								
0–3 symptoms	63	64	71	78	13	35	24	57
4 or more symptoms	36	36	20	22	23	64	18	43
Visits to doctor[b]								
1 or 2	43	46	46	51	15	46	15	38
3 or more	50	54	44	49	18	54	24	62

[a]Chi square between survivors and controls significant at the .05 level for
men and at the .01 level for women.
[b]Data not available for all respondents. Chi square between survivors and
controls not significant for men or women.

Source: Eaton, Sigal, & Weinfeld 1982.

   The 22–item scale is perhaps the most widely used (and criticized) mental
health scale in the field of psychiatric epidemiology (Meile 1972; Muller
1971; Seiler 1973; Shader, Ebert, & Harmatz 1971). Its flaws are well known:
it sometimes confounds physical and mental health symptoms, is subject to
response biases concerning the social desirability of symptoms and the tendency to respond affirmatively to questions, and is not useful for distinguishing between individuals in terms of psychopathology. On the other hand, it
is valid for distinguishing levels of mild psychiatric symptoms among
groups, and to our knowledge no other brief survey instrument has shown
itself markedly superior in this respect. The wide use of the Langner index
means that the size of the differences presented here can be compared with a variety of other studies, so that the magnitude of the effect can be judged.
   In the analyses of physical and psychiatric impairment that follow, immigrants who were not in Europe during World War II are used as the control
group.
   Table 4.1 presents the Langner scale scores and the number of visits to
the doctor for both sexes. Even 33 years after the war's end there was still
a moderately strong tendency for survivors to report more psychiatric
symptoms than did the controls. For the men, for example, 36% had four

or more symptoms, compared with 22% of the controls; there was a similar difference among the women. These differences were significant both for men and for women ($p < .05$ for men, and $p < .001$ for women), and were consistent with reports in the literature. With the sex categories collapsed, the difference between survivors and control subjects was also significant ($p < .01$). The Langner scale means were 3.9 for the survivor group and 2.9 for the control group. The questions defining the survivor and control groups and the Langner items were separated by literally hundreds of questions on community issues, so there seems to be no chance of the one influencing the other through a negative halo effect. The relationship between Langner scale scores and Holocaust experience cannot be attributed to a selective process of sampling, as in many other studies. These data provide the most conservative test of the hypothesis that the Holocaust experience produced harmful long-term consequences.

In Langner's original paper (1962) 60% of the sample of psychiatric outpatients reported four or more symptoms (mean sample score = 4.8), compared with 28% of a nonpatient sample (mean sample score = 2.7). Fifty percent of a former patient sample had four or more symptoms (mean sample score = 4.2). Our control group was roughly similar to Langner's nonpatient group (29% above the criterion level in Table 4.2), while the survivors were closer to the group of former patients (43% above the criterion level in Table 4.2).

Physical Impairment

The data on visits to the doctor during the previous year showed a much smaller difference. For example, 54% of the male survivors and 49% of the male control subjects had visited the doctor three or more times (difference not significant); the difference was in the opposite direction for women. The difference between Langner scale scores and visits to the doctor is in agreement with the study by Antonovsky et al. (1971) to the extent that one can consider visits to the doctor a measure of physical illness. In their study of menopausal women, Antonovsky et al. (1971) found no difference in physical health between survivors and a comparison group. The survivors, however, were significantly worse off on indices of mental health.

Psychiatric Impairment and Wartime Experience

We analyzed Langner scale scores according to the survivors' different types of experiences during the Holocaust. The most severe consequences were from the concentration camp experience, with 49% of 39 survivors above the criterion level of 4 or more symptoms. Of the 17 subjects who had been in hiding, 40% had 4 or more symptoms, followed by those who had been in resistance groups (38% of 13) and in labor camps (18% of 25);

there were various other idiosyncratic experiences (39% of 36 survivors with four or more symptoms). These different levels of impairment may reflect initial differences in individuals before the Holocaust, different situations and abilities influencing individuals' selection into one or another type of Holocaust experience, or the effects of the different types of experience during the Holocaust. Nothing in our data permits an explanation of them, and the limited sample size prohibits further analysis of them by even the simplest demographic categories.

Symptom Clusters

Table 4.2 presents subjects' scores on separate Langner scale items grouped into three clearly identifiable symptom clusters: depression, anxiety, and somatic complaints. Our own factor analysis of the items yielded depression and anxiety factors similar to factors reported by Engelsmann et al. (1972) but no comparable somatic factor. Table 4.2 also presents subscales as designed by Engelsmann et al. for the purpose of comparability. The general idea was to determine whether the findings regarding Langner scale scores were due solely to one or another cluster, since there has been speculation about all three of these clusters in the literature on Holocust survivors. In each case, the cluster cutoff points given in Table 4.2 are those closest to the median. There is no strong evidence in the table that the overall differences between survivors and control subjects are localized in any particular cluster.

Psychiatric Status and Age

Table 4.3 examines the effect of survivor status for men only, controlling for age. Taking account of age differences serves to minimize the effect of possible differences in age distribution between the survivor and control groups. In addition, if the Holocaust had had especially severe effects on individuals at a particular age level, that interaction would show up here. The age categories are quite crude, unfortunately, but they are as fine as possible with this number of subjects. The difference between survivors and controls was roughly the same at all three age levels: about 8%–23% more survivors were above the cutoff point than controls, and the three-way interaction was not statistically significant even at the .10 level. However, the effect of survivor status, with age partialed out, was still significant at the .03 level. The difference was slightly less strong for those who were in infancy or youth during the war (and were currently 35–60 years of age). This same pattern of findings occurred for both sexes together, but there were not enough respondents to present and statistically test data separately for women.

Psychiatric Status and Fear of Persecution

We also attempted to link the observed consequence of psychiatric impairment to the meaning of the Holocaust in terms of its specific persecution

Table 4.2
Holocaust Survivors and Comparison Subjects with Positive Responses to Langner Scale Items

Subscale	Survivors (N = 135)		Controls (N = 133)	
	N	%	N	%
Depression				
Couldn't get going	35	26	31	23
State of spirits	3	2	1	1
Nothing worthwhile	35	26	28	21
Feel apart	31	23	17	13
Things turn out wrong	16	12	12	9
Entire subscale[a]	65	48	53	40
Anxiety				
Restlessness	53	39	36	27
Worrying type	74	55	73	55
Nervousness	30	22	13	10
Hands tremble	3	2	5	4
Personal worries	42	31	33	25
Entire subscale[b]	11	8	44	33
Somatic				
Weak all over	39	29	24	18
Hot all over	23	17	23	17
Heart beating hard	9	7	9	7
Headaches	22	16	5	4
Fainting	4	3	3	2
Sour stomach	32	24	23	17
Cold sweats	3	2	3	2
Shortness of breath	9	7	7	5
Entire subscale[a]	81	60	55	41
Other				
Appetite poor	7	5	7	5
Trouble sleeping	23	17	21	16
Memory problem	20	15	15	11
Fullness in head	22	16	17	13
Entire scale	58	43	39	29

[a]One or more symptoms.
[b]Two or more symptoms.

Source: Eaton, Sigal, & Weinfeld 1982.

of Jews. The stress of the experience, in terms of the long-term severe physical deprivation and fear for the life of oneself and one's family, would seem to have been enough to produce disorders of at least a temporary nature, and perhaps more permanent disorders. But the symbolic quality of the persecution, and its focus on Jews and other specific groups, may also have contributed to impairment.

Table 4.3
Langner Scores for Male Holocaust Survivors and Controls, by Age Group

Langner Score	35–60 Years				61–70 Years				71–93 Years			
	Survivors N = 52		Controls N = 13		Survivors N = 31		Controls N = 26		Survivors N = 16		Controls N = 39	
	N	%	N	%	N	%	N	%	N	%	N	%
0–3 symptoms	36	60	10	77	18	58	21	81	9	56	29	74
4 or more symptoms	16	31	3	23	13	42	5	19	7	44	10	26

Note: Log linear analysis did not reveal a statistically significant three-way (age x survivor status x Langner score) interaction. However, with age partialed out, survivor status yielded a significant difference on Langner scores at the .03 level.

Source: Eaton, Sigal, & Weinfeld 1982.

If this symbolic quality is an important aspect of the psychiatric consequences of the Holocaust, a situation of renewed or reawakened feelings of
group persecution should emphasize or highlight the harmful consequences.
One of the survey questions was "Over the past five years, has prejudice
against Jews increased, decreased, or remained the same in Quebec?"

We found a dramatic interaction among perception of anti-Semitism,
Langner scores, and Holocust experience. Among the respondents perceiving an increase in anti-Semitism, 48% of the male survivors but only 12%
of the controls had four or more symptoms on the Langner index. Among
those perceiving no change or a decrease in anti-Semitism, there was no
difference between the male survivors and the controls (29% of each group).
This three-way interaction was significant at the .03 level.

The pattern of the data seems to indicate the presence of psychiatric
consequences that are reawakened by a situation of potential ethnic persecution, despite marked differences between the situation in Quebec and that
in Germany in the 1930s (Weinfeld 1977). We have presented the data so
that the perception of anti-Semitism appears as a causal factor, but there is
no way of establishing its causal priority with the data we have. It could
well be that certain Holocaust survivors suffered psychiatric consequences
that, in addition to affecting their responses to the Langner items, caused
them to exaggerate the perception of anti-Semitism; it is also possible that
both alternatives were operating in this population. What is clear is that the
psychiatric consequences of the Holocaust in this sample were associated
with fears of ethnic persecution.

There was a similar (though not statistically significant) pattern of interaction of survivor status, illness, and perception of anti-Semitism. Among
those perceiving an increase in anti-Semitism, 55% of the male survivors
but only 32% of the controls had three or more visits to the doctor (n.s.
at the .10 level). There was no such interaction among those perceiving no
increase, or a decrease, in anti-Semitism. Since the number of doctor visits
in the survivor and control groups was roughly the same (about 55% with
three or more visits in each group), one implication might be that the
psychiatric consequences led to visits to the doctor.

Stability of Coping Style

We elected to compare the data obtained from those who had been in
hiding and those who had been in armed resistance groups, to shed light
on the stability of coping styles. Thus, we focused on two groups that were
not in the concentration camps. We suggest that the respective preexisting
coping style of the members of these two groups were more likely to have
determined what happened to them during World War II than did the coping
styles of those who ended up in the camps. For those who were in the
camps, external factors such as the severity of their punishment and of the

other stresses to which they were subjected following their capture and incarceration played at least as important a role as their coping styles in determining the long-term consequences for their physical and mental well-being (Eitinger & Strøm 1973; Thygesen 1980).

We postulated that those who had been engaged in armed resistance typically used a more active coping style than those who were in hiding, and that they would continue to do so years after World War II. We are aware that the dividing lines are not clear. Even the act of finding a hiding place (sometimes a succession of them), coping with sometimes irritable, tense hosts, and successfully evading searchers often called for active coping. Nonetheless, in the spirit of Matussek's (1975) findings that the active copers tended to try to free themselves from incarceration more often, it is not unreasonable to suggest that there would be a higher probability of finding more of them among those in the resistance movement than among those in hiding.

The hypotheses examined were that, compared with those who were in hiding, those who were in armed resistance would

1. Be more upwardly mobile
2. Demonstrate greater Jewish identity
3. Perceive less anti-Semitism in Quebec (be less fearful) but would be more prepared to consider active responses to the likelihood of Quebec's move to independence from Canada, such as moving out of the province or taking a public stand on the matter.

Hypotheses 1 and 2 and the second part of hypothesis 3 are based on Matussek's observation that those who appeared to be faring well on follow-up adapted more actively to the guards, did not attempt to remain anonymous, and were more active in planning escapes. Thus, in a new country their initiative, if it persisted, might lead to upward mobility, a greater willingness to assert their identity, and a greater willingness to uproot themselves again in the face of a perceived threat. We also assumed that their successful experience with this active coping style would render them less fearful in situations of potential threat. Hence, the first part of hypothesis 3.

Because our examination of the psychiatric and health impairment of survivors revealed an interaction effect between the Langner 22-item scale scores and some of the variables we are exploring here, we also calculated the percentage in each of our two index groups who reported four or more symptoms on that scale, the cutting point commonly used to distinguish between distressed and nondistressed people. Lazarus (1976) suggests that either confrontation or avoidance may be appropriate following appraisal of threat, and each may lead to increased feelings of well-being if successful.

As a result, one might expect to find no difference between the two groups on measures of well-being. On the other hand, some clinicians have noted a tendency for people to develop psychosomatic symptoms when aggression cannot be turned outward. On the basis of this observation and the fact that the Langner scale is heavily loaded with psychosomatic items, a higher percentage of those who were in hiding might be expected to have more pathognomic 22-item scale scores.

Socioeconomic mobility was measured by subtracting the Blishen score (1967) of the respondents' first full-time occupation in Canada from that of the current one, or the usual one if the respondent was currently unemployed or retired. Upward mobility was defined by a positive difference between the scores. (The Blishen scores are a prestige ranking of occupations based on average levels of education and income associated in census data with specific occupations.) Closed-ended questions about the number of traditional Jewish rituals observed, the number of Jewish community organizations other than synagogues of which the respondent was a member, the number of Jewish business associates, self-definition as Zionist, and attitudes to Jewish intermarriage were used to tap Jewish identification. A closed-ended question was used to determine the respondent's willingness to take a public stand on political issues.

Findings. Table 4.4 shows the respondent's primary wartime experience cross-tabulated with the questionnaire items that dealt with the areas examined. Some of the items are paraphrased in the table to facilitate the presentation. The probabilities of finding each difference by chance are also indicated.

Few of the differences were statistically significant. So many were in the predicted direction, however, that we examined the probability that this was due to chance alone. The test proposed by Rosenthal and Rubin (1979) failed to reveal heterogeneity among the probabilities. We could, therefore, calculate the probability of the combined probabilities using the methods proposed by Fisher (1954, pp. 99–100) and by Stouffer et al. (cited in Mosteller & Bush 1954). According to both methods, the two groups were different at a highly significant level ($p < .0001$ and $p < .0001$ by the Fisher and Stouffer methods, respectively). The probability estimate obtained here by the Fisher method is a highly conservative one because the probabilities inn Table 4.4 are based on 2×2 contingency tables (Wallis 1942).

Discussion. With two exceptions, the differences are in the direction predicted. (Only one will be discusssed below, because only it even remotely approached statistical significance.) Furthermore, the Fisher and Stouffer tests revealed that when all the probabilities of differences between the groups on the individual items were combined, the differences between the groups were statistically highly significant in the predicted direction. Thus, while the individual tests of our general hypothesis provided only weak

Table 4.4
Percentage of Males in Hiding or Armed Resistance by Questionnaire
Item or Variable Chosen to Reflect Active or Passive Coping Style

	Hiding	Armed Resistance		
Questionnaire item or variable	N = 24	N = 13	χ^2	p^a
Upward mobility	50%	64%	0.24	0.32
Observance of at least 6 listed Jewish rituals	29	62	2.45	0.06
Belong to no community organizations				

apart from Synagogue	58	85	1.35	0.23[b]
Few or no business associates are Jews	47	17	0.57	0.23
Strong Zionist	33	70	3.05	0.04
"It's alright for a Jew to marry a non-Jew"				
- Strongly disagree	52	92	4.79	0.02
"Is there prejudice against Jews in Quebec?"				
- None	43	70	1.31	0.13
"Have you been a victim of prejudice because you're a Jew?"				
- Not at all or less than average	67	50	0.14	0.55[b]
"Has prejudice against Jews increased in Quebec in the past 5 years?"				
- Yes	60	25	1.35	0.11
"If referendum were in favor of independence from Canada, would you leave Quebec?"				
- Definitely or probably	36	67	1.39	0.12
"One should take a public stand regarding Quebec's independence from Canada and on election issues."				
- Agree	17	40	1.15	0.14

Table 4.4 (continued)

Questionnaire item or variable	Hiding N = 24	Armed Resistance N = 13	χ^2	p^a
"... first reason for leaving Quebec?"				
Economic	14	40	1.44	0.10
Anti-Semitism	33	15	0.57	0.21
22-item scale (Langner score 4 +)	60	38	0.35	0.56^b

aProbabilities are based on a one-tailed test except for the two items on which the groups scored in a direction opposite to the prediction (see below) and the 22-item scale, which are two-tailed. The combination of probabilities in this column using the methods proposed by Fisher (1954) and by Mosteller and Bush (1954) is significant at the .001 level.
bTwo-tailed test.

Source: Sigal & Weinfeld 1985a.

support for it, the general prediction for the stability of coping styles was strongly supported ($p < .001$). This support is striking, given the tenuousness of the links in the inferential chain on which our hypotheses were based.

These results must be viewed with caution, however, because of the very small sample size and because few differences between groups, when measured by individual items, were statistically significant. The small sample sizes obviously weaken any definite conclusions; the study can only be considered as a preliminary exploration. Nevertheless, our calculation and analysis of the combined probabilities served to strengthen our confidence in the general thrust of our findings.

The uncertainty as to whether the respondents' later coping styles were determined by the situations in which they found themselves during World War II, or by their styles prior to their falling victim to the Nazi persecution, is also problematic. The consistency of most of the findings with the hypotheses, the magnitude of the probability of an overall difference, and the presence of only one other study in this area based on adequate sampling procedures (Eitinger & Strøm 1973), however, suggest that they merit some consideration.

Contrary to our prediction, fewer of those in armed resistance movements belonged to community organizations than did those who had been in hiding. One possible interpretation, admittedly speculative, for this might be that among survivors of the Nazi persecution, particularly those who engaged in resistance, Jewish community organizations suffer from a poor reputation. This poor reputation derives from allegations of inadequately aggressive responses of European Jewish organizations to rising anti-Semitism, especially in Germany but in other countries as well. Similarly, Jewish organizations in North America have been criticized for insufficient militancy in an effort to save threatened Jews. Finally, the debate on the role of the Jewish Councils (*Judenraten*) in facilitating the implementation of Nazi anti-Semitic decrees may also have played a role in determining the attitudes of former participants in armed resistance to current Jewish organizations then. Thus, those in armed resistance may well have seen themselves as acting in a manner opposite to that espoused by the mainstream Jewish organizations then, and they may continue to be reluctant to affiliate with such organizations.

Krystal (1971), Matussek (1975), and Nathan et al. (1964), using very different methodologies, independently reached conclusions different from ours. They found no relationship between precamp personality and the long-term adjustment of Jewish concentration camp survivors. Jews with a variety of preexisting personalities suffered a deterioration in their functioning as a consequence of severity of the stress they experienced. Furthermore, the nature of the deterioration was not predictable from previous personality or background (Nathan, Eitinger, & Winnik 1964).

Why, then, did we find evidence for the persistence of personality traits in our groups? The first possible explanation is that our groups were not exposed to as severe stress as those in the camps. There can be no doubt about the severity of the stress experienced by all the persons we studied. Those in hiding, as well as those in the armed resistance, lived in continual fear of betrayal or of discovery (Wijsenbeek 1979). Askevold (1980), on the basis of his study of Norwegian wartime merchant fleet sailors, found that psychological stress alone was adequate to produce the concentration camp syndrome. In addition, those in the armed resistance were often involved in combat, which has been shown to result in long-term morbidity in some studies (Archibald & Tuddenham 1965; Nezu & Carnevale 1987; Stretch 1985). Yet, the stress experienced by our groups, though severe, may not have been great enough to annul the role of different coping styles, as was the case for the concentration camp survivors. The evidence here is equivocal.

The second possible explanation relates to the nature of the daily activities of the groups. Matussek (1975) found that the more arduous the labor that concentration camp survivors were exposed to, the greater the probability of long-term physical and psychological morbidity. Here is a much clearer difference between the two sets of groups. Those in hiding and armed resistance without doubt were not subjected to the unending forced labor endured by those in the POW camps in the Pacific theater during World War II, or those in the Nazi concentration camps; their psyches were not exposed to the consequences of this excessive physical duress.

This difference in daily activities is, therefore, the most likely explanation of the difference between our findings and those of the other investigators. This argument is supported by Matussek's findings with non-Jewish Germans who were political prisoners. For them, he did find a positive relationship between prewar home environment, or personality, and coping some 15 years after their release. As would be predicted from the above argument, they were not subjected to such stressful conditions as forced labor, severe malnutrition, or repeated, unpredictable verbal or physical assaults as were the Jews, for whom he found no such positive relationship.

The Langner 22-item scale results are interesting. Although, again, the difference between the two groups is far from significant, there was a tendency for more of those who were in hiding to have more pathognomic scores. If this difference proves to be replicable and significant in a larger sample, it would be consistent with the findings in our study of the entire sample of survivors and would offer further support for the inverse relationship between aggression directed outward and presence of psychosomatic symptomatology.

Adult Children's Perception of Their Survivor Parents

The way in which the parents present themselves to their children, whatever their degree of impairment, or the way the children perceive their

Table 4.5
**Percentage of Children of Holocaust Survivors (COS), of Other
Immigrant Jews (COI), and of Native-Born Jews (CON) Reporting
Effects of World War II on Their Parents and Themselves**

	COS	COI	CON	All Groups
A. Lasting effects on parents?				
Yes	98.3	63.5	39.2	70.2
No	1.7	36.5	60.8	29.8
N	242	74	204	520
B. Respondents affected by parents' experiences?				
Yes	86.9	39.2	17.5	52.8
No	13.1	60.8	82.5	47.2
N	238	74	200	511

Note: Chi square is significant at the .001 level for the three groups and for the COS-COI comparison for each question.

parents may determine the quality and nature of intergenerational effects. We therefore asked the children of survivors in our second survey three questions to tap this information:

1. Would you say that World War II had any lasting effect of any kind on your parents?
2. If yes, what were these effects, and how did you know about them?
3. Anything else?

For purposes of this chapter, answers to these questions provided us with another means of assessing the survivors' functioning and added a qualitative dimension to the assessment.

From Table 4.5, part A, we see that children of survivors were more likely to claim that World War II affected parents ($p < .001$) than were other comparable Montreal Jews whose parents were not survivors. Indeed, only four respondents out of 242 COS stated that World War II had no lasting effects on their parents.

The rest of this section deals with the responses of the survivors' children, describing their assessment of the effects of the war on their parents.

The following excerpts illustrate the nature of their responses.

1. "Father believes all non-Jews hate Jews; insists that his children marry Jews, and if not, he would literally disown us. My mother had the harder time, so she's kind of scared and tired in a way. If a similar situation ever arose again, I don't know if she'd be ready to fight back."

2. "Mother won't watch any TV show or read any book dealing with the war; she has claustrophobia because she was in a small, tiny place for three years. Mostly they're very, very loving, and the family is what they always want the best for."

3. "My father hates violence—he won't let my brother have a toy gun—and he hates to see any food wasted. He hates Germans—he won't buy anything German, Russian, or Polish."

4. "Both parents: There were always physical disorders due to psychological effects. They were very prejudiced toward various people. They were very demanding of me to fulfill an enormous variety of roles. The doctor told me at 13 to make my decisions and not let my parents tell me what to do or I'd be like them."

5. "My father was very sick—very nervous—constantly had nightmares—they talked about it all the time. My father lost his whole family. My mother gave up a son and is very hypernervous, anxious, makes a big thing out of nothing. She talked about it all the time. Pictures of the lost family plastered all over the house. We were not to forget."

6. "Mother: Her relationship to people—does not trust people, does not have faith in people, by saying so-and-so is bad, etc. I believe it has affected her social life and limited her desire to have any sort of social experiences, by that I mean hobbies, pastimes, etc."

7. "Father: Greater family sensitivity than most people—a greater passion for life and living. Mother: Strong sense of economical frugality and emphasis on being intelligent."

Each response was coded under one of 12 categories (see Appendix A) derived from the responses. Most of the children listed multiple effects on their parents, and some effects could be listed under two categories, though in general this was avoided. Each response was then rated as "positive," "negative," or "mixed." The terms "positive" and "negative" vary in meaning, depending on the specific category. In some cases they are clearly positive (such as better mental health), but in some cases they may denote an increase or decrease in a trait, where only value judgments can justify a label of positive or negative effect. Thus we have labeled an increase in Jewish identity as a positive effect, and continuing anti-German prejudice as a negative effect.

The effects on many aspects of the parents' lives and functioning as perceived by their children are presented in Table 4.6.

The direct relationship between increased exposure to the Holocaust and increased reports of being affected by it (Table 4.5, part B) argues for the credibility of our findings for survivors and their children. As one might

Table 4.6
Reported Percentage (number) of Effects on Parents by Coding Category

Category	0 None or Didn't state	1 Mother Pos. or increase	2 Mother Neg. or decrease	3 Father Pos.	4 Father Neg.	5 Both Pos.	6 Both Neg.	7 Mixed	
A. Physical health – only negative	90.0 (215)		4.6 (11)		3.4 (8)		1.7 (4)		100

Table 4.6 (continued)

Category	0 None or Didn't state	1 Mother Pos. or increase	2 Mother Neg. or decrease	3 Father Pos.	4 Father Neg.	5 Both Pos.	6 Both Neg.	7 Mixed	
B. Familial death	63.0 (150)		8.0 (19)		9.7 (23)		19.3 (46)		100
C. General mental health	47.3 (112)	1.7 (4)	5.5 (13)	3.8 (9)	8.4 (20)	8.4 (210)	15.6 (37)	9.3 (22)	100
D. Specific psychological symptoms - only negative	34.2 (81)		19.0 (45)		17.0 (40)	(1)	29.6 (70)		100
E. Familial attitudes	65.5 (156)	2.1 (5)	3.4 (8)	4.6 (11)	2.1 (5)	9.7 (23)	5.9 (14)	6.7 (16)	100
F. Outgroup	73.5		5.5		11.8		9.2		100

sentiment

Category									Total
(Germans, non-Jews)	(175)		(13)		(28)	(22)			100
G. Life course change	90.3 (215)	1.7 (4)	0.4 (1)		2.1 (5)	15.9 (14)	2.1	0.4	100
H. Adaptation to Canada	94.1 (224)	1.3 (3)	0.4 (1)		2.1 (5)	1.7 (4)	0.4 (1)		100
I. Religiosity	93.7 (223)	0.4 (1)	0.8 (2)	1.3 (3)	0.8 (2)	1.7 (4)	0.8 (2)	0.4 (1)	100
J. Israel	95.0 (226)	0.4 (1)		3.4 (8)	0.8 (2)				100
K. General Jewish identification	82.4 (196)	4.2 (10)	5.0 (12)			8.0 (19)	0.4 (1)		100
L. Unspecified	93.3 (222)	0.4 (1)	0.8 (2)	0.8 (2)	0.8 (2)	0.4 (1)	0.4 (1)	3.4 (8)	100
Total responses	(22)	(121)	(47)	(22)	(133)	(47)	(72)	(217)	(47)

Note: The 238 respondents reported a total of 659 effects on parents. Any parent might have had more than one effect. Percentages are calculated within each category.

69

expect, an increasing percentage of the respondents replied affirmatively when asked if their parents were affected by the events of World War II as one moves from CON to COI to COS. The same occurred in responses to the question concerning the effects of the parents' experience on the respondents.

Some aspects of the findings for the children's perception of their parents' functioning is also consistent with the findings of our first survey and reports of negative psychological repercussions derived from clinical interviews with, or questionnaire-based data on, survivors (Antonovsky, Maoz, Dowty, & Wijsenbeek 1971; Krystal & Niederland 1968; Levav & Abramson 1984). In the present study, of the 612 effects that could be coded as clearly positive or clearly negative, 77% were clearly negative (Table 4.6). Specific psychological symptoms (such as phobias, nightmares, depression) reported by 65% of the respondents were by far the most frequently observed of these negative effects. Not surprising to anyone who works with survivors or is familiar with the Holocaust experience, and also suggestive of the credibility of our findings, is that 37% continued to be involved with mourning or otherwise experienced a sense of loss of dead family members.

That only 10% of the parents were reported to be experiencing poor physical health appears to be discrepant from reports based on objective data. Eitinger and Strøm (1973, 1981) in follow-up studies of non-Jewish survivors of the Nazi concentration camps, and Beebe (1975), in a follow-up study of ex-POWs of the Japanese internment camps of World War II (who also were subject to beatings, forced labor, and malnutrition), report much higher rates of physical than of psychological morbidity. Because of the consistency of our other findings with those reported previously, it is unlikely that this discrepancy is due to faulty or biased reports by our respondents.

The apparent discrepany may be due to the different criteria for psychological morbidity used in their studies and the present one. For the most part, they used standard clinical criteria such as rates of hospitalization. Our criteria most closely resembled those used by Antonovsky et al. (1971), who found no increased risk on physicians' ratings of physical health, but a significantly greater risk on ratings of emotional health in (female, menopausal) survivors.

A second possible explanation for the discrepancy may be inferred from the fact that non-Jewish survivors of the Nazi concentration camps and ex-POWs who had been interned in the Japanese concentration camps during World War II had higher mortality rates on follow-up (Eitinger & Strøm 1973, 1981; Keehn 1980). Those Holocaust survivors who were ill may have died prematurely, leaving only the physically hardier ones to survive. A finding that survivors who lived to be 65 or older have a greater life expectancy than comparison groups (Grauer, Mueller, & Zelnicker 1984) supports this hypothesis.

A final possibility is that because there was a wide range in the severity and duration of the stresses experienced by the parents, the mean stress level of the group, while great and prolonged, was lower than that experienced by Jews, Gypsies, and the ex-POWs in the Nazi concentration camps, or by civilians and military personnel in the Japanese camps during World War II and the North Korean camps. (In addition to concentration camp survivors, our respondents' parents included people who were in hiding, in the ghettos, or in the partisans.) Consistent with this hypothesis is the fact that combat-fatigued troops, who may be presumed to have experienced the stress of combat for a briefer period of time than concentration camp survivors or ex-POWs, like our group of parents, were found to suffer primarily from psychological, not physical, morbidity in a long-term follow-up study (Archibald & Tuddenham 1965).

The effects coded as positive, found in up to one-third of the survivor parents (see Table 4.5), should not go unnoticed. With rare exceptions (Kestenberg 1972; Klein 1971; Ornstein 1985, 1986; Pilcz 1975; Zlotogorski 1983) the scientific and clinical literature has failed to suggest any positive effects. The failure is probably due to the fact that clinicians and other research workers, understandably, are generally oriented toward examining psychopathology, particularly if they are studying the consequences of tragic or traumatic events.

In this context, one might also observe that only 26% of the parents were reported to continue to harbor hostility toward Germans or other non-Jews. It appears that exposure to even the extreme persecution and threat of genocide experienced by the parents did not necessarily lead to a generalized attribution of danger or hatefulness to the world. Our findings concerning the possible positive effects of exposure to prolonged, excessive stress should not be taken as an endorsement of the value of such experiences. Rather, they reflect the remarkable resilience of some people in the face of catastrophe.

Individual Differences Among Survivors

Not all survivors are physically impaired. Even among those who are, not all developed the same physical illness. Similarly, not all survivors manifested psychological impairment, and the data from the previous sections suggest that the long-term consequences of the persecution might differ from one person to the next.

As we indicated earlier (Chapter 2), Danieli (1981, 1982) has proposed that there are at least four identifiable personality types among survivors, labeled the Numb Ones, the Victims, the Fighters, and Those Who Made It.

The first three of these descriptions will be recognized by clinicians who work with people exposed to any of a variety of traumata—combat, torture, rape, fire, or flood.

Until now these descriptions have remained impressionistic. Can their presence and independence be established by standard quantitative methods? Our access to a randomly selected community sample permitted us to answer this question.

Method. We culled a list of 47 adjectives and phrases from Danieli's (1981, 1982) descriptions of the four types of parents. The adjectives and phrases were scrambled, and all respondents in our study of the second generation were then asked to indicate (true or false) whether each adjective described their parents well or not. They rated each parent separately.

Principal component analyses were performed separately for mothers and fathers, first within the COS and then within the two comparison groups combined, that is, we performed four analyses. Each yielded four factors. Since the same factors emerged in each of the four groups, we selected only those items with loadings of .40 or higher on at least three of the four factor analyses for any given component. We then submitted the lists of variables to two separate groups of raters for labeling.

Rich, who wrote a dissertation based on Danieli's categories (Rich 1982), and Danieli comprised the first group of raters. They were asked to indicate to which, if any, of the Danieli categories each factor belonged.

Ten senior psychiatrists, the second group of raters, were each given the same lists and asked to name the personality, character, or disorder that would best fit each list. For them, each list of variables was subdivided into subgroups labeled "highest loading (most typical characteristics)" and "lower, but still relevant loadings." A mean factor loading of .50 was used as the dividing line.

In order to determine the generalizability of Klein, Zellermeyer, and Shanan's (1963) observation of greater severe psychopathology among hospitalized patients who were in the ghettos, in concentration camps, or in hiding than among those who were in the labor camps or in the partisans, we compared the scores of these groups on the factors revealed by the preceding analysis. We did not include those parents who were primarily in the ghettos since their numbers were too small because of our inclusion requirement that both parents had to have been in the same primary situation.

Findings. The factors and mean factor loadings for each of the items are presented in Table 4.7. The four factors explained at least 90% of the variance in each factor analysis. Alphas for the four factors, using unit weight for the variables, were .58, .78, .80, and .77, respectively.

Danieli and Rich were in complete agreement on their labeling of the four factors. They labeled Factor I Numb, Factor II Victim, Factor III Victim/Numb, and Factor IV Fighter/Those Who Made It.

Factor I was labeled Schizoid Personality and Factor II Paranoid Personality by nine of the ten psychiatrists. Factor III was labeled Depressive Character by five of the ten, and Masochistic by three more. Factor IV yielded the widest scatter in ratings. They can best be typified as Type A/ Normal Aggressive, given in various forms by six of the ten psychiatrists. The remainder clustered around the Obsessional/Compulsive category.

Two-way 3 × 2 (group × sex of respondent) ANOVAs computed separately for each of the four factors revealed significant group effects on Factor II (Paranoid Personality) ($p < .01$) and Factor III (Depressive/Masochistic ($p < .01$) for the fathers, and on Factor I (Schizoid Personality) for the mothers ($p < .02$). Subsequent t-tests revealed that on Factors II and III, the scores of the fathers who were in the resistance were significantly higher than those of fathers who were in hiding ($p < .02$ and $p < .001$, respectively). Those who were in the resistance also had higher scores on Factors II and III than those who were in concentration camps ($p < .002$ and $p < .01$, respectively). The mothers who had been in the resistance also scored significantly higher on Factor I than those who had been in the concentration camps ($p < .01$).

Discussion. The quantitative analysis has confirmed and sharpened Danieli's original clinical perceptions. We were able to confirm the existence of at least four personality types that may result from exposure to severe, prolonged stress: schizoid, paranoid, depressive/masochistic, and Type A/ normal aggressive personality types. These correspond roughly to Danieli's categories of Numb, Victim, Victim/Numb, and Fighter/Those Who Made It, respectively.

These factors do not necessarily exhaust the personality types that derive from such experiences; our findings are constrained by the list of adjectives we offered the respondents. Furthermore, these factors describe pure types, which are rare even in clinical settings. While any individual might be typified by one of the labels attributed to the factors, most people will possess some characteristics belonging to the other factors as well. The reader should also note that even high scores on any of these factors are not necessarily indicative of psychopathology. The determination of cutting points for psychopathology would require different methodologies than the ones used for these studies.

We used these categories to explore the possible different long-term effects of surviving concentration camps, labor camps, hiding, or the partisan experience. Our findings that those who were in the resistance, particularly the men, were significantly more marked by their experience than those who were in hiding or in the concentration camps should be accepted with caution for three reasons. First, the reliability of this finding is open to question because of the relatively small number of parents in the four subgroups. Second, those survivors who were most severely affected may either have died by the time the study was conducted (almost 40 years after the end of World War II) or be hospitalized for their illness and, hence, not

Table 4.7
Mean Factor Loading of Items Used for Respondents' Ratings of Their Parents' Personalities

Description	I	II	III	IV
		Factor		
Schizoid Personality				
Distant	.64	.06	.17	.06
Hard to get to know	.63	.16	.15	.00
Rarely shows feelings	.62	.03	.02	.05
Withdrawn	.59	.29	.16	.10
Not open	.58	.19	.10	.10
Cold	.57	.29	.03	.05
Secretive	.54	.19	.10	.10
Silent	.53	.02	.31	.08
Doesn't like others to show feelings	.43	.22	.06	.02
Paranoid Personality				
Quarrelsome	.10	.62	.30	.10
Always angry	.08	.55	.14	.00
Suspicious	.09	.55	.17	.02
Untrusting	.18	.53	.16	.02
Resentful	.18	.53	.26	.01
More interested in self	.23	.49	.07	.06
Manipulative	.10	.46	.05	.22
Demanding	.02	.45	.14	.35

Table 4.7 (continued)

Description	Factor			
	I	II	III	IV
Depressive/Masochistic				
Frightened	.01	.00	.66	.12
Nervous	.03	.13	.58	.16
Suffers	.08	.18	.54	.06
Worries	.04	.01	.54	.04
Many physical complaints	.04	.23	.54	.00
Self-pitying	.00	.20	.49	.13
Afraid of change	.17	.02	.45	.15
Shaky	.10	.01	.45	.06
Type A/Normal Aggressive				
Tough	.02	.08	.17	.67
Strong personality	.08	.00	.19	.63
Fighter	.12	.17	.03	.61
Aggressive	.04	.23	.04	.57
Driven to achieve	.03	.04	.05	.49
Always on the go	.18	.14	.04	.47
Succeeded in making it	.04	.14	.10	.47
Heroic	.05	.17	.10	.46
Alpha	.58	.78	.80	.77

Note: Only those of the original 47 items that had loadings of .40 or higher on at least three of the factor analyses performed on each of the four ratings of parents are included in this list. Mean loadings are based on the three highest of the four loadings. Factor labels as those ascribed by psychiatrist raters. Underlining indicates items used to arrive at factor scores.

be included in our study; in other words, our samples of these subgroups may contain an unknown bias. Third, consistent with the second point, the findings on Langner's 22-item scales (see Table 4.4) suggest that even though the differences we found are significant, the actual scores are still within the range of normality.

We used these categories in another way: to determine the sources of the discrepancies between our findings and those of clinicians concerning the mental health of COS. The success of this attempt, described in the next chapter, suggests the validity and clinical utility of the four factors for the description of long-term psychological impact of the Holocaust on survivors. These categories may also be useful in investigations of the psychological consequences of other types of potentially traumatic situations, such as floods, earthquakes, or assaults. Minimally, they should alert historians, clinicians, and empirical reserachers to consider the heterogeneity of possible long-term consequences of psychosocial trauma.

ECONOMIC AND SOCIAL ADAPTATION

We compared the survivor group with the controls on a variety of social outcome measures that we would reasonably expect to be affected by the survivor experience: economic achievement; segregation in the community; perception of anti-Semitism; satisfaction with economic and political conditions; intention to leave Quebec. (See Appendix B for construction of these indices.)

We shall present the data in tabular form, with chi-square analysis when it is appropriate. In addition, regression analysis will be used to clarify the relationship among the variables. The regression analysis is confined to respondents who are foreign born, over 40 years of age, and of European (Ashkenazi) origin. A "dummy" variable differentiated survivors from other respondents. Since the survivor and immigrant groups differed in age, age is controlled in the regression analyses reported here. Furthermore, ANOVAs yielded substantially the same results as the regression analysis. For the sake of ease of communicating the results, therefore, only the results of the regression analyses will be reported. Tests for interaction effects were conducted by creating new variables for inclusion as independent variables in their regression analysis. The beta coefficients of all these variables (the product of dummy variables for being a survivor with age, sex, etc.) were not statistically significant, and so will not be reported.

Economic Achievement

Journalistic accounts of survivors in America highlight cases of dramatic entrepreneurial success (Rabinowitz 1976). Yet scientific studies with control groups (Eitinger 1964) and without (Matussek 1975) have described

Table 4.8
Economic Achievement: Comparison of Survivors, Immigrants, and Natives (percent)

		Categories			
		Survivor	Immigrant	Native	Total
A.	**Family Income[a]**				
	Less than $20,000	70	70	33	53
	More than $20,000	30	30	67	47
	N	98	91	160	349
B.	**Occupational Status[a]**				
	Low	72	65	49	60
	High	28	35	51	40
	N	102	98	178	378
C.	**Intragenerational Mobility[b]**				
	Downwardly mobile	9	13	15	13
	Immobile	47	39	35	39
	Slightly mobile	20	28	31	27
	Highly mobile	25	20	20	21
	N	113	108	156	377

[a]Chi-square probability is significant at the .001 level for the three-group comparison, but not for the survivor-immigrant comparison.
[b]Data are derived from the differences between the Blishen scores (Blishen & McRoberts 1976) of respondents' present job (last or usual job if unemployed) and their first job in Canada. Percentages do not sum to 100, owing to rounding. Chi-square comparison of the three groups of survivor with immigrant revealed no significant differences.
Source: Weinfeld, Sigal, & Eaton 1981.

impairment in economic achievement for concentration camp survivors. Survivors have experienced interrupted education and training, the erosion of skills, and the destruction of careers or business in full bloom, all of which could adversely affect subsequent life chances. This is quite apart from the obvious physical and mental strain of the experience, which might also affect economic achievement.

Findings. Table 4.8 presents comparative data for three indicators of eco-

Table 4.9
Standardized Betas: Independent Effects of Being a Holocaust Survivor
(regression control for age, sex, education, religiosity)

Dependent Variable	Standardized Beta
Perceived anti-Semitism	.04
Level of satisfaction	.10
Social segregation	.16[b]
Probability of migration	-.10
Family income[a]	-.27[b]
Occupational status	-.19[b]
Mobility	.00

Note: computations are for foreign born respondents, over 40, of Ashkenazi origin.
[a]The equation for family income also controlled for presence of a working spouse.
[b]F-test probability is significant at the .05 level.

Source: Weinfeld, Sigal, & Eaton 1981.

nomic achievement. Occupational status is measured by the Blishen Index (Blishen & McRoberts 1976), which is a measure of socioeconomic status derived from average levels of education and income associated with given occupations (in the Canadian census) as well as prestige rankings from survey data.

Looking first at the measures of family income and occupational status, we note large gaps between the native group and the other two groups. The advantage of the native-born respondents is a result of this group's youth (implying earned incomes rather than retirement pensions) and their higher educational level. The data do not show the survivors to be substantially worse off than the immigrant controls for these two variables (see Table 4.8, A and B), and as we noted in Chapter 3, the two groups are comparable in educational attainment. The regression analysis, however, reveals that survivors do seem to be significantly, and adversely, affected by their experience compared with other immigrants (standardized betas of −.27 and −.19 for income and occupational status, respectively) (Table 4.9). Still, both this and the tabular data suggest that large numbers of survivors were indeed able to make satisfactory economic adjustments.

Support for this view is seen in the patterns for intragenerational mobility observed for the three categories, presented in Table 4.8, C. The measure in question is based on the difference in Blishen scores of respondents' first full-time job in Canada and their current one, or their last or usual one if they were currently unemployed. There is no significant difference among any of the groups. If anything, survivors are slightly (if insignificantly) more likely to be highly upwardly mobile and less likely to be downwardly mobile. This is supported by the low Beta coefficient (.00) in Table 4.9.

Discussion. Many of those in the survivor group may have begun their occupational careers in Canada as refugees, at positions far below their abilities, and thus the subsequent upward mobility would reflect the temporary effects of their desperate initial condition. The phenomenon of initial loss of occupational status is common to many immigrants, and can be assumed to be even more acute for refugees. Yet the survivors revealed little cumulative or prolonged loss of occupational position, as indicated by the mobility data. Stated simply, they seem to have made the best of a bad situation.

Segregation within the Jewish Community

Sociological theory has argued that the experience of out-group hostility contributes to development of solidarity among the in-group (Coser 1956; Levine & Campbell 1972; Sherif & Sherif 1953; Simmel 1955). This formulation may be based either on seeing self-segregation as an adaptive resonse to hostility (or a rational strategy in cases of conflict) or on the fact that out-group discrimination eliminates opportunities and restricts the freedom of in-group members, imposing the segregation by design. Wirth (1928) applied both perspectives to his classic study of American Jewry, stressing the effect of anti-Semitism in sustaining Jewish identity. This view of ethnic segregation has been challenged by an emphasis on a voluntaristic approach on the part of the minority groups. Thus, we find there are adaptive functions of ethnic communities for the integration of immigrants (Breton 1964), and even apparent preferences among native-born members of minority groups for residential segregation (Kantrowitz 1973; Richmond 1972).

Jews have remained highly segregated both residentially and socially in North American cities (Richmond 1972; Sklare 1971). One might reasonably expect that, whether by choice or by necessity, survivors might be more segregated within the Jewish community (being both immigrants and victims of extreme out-group hostility).

Findings. Table 4.10, A, presents the distribution for an index of segregation that combines data on both social (friendship networks) and residential segregation (see Appendix B). Survivors do not seem more segregated within the Montreal Jewish community than other Jews. The regression analysis (Table 4.9), however, reveals a modest (Beta = .16) and sttistically significant ($p < .05$) relation between survivors and greater social segregation compared with other immigrants. Thus, having experienced the Holocaust may lead to a somewhat greater segregation.

Table 4.10
Segregation by Respondent Group and by Perceived Level of Anti-Semitism

A. Segregation (Social and Residential) (%): Comparison of Survivors,
    Immigrants and Natives

	Group			
Segregation	Survivor	Immigrant	Native	Total
Low	26	29	28	28
Medium	39	43	38	39
High	35	28	34	33
N	119	119	133	431

B. Perceived Anti-Semitism by Segregation (%)

	Perceived Level of Anti-Semitism		
Segregation[a]	Low	High	Total
Low	29	26	27
Medium	38	40	39
High	34	33	34
N	210	191	401

Note: See Appendix B for construction of index of segregation.
[a]Not all percentages sum to 100, owing to rounding. Chi square
comparisons revealed no differences.

Source: Weinfeld, Sigal, & Eaton 1981.

Discussion. As demonstrated, survivors do not perceive more anti-Semitism than nonsurvivors. Levine and Campbell (1972) have suggested that
the perception of threat may be as effective as real threat in developing
feelings of in-group solidarity. A brief digression is revealing. Table 4.10,
B, presents data for both the survivor group and the two controls combined,
relating perceived anti-Semitism and social segregation (for the discussion
of perceived anti-Semitism, see below). We find no relation between the
two. Those perceiving little anti-Semitism are as likely to be segregated as
those who perceive much. While further research is necessary, it may be

that the experience of anti-Semitism, not its perceived existence, makes a greater difference in the segregation of Jews. Our survey also found, for example, that far more respondents perceived at least "a bit" of anti-Semitism in Montreal (86%) than had been victimized by it personally (50%).

The weak effect of perceived anti-Semitism suggests that some portion of Jewish social segregation is voluntatry. For example, this survey revealed a general relation between religiosity and segregation: Jews who are more religious tend to be more socially segregated ($r = .25$). While this may reflect non-Jewish exclusion of those Jews who are more religious, voluntary factors must not be discounted. The strictures of Orthodoxy, such as the requirements of walking to synagogue on the Sabbath, the dietary requirements, inhibition of interfaith socializing, proscriptions against intermarriage, limit the potential of interaction with non-Jews.

Perception of Anti-Semitism

A review of the literature failed to reveal any empirical investigations of the long-term effects of a previous experience of severe victimization, due to minority group status, on victims' current perception of discrimination. One possible effect of such a prior episode might be an oversensitivity to possible victimization, leading to continuing perceptions of prejudice and discrimination after a negative stimulus has been removed, and a transfer of such perceptions from a threatening to a nonthreatening environment. Such hypersensitivity is a popular stereotype of both Jews and blacks, and might be considered a component of the paranoia described as an element of the psychological profile of survivors analyzed in previous clinical and other studies (Krystal & Niederland 1968; Matussek 1975). Shuval (1957) studied "mistrust, suspicion and perception of hostility to the outside world" of Jewish survivors in Israel, their attitudes to the physical environment there, and the difficulties in immigrant adjustment in Israel. She found no difference between survivors and controls. The generalizability of her findings is questionable, since the majority of the population in Israel is Jewish. She could not, therefore, measure the level of anti-Semitism that survivors perceive to be held by a gentile majority.

Findings. Table 4.11 presents the distributions for an index of perceived anti-Semitism. The proportions of those who perceive a high level of anti-Semitism are similar in survivor and control groups (Table 4.11, A). Survivors did perceive an increase in anti-Semitism in Quebec over the past five years (Table 4.11, B). Yet this perception of increasing anti-Semitism by survivors has not produced a significantly higher level of perceived anti-Semitism in the present. (Perhaps five years earlier, survivors perceived lower levels of anti-Semitism than others.) From the regression equation (Table 4.9) we note the low and insignificant Beta (.04) for the anti-Semitism

Table 4.11
Level of Perceived Anti-Semitism: Comparison of Survivors,
Immigrants, and Natives (percent)

		Group		
	Survivor	Immigrant	Native	Total
A. Level of Perceived				
Anti-Semitism				
Low	54	54	51	53
High	46	46	49	47
N	105	113	189	407
B. Extent Change in Anti-				
Semitism in Past 5 Years				
No Anti-Semitism	3	4	2	3
Decreased	5	6	12	9
Same	45	55	59	55
Increased	47	35	27	34
N	75	83	156	314
C. Possibility of Anti-Semitism				
Not mentioned	64	57	69	64
Mentioned	36	43	31	36
N	111	111	190	412

Note: Not all percentages sum to 100, owing to rounding. Chi-squares for the three-group and survivors-immigrants are not significant.
Source: Weinfeld, Sigal, & Eaton 1981.

variable, suggesting no greater level of perceived anti-Semitism for survivors compared with other foreign-born respondents.

Respondents were also asked to select from among other several possible reasons those for which they would (hypothetically) leave Quebec. Survivors were not found to be more likely than native control groups to select "possibility of anti-Semitism" as a first or second reason (Table 4.11, C).

Discussion. Why do survivors not seem to perceive higher levels of anti-Semitism? One explanation may be that their experiences have inured them

Table 4.12
Political and Economic Satisfaction: Comparison of Survivors,
Immigrants, and Natives (percent)

Level of Satisfaction	Categories			
	Survivor	Immigrant	Native	Total
	N = 107	N = 116	N = 193	N = 416
Low	47	53	58	54
High	53	47	42	46

Note: See Appendix B for construction of satisfaction. Chi square for
the three groups and Survivors-Immigrants is not significant.

Source: Weinfeld, Sigal, & Eaton 1981.

to subsequent developments. This explanation is roughly analogous to Shuval's (1957) claim that survivors were more hardened than controls to new sources of strain in their environment. In her study, hardening was operationalized to mean a smaller shift from optimistic to pessimistic attitudes when confronted with strain. A similar pattern emerged in a recent study of crime victims, while found that victims and nonvictims do not seem to differ in the degree of their concern about crime (Thomas & Hyman 1977). A second explanation is that survivors who might perceive a higher level of anti-Semitism had already left Quebec. In any event, we found no evidence of greater paranoia-like fear of majority-group hostility on the part of thè survivors.

Satisfaction with Economic and Political Conditions

The clinical literature on survivors has identified the symptoms of anxiety, worry, and generalized dissatisfaction as typical (Krystal & Niederland 1968). Antonovsky et al. (1971), in a study done some 25 years after the war, found that female survivors in Israel were more given to worry than a control group. As indicated earlier, Shuval (1957) found survivors in Israel to be generally more pessimistic about their future (when not subject to particular strain) than controls. Did our data confirm these findings?

Table 4.12 presents the distribution for our three groups on an index of satisfaction with economic and political conditions in Quebec. To be sure, this index does not measure personal worry or anxiety, but sociopolitical attitudes. Yet, given the uncertainties in the political and economic environment in Quebec, these are of interest. We find no evidence to suggest that the survivors are less satisfied than the controls. Thus, even if survivors do suffer from personal anxieties, as suggested by the clinical literature, they do not seem to have been generalized to affect assessments of socio-political conditions.

This is confirmed by the regression analysis (Table 4.9); the unique effect of being a survivor shows no association with satisfaction. Among some survivors, evaluation of present conditions may involve comparison with the far greater misery or dangers of the past. Our next analysis provides further support for the above findings.

Intention to Leave Quebec

Historians have noted the failure of German Jews to recognize and then deal adequately with the incipient dangers of the Nazi threat (Poppel 1977). Their well-known attachment to Germany, blinding them to the mounting danger, is often cited as a major contributing factor. If minority groups learn from the experiences of their collective past, then the dangers of inertia and procrastination are one such Jewish lesson from the Holocaust. As we have indicated, no objective parallels can be drawn between Germany in the 1930s and Quebec today. Nor did anti-Semitism loom large as a factor in the thinking of respondents about possible emigration from Quebec. Yet in view of publicized concern over the exodus of anglophones, including Jews, it was of interest to examine whether survivors were more likely to consider emigration than were other Jews, regardless of the specific causes at work. Our findings could throw further light on the level or manifestations of anxiety and mistrust among survivors. Respondents were asked to estimate the probability of their being in Montreal in five years' time, under a "status quo" assumption and under the assumption of clear support for Quebec's independence in the upcoming referendum (since rejected). The responses were combined to form an index of propensity to emigrate (see Appendix B).

As seen in Table 4.13, the native group has the highest proportion of those most likely to emigrate. In large part this is due to their younger age. We found no difference between the survivor and immigrant groups. This is confirmed by the regression analysis (Table 4.9). This finding is not surprising, given our inability to document either a greater perception of anti-Semitism or lower levels of satisfaction on the part of survivors.

SUMMARY

Consistent with the findings of community studies of military personnel and clinical studies of survivors, we found evidence for psychological impairment in survivors as a group 33 years after the end of World War II. The evidence was derived from an examination of scores on the 22-item index, which records psychological and physical symptoms of stress, and

Table 4.13
Probability of Emigration within Five Years: Comparison of Survivors, Immigrants, and Natives

Probability of Migration	Categories			
	Survivor[a]	Immigrant	Native	Total
	N = 85	N = 90	N = 162	N = 337
Low	44	44	26	35
Medium	38	37	48	42
High	19	19	26	22

[a]Percentages do not sum to 100, owing to rounding. Chi square probability is significant at the .02 level for the three group comparison, but not significant for Survivor-Immigrant comparison.

Source: Weinfeld, Sigal, & Eaton 1981.

from the significant interaction effects between respondents' scores on the 22-item scale and their perception of external threat.

It is important to note, however, that not all survivors were found to be impaired. Indeed, our analyses clearly indicated that it is a mistake to consider survivors to be a homogeneous group. We were able to identify four personality types, and to find some evidence to suggest the stability over the years of two distinct personality traits among survivors.

5

The Second Generation

In this chapter we report the findings of our community study of children of survivors (COS). We first examine the evidence for the generalizability of the clinical and anecdotal reports of familial distress and personal dysfunction in this group. Next, we examine their occupational achievements. Finally, we examine whether historical events are remembered, and how the experience of extreme persecution may affect the sociopolitical attitudes of the subsequent generation.

FAMILY RELATIONS

Relationships with Parents and Siblings

As we noted in Chapter 3, the clinical literature suggested serious problems in relationships and communication in the families of survivors. The parents were seen to pressure the children to achieve goals that did not necessarily match the children's wishes or their abilities. They were also seen to be excessively involved with their children or distant from them, to be excessively controlling or preoccupied and not setting adequate limits on their behavior. The children, for their part, were reported to be either rebellious or excessively dependent on their parents. In brief, in psychodynamic terms the members of the families were reported to be symbiotically tied to each other and not to have achieved separation-individuation (Mahler, Pine, & Bergman 1975), or to be enmeshed or disengaged in terms of structural family theory (Minuchin 1974).

We used multiple-choice questions to explore the respondents' perceptions of interactions in the family and their perceptions of the affective, attitudinal, or behavioral consequences in many areas. In the discussion that follows, we situate the questions we included in this part of the questionnaire within the conceptual family framework proposed by Minuchin (1974), particularly his concept of enmeshment-disengagement. Their relevance for the psychodynamic understanding of individual and family function will be obvious to the psychoanalytically oriented reader.

Minuchin refers to overcontrol and intrusiveness as characteristics of the enmeshed family. Accordingly, we included questions on how involved or detached, cold or warm, and permissive or strict the respondents perceived each parent to be when they were growing up, and currently, and how they felt about it then and now. As a further test of the degree of overcontrol or intrusiveness in the family, and to test Rakoff's (1966) clinical observation that the children were pushed to achieve, we asked whether the respondents perceived such a pressure in a number of areas of their lives and how they felt about it.

Minuchin proposes that the presence of poorly defined, diffuse, permeable boundaries or excessively rigid boundaries indicate, respectively, enmeshed and disengaged families. We used several indices to determine the nature of the families' boundaries as perceived by our respondents. We inquired about how strong differences of opinion were expressed. Among the options offered we included hitting or slapping and silence. These questions also enabled us to verify the clinical observation that there was a problem in the control of aggression in survivors' families. We also attempted to examine the question of boundaries by asking those respondents who no longer lived with their parents, but lived in the same city, how far they lived from them, and how frequently they spoke to each other. We considered the latter two indices to be measures of the respondents' autonomy, an aspect of personal functioning that is related to the enmeshment and boundary issues within the Minuchin framework, and considered to be at risk among the COS, according to clinical observations. The degree to which respondents felt they made decisions to please or to defy their parents was assumed to be another measure of autonomous functioning.

To round out the picture of relationships within the family, we also enquired about the nature of the respondents' relationships with their siblings, in the past and currently. Responses to this question served not only as further indices of enmeshment or alienation but also to test Sigal's (1972) clinical observation of excessive sibling rivalry in families of survivors.

Method. We asked whether the respondents felt pressured to achieve academically, socially, occupationally, to get married, and to have children. Because a person's affective response to pressure to achieve reflects whether it is seen as consistent with or alien to his or her own aspirations, we also asked how the respondents felt about the pressure in each of these areas.

To tap the family atmosphere and the degree of enmeshment or autonomy and boundaries in the family, we asked the respondents about the degree of friction they perceived between themselves and each parent, whether they were frightened of either parent, or either parent was frightened of them, whether they were worried about each other, about guilt over letting their parents down, about submission, and about defiance. The precise nature of the questions and the scales used for the responses are in Table 5.1.

We based the questions concerning the respondents' subjective experiences of their relationships with their parents primarily on Becker's (1964) model, paraphrasing some of his terms so that they might not seem prejudicial when we asked respondents to describe their parents. The dimensions, paraphrased, were involved-emotional vs. calm-detached, warm vs. cold, and strict vs. permissive. For each dimension we asked respondents to rate each parent as they saw him or her when they were growing up; to state whether they wished then that the parent would be more, or less, that way; and whether they would prefer the parent now to be more or less that way. Ratings were on four-point scales for perceptions (such as very strict, strict, permissive, very permissive) and on five-point scales for reactions (such as from "prefer very much more strictness" to "prefer very much more permissiveness").

Findings. The only statistically significant differences between the groups occurred in the area of perceived parental discipline and the respondents' reactions to it. Male COS perceived their mothers to be currently strict more often than did the control groups ($p < .05$). For example, 31.4%, 16.7%, and 12.7%, respectively, of the COS, COI, and CON rated their mothers as strict or very strict. Although the male COS did not differ from the control group in their perceptions of their mothers' strictness in the past, they did more often report that, when they were growing up, they wanted their mothers to be more permissive ($p < .05$), and currently they still tended to feel that way more often ($p < .10$). For example, 57.3%, 33.3%, and 45.1%, respectively, of COS, COI, and CON reported tht they wanted their mothers to be more or much more permissive when they were growing up; and 30.7%, 5.3%, and 7.9%, respectively, continued to feel that way currently. Furthermore, more male COS currently wanted their mothers to be less involved with them ($p < .01$). For example, 25.8%, 13.6%, and 7.9%, respectively, reported wanting their mothers to be more or much more detached.

Female COS more often than female COI and CON reported that their fathers were strict when they were growing up ($p < .01$), that they wished their fathers had been more permissive then ($p < .05$), and, in retrospect, tended to continue to feel that way ($p < .10$). For example, 68.8%, 48.5%, and 52.6% of the female COS, COI, and CON, respectively, remembered their fathers as strict or very strict when they were growing up; 50.9%,

Table 5.1
Percentage of Specified (underlined) Responses to Some Measures of the Relationship between Respondents and Their Families

Variable	Response Rate $\%^a$			d.f.	χ^{2b}
	COS	COI	CON		
Communication with parents					
R would confide in parents if troubled (Yes No)	62.9	38.9	72.5	2	16.115**
Parents would confide in R if troubled (Yes No)	88.4	79.4	80.7	2	4.588
Pressure to achieve					
R felt pressured by parents to achieve: (Yes No)	76.0	66.2	68.6	2	4.317
Academically	39.3	42.0	37.8	6	1.911
Socially 4-point scale from	18.5	6.0	17.5	6	6.700
Occupationally very little to very	30.6	27.1	27.7	6	3.123
Marriage much	25.0	16.0	16.5	6	6.393
Have children	16.2	12.8	7.6	6	5.738

Friction (in past three months, unless otherwise stated)

(On 6-point scale ranging from none to extreme)

Friction with mother?	49.1	53.3	43.0	10	5.499
with father?	52.3	66.7	54.6	10	9.128
with sibling nearest in age, when growing up? (N = 197, 69, and 191, respectively)	14.7	18.8	12.0	10	11.562
and in past three months? (N = 178, 59 and 80, respectively)	56.2	69.5	56.9	10	9.224
Fear, worry, guilt (in past three months)					
R afraid of any family member? (Yes No)	25.3	9.7	17.3	2	9.959**
of mother?	69.8	33.0	60.0	2	2.092
of father?	60.0	0	56.3	2	4.114

Table 5.1 (continued)

Variable	Response Rate %[a]			d.f.	χ^2[b]
	COS	COI	CON		
Any family member afraid of R? (Yes No)	19.3	13.9	12.8	2	3.742
mother?	70.0	83.3	66.7	2	0.648
father?	45.2	66.7	47.8	2	0.511
R worried about any family member? (Yes No)	75.4	76.4	79.3	2	0.990
about mother?	81.1	76.9	74.8	2	1.596
about father?	74.8	75.0	65.2	2	3.300
Family member worried about R? (Yes No)	43.9	13.5	42.5	2	4.734
mother worried about R?	97.3	90.0	9.33	2	2.984
father worried about R?	80.4	83.3	72.2	2	2.744

R feeling guilty about letting parents down or
being unfair to them? (6-point scale ranging
from none to extremely guilty)

in relation to mother?	50.0	48.3	56.1	10	5.410
in relation to father?	55.4	63.0	60.0	10	4.672

Submission, defiance

Degree to which R made decisions and chose lifestyle

to please parents more than self?

(6-point scale ranging from none to extreme

compliance)

Table 5.1 (continued)

Variable	Response Rate %[a]			d.f.	χ²[b]
	COS	COI	CON		
to please mother?	42.9	55.2	42.1	10	8.206
to please father?	42.9	57.7	39.7	10	4.516
R made decisions to rebel against or to					
defy parents? (6-point scale ranging					
from none to extreme defiance)					
against mother?	77.5	82.5	76.7	10	4.516
against father?	80.4	85.2	77.1	10	5.938

Overall relationship to parents compared with other families R knows? (5-point scale ranging from much better and better to much worse)	60.7	49.3	60.5	8	11.360
Physical proximity to and frequency of contact with parentsc					
Distance between dwellings if R not living at home (5-point scale ranging from next door to more than 12 blocks away)	69.2	88.1	76.7	8	10.597
Frequency with which R speaks to parents (7-point scale ranging from several times/day and daily to less than once/year)					
to mother?	84.2	65.0	77.0	12	23.231*
to father?	70.8	60.9	65.2	12	7.633

Table 5.1 (continued)

Variable	Response Rate %[a]			d.f.	χ^{2}[b]
	COS	COI	CON		
R's satisfaction with frequency of contact (3-point scale – too frequent; about right; <u>too infrequent</u>)					
with mother?	6.8	11.9	9.1	4	3.616
with father?	13.3	17.4	20.1	4	5.264

Note: Where mother or father not specified, N ranges from 199 to 230 for COS, from 150 to 174 for COI, and from 273 to 296 for CON. When mother or father is specified, data refer to families in which both parents are survivors, or immigrants in the COS or COI groups, respectively: For COS, N then ranges from 134 to 178, and for COI from 23 to 36, and from 173 to 196 for CON. Within-group differences in N's are due to nonresponse or unscoreable response.

[a]Percentge of respondents giving underlined response(s).
[b]Ch-square is based on entire contingency table for each variable.
[c]Question asked only if parents live in same city as R. N = 146, 42, and 102 for COS, COI, and CON, respectively.
*p < .05.
**p < .01.
Source: Sigal & Weinfeld 1987.

24.3%, and 31.0%, respectively, remembered wishing that their fathers were more or much more permissive in the past; and 50.9%, 24.3%, and 31.0%, respectively, continued to feel that way about their fathers' behavior in the past.

Table 5.1 shows the remaining findings. The reader will note that, as one might expect from the clinical reports, a high percentage of COS (76%) did report they were pressured to achieve, suggestive of enmeshment. A similar, high percentage (over 80%) reported being in touch with their parents at least several times a week and that their parents worried about them, again suggestive of enmeshment. But the percentages were equally high in at least one of the comparison groups. The results are similar for almost all of the other variables we examined. In the approximately 40 remaining comparisons, only three resulted in statistically significant differences, all due to deviant scores by COI. Controlling for age did not alter the findings.

Discussion. We failed to find any overwhelming evidence for enmeshment or alienation among young adult COS. It was only in the perception of the parenting they received that some consistent findings emerged. Male and female COS recalled having more difficulties with discipline by the cross-sex parent when they were growing up. Female COS, or their fathers, appear to have resolved these difficulties, since female COS's reports did not differ from the control groups in this area at the time of the study. The fact that male COS, more often than the control groups, found their mothers to be too involved with them in the past and continued to find them too strict suggests that they, or their mothers, may not have resolved some issues related to the COS's autonomy.

Whatever issues remained unresolved do not appear to have significantly affected the COS's relationships to their mothers or siblings in the many other areas of the parent–child or the intersibling relationships that we examined. The importance of even the differences that we did find should be assessed in the light of the fact that 15 differences might have emerged for males and for females separately in their reports of the parenting they received and their assessment of it; we found only 3 for each. This is more than might be expected by chance alone, but its relevance as a test of the generalizability of the clinical observations, or for the work of clinicians, is open to question.

Because there are so few controlled studies of community samples, findings contrary to ours are worthy of mention. In one study, COS were found to have lower Autonomy Scale scores on the Adjective Check List than controls (Ofman 1981). In the same study, female COS were found to have lower boundary differentiation scores on three of four measures derived from drawings of the person, and of the person in his or her family; on the fourth, female COS were more differentiated.

In a second study, COS were found to be more concerned about their mothers' physical and emotional health and more often to judge this concern to be unrealistic (Podietz et al. 1984). This study also found tht COS phoned their parents more frequently when they first moved away from home; our data suggest that the phenomenon did not persist.

In a third study, COS gave more responses to the Rosenzweig Picture Frustration test that were judged to indicate less emotional openness with their parents, a feeling of more indebtedness to them, a greater obligation to fulfill the parents' expectations, and a greater feeling of responsibility for their well-being (Nadler et al. 1985).

These three studies were based on nonrepresentative samples. They demonstrated, nonetheless, that in some samples, evidence may be found to support the clinical and anecdotal literature. Our findings question the validity of this evidence for the general population of COS.

Relationship with Spouse or Partner

With minor exceptions, the many indices of troubled family relationships we used failed to reveal differences between the families of survivors and the comparison groups. Our questions simply may not have addressed the issue well enough. Therefore, we examined the responses to another set of questions that we had included to address the question of the alleged maladaptive functioning of the COS from another angle, the respondents' relationship to their spouses or persons with whom they were living.

Difficulties in relating that derive from role modeling, identifications, or projective identifications in a person's family of origin may not manifest themselves until the person is involved in an intimate adult relationship. Insecurities, unresolved conflicts, earlier defeats or triumphs, reactions to being burdened by parents' problems or conflicts, expectations, and even satisfactions may determine the person's expectations of the partner or spouse. More troubled family backgrounds are likely to leave a person with a residue of deficit in modeling spousal behavior or with identifications and introjections that result in disharmony in the person's adult relationships. Troubled backgrounds have been shown to result in higher divorce rates and other marital difficulties. We therefore examined the divorce/separation statistics for our groups and, for those cohabiting or married, explored many aspects of the relationship between them and their partners. If COS have the emotional problems and the difficult family relations suggested by the clinical literature, we would expect these difficulties to manifest themselves in their marital relationships.

A question about the current and past marital status of our respondents provided information about divorce/separation rates. Questions constructed by Piper, Debbane, Bienvenu, and Garant (1984), based on the subscales that address marital relationships in the Structured and Scaled Interview to

Assess Maladjustment (Gurland, Yorkston, Stone, Frank, & Fleiss 1972) provided information about the relationship between our respondents and their partners. The questions addressed the amount of friction there was between the two; the degree of the respondents' openness in expressing their feelings to their partners; their dependence on their partners and their feelings about it; the degree of their compliance with their partners' wishes when they disagreed; their assertiveness with their partners; their need for warmth, affection, or attention from their partners, and whether their partners have expressed the need for more of these from the respondents. All responses were to be given on a six-point scale ranging from the total or extreme presence of the quality to complete or extreme absence of it. The points on the scale were the odd numbers ranging from 1 for none or total absence to 11 for the extreme presence. The respondents were asked to focus on the previous three months when answering these questions.

Next, we asked questions of a more general nature, with responses coded on a four-point scale ranging from "a great deal" (scored 4) to "not at all" (scored 1). We asked the rspondents how much they were troubled by any problems they and their partners had; how much they were troubled by any shortcomings their partners had, and vice versa; how much they were troubled by their own shortcomings in the relationship; and how satisfied they were with their marriage (cohabitation).

Findings. Means and standard deviations for answers to the above questions are shown in Table 5.2.

A 3 × 2 (group × sex) ANOVA revealed main effects for groups in the degree of friction with the partner ($p < .03$) and the frequency of compliance with partner's wishes ($p < .04$). There were many significant sex differences (main effects), but they are not relevant to the issue at hand.

Main effects for group were found for the degree of the respondents' openness in their feelings with their spouses (partners), and the frequency of the respondents' compliance with them ($p < .001$, and $p < .04$, respectively). Subsequent t-tests revealed that in neither case did the COS differ from both the COI and the CON. We conclude that their relationship to their spouses (partners) did not differ from that of the comparison groups.

In brief, the comparisons of the COS's relationship to their spouses or partners did not reveal any evidence of psychopathology in them.

PSYCHOLOGICAL WELL-BEING

Clinicians have reported problems in the control of aggression, anxiety, and depression, and problems in self-esteem among children of survivors.

In the course of determining the degree to which these observations were descriptive of the general population of COS, we inquired about problems that some clinicians might consider to be other manifestations of problems

Table 5.2
Means and Standard Deviations for Questions Dealing with Marital Relations

Variable	Group		
	COS	COI	CON
1. R's openness with feelings to partner			
M	2.333	2.069	2.743
SD	2.015	1.990	2.361
2. Friction between R and partner			
M	3.647	3.379	4.228
SD	2.203	2.068	2.245
3. R's dependence on partner			
M	7.058	6.965	6.960
SD .	2.355	2.609	2.366
4. R's feeling re dependency			
M	1.692	1.836	1.633
SD	1.596	1.951	1.509
5. R's compliance with partner's wishes			
M	5.876	5.966	5.356
SD	2.126	1.686	2.047
6. R's assertiveness with partner			
M	6.897	7.351	6.922
SD	2.222	2.040	1.968
7. R's need for warmth and affection from partner			
M	6.794	7.103	7.274
SD	3.072	3.210	2.641

Table 5.2 (continued)

	Group		
Variable	COS	COI	CON
8. Partner's need for more warmth and affection from R			
M	5.824	5.897	6.118
SD	3.333	3.183	3.026
9. Distress caused by problems between R and partner			
M	2.180	2.224	2.267
SD	.912	.839	.799
10. Distress caused to partner by R's shortcomings			
M	2.090	2.155	2.226
SD	.690	.834	.612
11. Distress caused to R by partner's shortcomings			
M	2.188	2.155	2.235
SD	.679	.745	.678
12. R's general satisfaction with marriage (cohabitation)			
M	3.623	3.621	3.564
SD	.642	.524	.639

Note: All answers were on a 5-point scale consisting of the odd numbers ranging from 1 to 11 for item 1-8 and on a 4-point scale from 1 to 4 for items 9-12. Higher scores represent more of the quality or characteristic, except for items 5 where it represents less, and item 4 where it represents a higher degree of being troubled by the quality. N ranges from 133 to 138 for COS, 55 to 58 for COI, and 98 to 102 for CON. t-tests following significant F tests failed to reveal any differences between COS and the two comparison groups on any variable.

Source: Sigal & Weinfeld 1987.

in the control of aggression: phobias, problems in dealing with death, and suicide.

Control of Aggression, Depression, Anxiety, and Self-Esteem

We selected the Psychiatric Epidemiology Research Instrument (PERI) (Dohrenwend, Shrout, Egri, & Mendelsohn 1980) as the source of our principal measures of personality rather than a variety of separate scales for a number of reasons: It contains scales for most of the personality and affective variables we wished to measure; the subscales were developed with the aid of a panel of clinicians; they were uniformly standardized; and they have adequate internal consistencies (alphas range from .64 to .72 for the scales we used). The subscales chosen were Active Expression of Hospitality, Passive-Aggressive Behavior, and Rigidity. We included three other PERI subscales—Guilt, Sadness, and Low Self-Esteem—that could reflect the negative consequences of either over- or undercontrol of aggression. In addition, in another part of the questionnaire, we asked respondents whether they had experienced anxiety or depression within the past 12 months. Responses to each of these latter two items were on a Yes or No scale.

Findings. For the following analyses, the PERI scale labeled Low Self-Esteem was scored as a high self-esteem scale, because the majority of the questions inquire about a positive sense of self-worth. It will, henceforth, be referred to as the Self-Esteem scale. A higher score on it is indicative of greater self-esteem. The means and standard deviations for each of the PERI subscales used in this study are shown in Table 5.3.

A 3 × 2 (group × sex) ANOVA of the PERI subscales revealed a significant main effect for groups on the Rigidity scale ($p < .02$), and for sex on the scales for Sadness ($p < .001$), Passive-Aggressive behavior ($p < .05$), and Self-Esteem ($p < .001$). There were no other significant main effects, nor any sex × group interaction effects. COS did not differ significantly from the two comparison groups on the rigidity scale.

Discussion. Despite our failure to find that the COS differed from the two comparison groups on the total score of the PERI subscales, there could be a higher proportion of deviantly high scorers among the COS. The PERI, however, has not been calibrated for the detection of psychopathology in the local population. Community studies quite consistently find the 20% of the population is moderately to severely psychologically impaired (Neugebauer, Dohrenwend, & Dohrenwend 1980). In the absence of any other suitable criterion, we therefore chose as our cutting points for the detection of psychopathology the scores on each of the PERI subscales that most closely separated the highest 20% of the three groups combined from the remainder, separately for males and females.

The percentage of each group scoring above these cutting points is shown

Table 5.3
Means, Standard Deviations, and Percentages of Subjects Falling Above Cutting Point for PERI by Group and Sex

PERI Scale	COS	COI	CON	% Above Cutting Point[a] COS	COI	CON
Active Expression of Hostility						
Men						
M	16.20	16.32	15.07	22.4%	24.3%	17.6%
SD	4.52	4.13	4.30			
Women						
M	16.33	16.78	16.48	25.2	27.0	23.3
SD	4.75	4.85	4.68			
Passive-Aggressive Behavior						
Men						
M	4.87	4.24	4.62	25.0	10.8	14.9
SD	2.24	1.86	2.08			
Women						
M	4.49	3.94	4.25	18.6	5.7	13.0
SD	2.17	2.00	2.01			
Rigidity						
Men						
M	21.46	19.13	22.54	18.3	7.8	22.5
SD	8.23	7.09	7.76			
Women						
M	21.57	20.30	22.74	20.0	16.2	20.7
SD	8.43	8.47	7.46			
Sadness						
Men						
M	5.02	4.97	5.48	9.0	7.8	12.1
SD	2.94	3.03	3.21			
Women						
M	6.63	6.38	7.05	21.7	18.9	30.9
SD	3.38	2.97	3.55			
Guilt						
Men						
M	3.93	3.97	3.85	25.8	29.7	24.4
SD	2.80	2.74	3.04			
Women						
M	3.99	3.35	3.83	26.6	13.5	23.9
SD	2.76	2.49	2.55			
Self-Esteem						
Men						
M	7.56	8.37	7.63	24.1	23.7	25.8
SD	4.05	4.77	4.05			
Women						
M	9.33	8.22	9.45	14.7	24.3	9.6
SD	4.35	4.29	4.24			

Note: N varies for COS from 108 to 120, for COI from 35 to 39, and for CON from 93 to 110.

[a]The cutting point was that which was closest to identifying the upper 20% of respondents on each scale for the three groups combined.

Source: Sigal & Weinfeld 1987.

in Table 5.3. Tabulations of the number of respondents above and below the cutting point in each of the groups for each PERI subscale revealed only one difference, and it fell short of statistical significance: more female COS than COI or CON tended to score above the cutting point on the Self-Esteem scale ($p < .07$).

We did not find statistically significant differences between the groups when respondents were asked directly if they had experienced anxiety or depression in the last 12 months, or in the frequencies of suicidal ideation reported by the three groups. In the COS, COI, and CON groups, 30.8%, 32.9%, and 37.9%, respectively, answered Yes to the question about anxiety, and 18.9%, 20.3%, and 25.7% to the question about depression.

In summary, the one statistical difference we did find that was consistent with clinical observations, on the Rigidity scale, is unlikely to be of any clinical significance because the mean score of the COS lies between that of the CON and COI, and differs from them by less than a third of a standard deviation. Thus, although one cannot prove the null hypothesis (that groups do not differ), the evidence in favor of it with respect to problems in the control of aggression in the broader community of COS is compelling.

Phobias

Since, within a psychodynamic context, phobias may be considered the consequence of poorly controlled hostility, we constructed a phobia scale. For this purpose we chose the items referring to specific situations in the phobic anxiety factor found by Fleiss, Gurland, and Cooper (1971) (staying at home alone, going out alone, being in closed spaces, being in crowds) and added to them four situations that the senior author (John Sigal) had frequently found problematic for COS in his contacts with them: wearing a seat belt when riding in a car, traveling by plane, a parent's going out of town, a spouse's going out of town. We asked respondents to rate the degree to which each of these situations made them anxious on a five-point scale ranging from "Very often" to "Never." We concluded this section by asking respondents if any other situations made them anxious, and if so, to give details.

We found no difference among the groups on 10 of the 12 items in the phobia scale. The COS reported that they were less anxious in closed spaces: 3.8% (9), 11.8% (9), and 11.6% (23) of the COS, COI, and CON, respectively, reported having this anxiety fairly often or very often ($p < .01$) for the complete cross-tabulation of the five categories of response for each of the three groups. Similarly, 12.7% (19), 25.9% (15), and 18.8% (22) in the three respective groups reported being anxious fairly often or very often when their spouses left town, ($p < .02$ for the complete cross-tabulation).

When differences did occur, therefore, the COS were *less* phobic than the other groups.

Psychosomatic Complaints

Because some investigators have argued that aggression turned against the self may result in psychosomatic symptoms, we included Langner's (1962) 22-item scale, which is a measure of nonspecific psychological stress containing a large number of items referring to stress-related somatic symptoms. We also asked the respondents if, in the past 12 months, they suffered from any of a list of problems that might be considered psychosomatic: asthma, allergies, sinus problems, blood pressure, eczema and skin disease, ulcers, backaches or sciatica, arthritis, a cough lasting more than two weeks. We included the question "Over the past five years, has prejudice increased, decreased, or remained the same in Quebec?" in another part of the questionnaire to permit a comparison with findings from the study of survivors in which we found an inverse relationship between responses to this question and Langner scale scores for control subjects but a direct one for survivors (see Chapter 4, section "Psychiatric Status and Fear of Persecution").

Chi-square analysis failed to reveal any differences among the groups on eight of the nine items in the checklist of psychosomatic items or in the percentage of subjects reporting two or more such problems. There was a difference in the reports of back problems or sciatica, CON reporting the most (26.6%), followed by COS (18.9%) and COI (12.0%) ($p < .02$). The difference between the CON and COS approached statistical significance, ($p < .07$).

Chi-square analysis within each group of respondents scoring 4+ on the 22-item scale (the standard cutting point used to discriminate between clinic and nonclinic populations) versus the remainder, and the responses of "the same" or "decreased" versus "increased" to the question concerning perceived change in anti-Semitism in the past five years, showed no significant relationship.

Again, where differences did occur, the COS were not the most adversely affected group.

Dealing with Death

Our clinical observations led us to believe that some COS were unable to deal with death for two reasons. The first was because their parents could not provide them with an adequate role model for doing so, since the parents had not been able to cope with the killing they had witnessed, or had suffered through the deaths of their family members and friends. The second was that the COS had not been able to master their own aggressive wishes or destructive fantasies because their parents could not tolerate or respond adequately to the children's developmentally normative expressions of aggression, due to the parents' depression or ego depletion resulting from their concentration camp experiences (Rakoff, Sigal, & Epstein 1966; Sigal 1972). Accordingly, we asked, "Do you have more difficulty than most in dealing with funerals, shivas (ritual mournings), or memorial services?" and, in another part of the questionnaire, whether they had seriously considered committing suicide ever, and in the past 12 months. Responses to each of these questions were recorded on a six-point scale ranging from Never to Often.

The differences we found with regard to the respondents' difficulty in dealing with funerals, shivas, or memorial services were in the predicted direction: 27.2%, 19.4%, and 18.4% of the COS, COI, and CON, respectively, reporting such difficulties, but the difference falls far short of statistical significance. In the COS, COI, and CON, respectively, 84.0%, 87.8%, and 86.0% answered Never to the question about lifetime thoughts of committing suicide, and 76.8%, 83.3%, and 82.2% to the question about suicidal thoughts in the last 12 months.

Here, then, we found no differences among the groups.

Unnatural Deaths

Survivors of the Nazi concentration camps and ex-POWs from the Japanese and Korean camps are at increased risk for violent death (suicide, homicide, or accident) (Eitinger & Strøm 1973; Keehn 1980, Nefzger 1970). Clinical observations by the senior author suggested the same might be true for COS. Accordingly, we asked, "Has anyone in your immediate family ever died of unnatural causes (accident, suicide, homicide)?" and, if the response was affirmative, how the person was related to the respondent and what was the cause of death. Counting only postwar deaths, of the 33 respondents who answered Yes to the question concerning deaths in the family by natural causes, 63.6% (21) were COS, 9.1% (3) were COI, and 29.0% (9) were CON. Siblings accounted for 19.0% (4/21) of these deaths among the COS (one as a result of an accident, one by suicide, two by homicide), none among the COI, and 11.1% (1/9) among the CON (as a result of an accident). The difference is not statistically significant. However, the COS came from smaller families than the CON; 39.7% and 64.5% of them, respectively, reported having two or more siblings ($p < .01$).

Our sample, though much larger and more representative than those of previous studies, was too small to reliably detect differences in suicide rates or in rates of what we termed death by unnatural causes. The suicide rate for Quebec, the province in which Montreal is located, is 0.85 per 1,000 for people aged 20–34 (Statistics Canada 1983b). If our findings were replicated in a larger sample, they would represent a rate of approximately 5 per 1,000 for the CON and 16 per 1,000 for the COS, who, in addition, came from smaller families. This finding is noteworthy; the suicide rate among COS may be higher than in the other groups.

RESPONDENTS' PERCEPTIONS OF INTERGENERATIONAL EFFECTS

In Chapter 4, we reported the respondents' perceptions of lasting effects of World War II on their parents. Here we report the respondents' perceptions of how they, the respondents, were affected by their parents' experiences. We obtained their reports of intergenerational effects from the following questions:

Do you think that you today are affected by your parents' experience during World War II?

If yes, how are you affected?

Responses were recorded verbatim and coded subsequently.

Findings

The COS responded Yes to the first question much more often than the other respondents ($p < .001$). Indeed, few said they were not affected (see Table 4.5, B).

The rest of this section is devoted to a within-group analysis of COS's reponses. The following excerpts illustrate the nature of their replies, which provided the data base for coding their responses to the second question:

1. Feels guilty; feels she owes parents something because they suffered so much. So big effect on R's life—she does things that make parents pleased. If she ever does do things for herself, she'll feel guilty (and parents will make her feel even more guilty).
2. "They make me feel guilty and they put you through the guilt mill. They were very giving but I knew what was expected of me."
3. "I'm very sensitive about family ties. Family is number one, very close knit. I've suffered emotionally with them, hearing all the stories. I feel very deprived that I never had grandparents—I don't even have a picture of them."
4. "Made me feel close to what family I had left. I also feel very strongly about marrying a Jewish girl. I observe Jewish customs and traditions."
5. "Just listening to all their stories and their experiences has made me more sensitive to the suffering people can go through and still survive. They've made me aware of today's political situation and how things can go sour very quickly as happened in World War II."
6. "It made me aware of how mankind can treat their fellow man and I am on guard. Made me vigilant, more politically aware of what is going on around and in the world. I do not really accept things as they are."

Table 5.4
Reported Percentage (number) of Effects of World War II on COS by Coding Category

Category	0 None or Didn't State	1 Positive Effect or Increased	2 Negative Effect or Decreased	3 Mixed	
A. Loss of family	84.7 (172)		14.8 (30)	0.5 (1)	100
B. General mental health	37.6 (76)	28.7 (52)	21.3 (43)	14.9 (30)	100
C. Specific psychological symptoms (always neg.)	79.8 (162)		20.2 (41)		100
D. Familial attitudes	66.5 (135)	19.7 (40)	7.9 (16)	5.4 (11)	100
E. Out-group sentiments (Germans, non-Jews)	82.8 (168)		17.2 (35)		100
F. Life course change	97.0 (197)	1.0 (2)	1.0 (2)	1.0 (2)	100

G. Religiosity	94.6 (192)	6.5 (7)	1.0 (2)	1.0 (2)	100
H. Israel	93.6 (190)	6.4 (13)		(2)	100
I. General Jewish identification	65.5 (133)	34.0 (69)		0.5 (1)	100
J. Other (political attitudes) unspecified	91.6 (186)	2.0 (4)	3.0 (6)	3.11 (7)	100
Total		(187)	(175)	(54)	

Note: The 203 respondents reported 416 effects. Any respondent could report more than one effect. Percentages are calculated within each category.

Source: Sigal & Weinfeld 1987.

7. "MuBwith Jewish community and traditions. My sensitivity to people was an outgrowth of the discussion and experiences in the household, relating to the Holocaust."

Table 5.4 presents the coded data for the respondents. The list of coded categories for respondents and their parents is almost identical, the only difference being that responses in the categories Physical Health and Adaptation to Canada (Table 4.6, rows A and H, respectively) for the parental effects were not found in their children.

Significantly fewer respondents reported specific psychological symptoms for themselves than for their parents ($p < .001$), and marginally more reported more positive effects for themselves ($p < .10$).

Discussion

The direct relationship between our respondents' reports of increased exposure to the Holocaust (COS < COI < CON) and reports of being affected by it (Table 4.5) argues for the credibility of our findings for survivors and their children. As one might expect, an increasing percentage of the respondents replied affirmatively when asked if their parents were affected by the events of World War II as one moves from CON to COI to COS. The same occurred in responses to the question concerning the effects of the parents' experiences on the respondents.

Any inferences we make concerning the transmission of the impact of the parents' experiences to the second generation is based on the assumption that it is primarily via the parents that the respondents were affected by World War II. This is not an unreasonable assumption, given that all our respondents were born after 1945, the overwhelming majority in Canada or the United States. (Any possible impacts of schools, other relatives, or the community at large are not considered by this assumption.)

Most striking is the fact that although some 65% of the respondents reported that at least one parent had specific symptoms of a psychological nature deriving from World War II, markedly fewer—some 20%—reported that they were so affected. On the other hand, they reported marginally more positive effects for themselves, principally in the area of general mental health and, consistent with the findings of others (Heller 1982; Klein 1973; Pilcz 1975), also in the areas of Jewish identification and familial attitudes (Table 5.4, column 1).

Three interpretations for the significant reduction in negative psychological consequences from one generation to the next might be entertained. One is that respondents are less likely to reveal negative psychological traits about themselves than about their parents, particularly in a face-to-face interview. The second is that they may have exaggerated the psychological problems of their parents. The third is that their parents did indeed experience more effects of the Holocaust of all types, particularly negative symptomatology, but these have not reappeared to the same degree among the second generation.

While the first two hypotheses are tenable, our findings (reported in Chapter 3 and earlier in this chapter) and other research reports based on randomly selected community samples (Levav & Abramson 1984) clearly favor the third interpretation; as a group the parents are impaired. Our respondents' responses to standardized and other questionnaires suggest that they do not have more psychological difficulties than adult children of native-born parents.

It should be noted that our questions that elicited these negative effects focused on the effects of the events of World War II. It is possible that respondents refrained from revealing other negative traits or symptoms because they were not associated in their minds with those events. One might, therefore, argue that the responses analyzed here represented a partial inventory of psychological impairment—that portion which the respondents associated with the Holocaust. However, our data on family relations and the various indices of psychological well-being do not support this hypothesis; the levels of mental health in the children of survivors fell within normal limits.

ARE CHILDREN OF SURVIVORS EMOTIONALLY DISTURBED?

The vast array of familial, attitudinal, affective, and personality variables we have examined so far has failed to reveal any meaningful differences between COS and the comparison groups. Consistent with this finding is the fact that about the same percentage of COS (25.7%) as those in the comparison groups (33.8% and 36.2% of the COI and CON, respectively) said that they had seen a professional person "for help with an emotional problem or for [their] nerves" at some time in their lives. (The differences between the groups is not statistically significant.) Among those respondents who did seek help, a higher percentage of COS than CON sought help for marital problems (33.3% vs. 18.3%). The fact that about the same percentage of COI (32.0%) as COS sought help for marital problems suggests that this may be a distinguishing feature of children of immigrant Jews, not of children of survivors.

Why the discrepancy between our findings and those of earlier studies? Our data permitted us to examine several possible explanations. All of them can be subsumed under the rubric of the assumption of heterogeneity— whether it is heterogeneity of the parents' persecution experience; heterogeneity of survivors' personalities; heterogeneity of relationships between the parent survivors and with their children; or heterogeneity in the way in which the parents communicated their persecution experiences to their children. We shall examine each of these assumptions in turn for their ability to explain the discrepancies between our findings and the earlier clinical and anecdotal reports and some of the other research findings.

Since much of the clinical literature focuses on children of parents who were in the concentration camps, we will first examine our data to determine if they had greater problems in the control of aggression, even though we were not able to find an excess of problems in this area for COS in general.

Then we will determine if any of the background variables described above discriminated between those COS who said that they had sought professional help for an emotional problem or a problem with nerves and those who did not.

Children of Concentration Camp Survivors (COCCS)

We have defined survivors in the broadest terms: as all those who were subjected to the Nazi persecution. Some studies have limited themselves to concentration camp survivors and their children. One set of investigators failed to find differences between COCCS and comparison groups on any personality measures in a nonclinic population (Leon, Butcher, Kleinman, Goldberg, & Almagor 1981). Nadler, Kav-Venaki, & Gleitman (1985), however, using Rosenzweig's Projective Test of Reaction to Frustration, found evidence for a lesser degree of externalization regression and a greater degree of guilt among COCCS than in a control group, and COCCS tended to report more guilt ($p < .06$) on a questionnaire in another study (Weiss, O'Connell, & Siiter 1986).

In these studies, subjects were of approximately the same ages as ours—young adults. But the parents in the Nadler et al. (1985) study were much more homogeneous with respect to their experience of the Nazi persecution. They were all in Nazi concentration camps for at least six months, whereas at least one parent in the other two studies could have been in any of a variety of situations, including concentration camps, labor camps, in hiding, or in partisan groups. Since the potential negative consequences of externalization of aggression were generally much more immediate and visible in the concentration camps than in the other contexts, survivor parents may continue to be wary of overt expression of their aggression and foster the same attitude in their children. On the other hand, the study by Nadler et al. (1985) and the other two studies (Leon et al. 1981; Weiss et al. 1986) were based on very small, potentially biased samples, so generalization from them is problematic.

We used data from our community sample, which happens to be in the same age range as that of Nadler et al., to examine the issue. As in Nadler et al.'s study, the parents of the COCCS group in the present study were in concentration camps for at least six months, but we chose respondents from our sample of COS whose two parents were concentration camp survivors. We thereby reduced the possible confounding or mitigating effect of the experience of the other parent. We were able to obtain 40 such COCCS (mean age = 29.4, s.d. = 5.06). Like Nadler et al., we had a control group of children from families in which both parents were natives of the countries that were occupied by the Nazis during World War II, but who came to Canada prior to the occupation (COI; N = 39, mean age = 33.9, s.d. = 3.26). Our CON served as the second control group. The PERI scales used in our study of COS were used for the present analysis as well.

Findings. Two-way (group × sex), age-controlled ANCOVAs revealed only one significant group difference in the six tests—on Rigidity ($p < .04$). Post-hoc analysis using Scheffé's test failed to reveal a difference between the adjusted means of the COCCS and each of the comparison groups. The only significant difference found was between the COI and CON ($p < .05$).

Discussion. There are five essential differences between our method and that used by Nadler et al. (1985): sample selection; sample composition; sample size; sociopolitical context; and measures.

By sampling criteria alone, our findings are more valid than those of Nadler et al. for the following reasons:

1. We used random sampling methods in the general community; they used a referral-by-friends method for some of their subjects, but did not say how they obtained the rest of their sample. Their entire sample consisted of university students.
2. Our sample of COCCS was fourfold larger than theirs, and our comparison groups were, respectively, approximately 50% and 100% larger.
3. In our index sample both parents were concentration camp survivors; in theirs, this was so for only two of their index subjects.

The fact that Nadler et al. (1985) conducted their study in Israel, and we in Canada, suggests one possible source of the difference between our respective findings. It is likely that all of their subjects had completed the two or three years of military service that are compulsory for female and male Israelis. Some may even have been in combat. All certainly lived in an environment in which there is a continual awareness of the possibility of war. None of our subjects had such experiences. This sociopolitical difference may have interacted with the effects of the parents' wartime experiences to produce the difference in the two sets of findings.

The two studies employed different measures. Nadler et al. used responses to a projective test and to a set of open-ended questions that were rated by judges to determine the degree to which their subjects externalized aggression. In contrast, we used subjects' self-reports (given on Likert-type scales) to the kinds of questions clinicians might ask when attempting to determine problems in the control of aggression and their consequences. Even if the findings of Nadler et al. were confirmed in an equivalent community-based sample in Canada, one might, therefore, at most conclude that COCCS externalize aggression in *fantasy* less than do control groups. Our data would suggest that these fantasies are not of sufficient intensity to challenge the respondents' defenses to the point of creating problems in the control of aggression, excessive guilt, or self-esteem.

Similarly, in Israel, if the PERI subscales were to reveal problems in the control of aggression, and the findings of Nadler et al. were confirmed in a probability sample, the statement that COCCS have problems in the control of aggression would still be imprecise unless it specified the socio-political context.

The arguments advanced above concerning the comparative merits of the sampling procedure and sample size and composition suggest that our findings are more generalizable than those of Weiss et al. as well.

The contention that the community of young adult COCCS have problems in the control of aggression is not supported by current evidence. So this variable does not explain the discrepancy between our findings and the clinical and anecdotal literature.

Correlates of Heterogeneity in Parents' Personalities

In Chapter 4 we confirmed the existence of four distinguishable personality factors among survivors: the schizoid (Numb), the paranoid (Victim), the depressive/masochistic (Victim/Numb), and the Type A/normal aggressive personalities (Fighter), to use the labels given by our psychiatrist raters (Danieli's labels in parentheses). Is it possible that one type of parental personality in a survivor is more likely to result in tensions and emotional problems in the offspring than another? If this were found to be so, it would be reasonable to speculate that clinicians were basing their reports on one or more unrepresentative types of COS.

We used one-way ANOVAs to compare the factor scores of the parents of those 61 COS who sought help for emotional problems or distress with those who did not on each of the parental personality factors.

Table 5.5 shows the means and standard deviations of the factor scores on each of the parental personality factors for the two groups of COS. F-tests revealed that the fathers of the COS who sought professional help for their personal problems scored significantly higher on the factors labeled schizoid personality (Numb) ($p < .05$) and paranoid personality (Victim) ($F = 4.083$, d.f. $= 1.226$, $p < .05$). The mothers scored significantly higher on the factors labeled schizoid personality (Numb) ($p < .007$), paranoid personality (Victim) ($p < .05$), and depressive/masochistic pesonality (Victim/Numb) ($p < .004$).

The parents' personality, therefore, did play a role in determining the respondents' help-seeking behavior, and the types of personalities that played such a role overlapped, but were not identical, for the mothers and fathers of the COS.

Correlaters of Heterogeneity in Parents' Persecution Experience

There are some suggestions from the present study and that of others (Klein, Zellermayer, & Shanan 1963) that although survivors as a whole were exposed to severe, prolonged stress, some situations were more stressful than others. This differential stress could have a differential effect on the parents and, in turn, on the children. We therefore used chi-squares to test our data for evidence that those COS who sought professional help for emotional problems were more likely to have had two parents who had been subjected to the more stressful of the wartime experiences—for example, being in a concentration camp or in hiding in contrast with being in a ghetto or in the partisans.

For purposes of this analysis, we used only famiiles in which both parents were in the specified situation. There were fewer than five families in which both parents were primarily in a ghetto, so we did not include them in the analysis. Of the remainder, 27% (out of 37), 57.9% (out of 19), and 21.1% (out of 133) COS with two parents who had been in hiding, in the resistance, or in the concentration camps, respectively, had sought professional help. The difference is highly significant ($p < .001$); inspection of the above results makes it apparent that children with two parents who had been in the resistance were overrepresented among those seeking help. This finding, though unexpected, is consistent with the findings of the preceding analysis, because those in the resistance had higher scores on the paranoid and depressed/masochistic factors than those who had been in hiding or in concentration camps (see Chapter 4, section "Individual Differences Among Survivors"). We have now established a second possible explanation for the difference between our findings and those of previous reports; the persecution experienced by the parents of those seeking help may differ from that of the parents of the COS who did not seek help.

Correlates of Heterogeneity in Relationship Between the Parents

The nature of the parents' relationship to each other is a third possible explanation of the discrepancy. A poor relationship between parents is known to give rise to psychological problems in children (Rutter & Madge 1976 review this literature). Did our group of COS who sought professional help for emotional problems have parents with a poorer relationship to each other than the COS who did not?

Table 5.5

Means and Standard Deviations of Personality Factor Scores of Survivor Parents Whose Children Did and Did Not Seek Professional Help for Personal Problems, by Parental Personality Type

Parental Personality	Fathers		Mothers	
	Child Sought Help	Child Did Not	Child Sought Help	Child Did Not
I Schizoid (Numb)				
M	3.186	2.639	2.083	1.538
SD	2.004	1.778	1.510	1.264
II Paranoid (Victim)				
M	2.103	1.553	2.186	1.622
SD	2.125	1.664	2.129	1.700
III Depressive/Masochistic (Victim/Numb)				
M	3.172	2.765	4.649	3.563
SD	2.528	2.414	2.453	2.458

IV Type A/Normal Aggressive

(Fighter/Those Who Made It)

M	4.321	3.935	3.692	4.000
SD	2.643	2.462	2.201	2.332

Note: N = 61 for those who did seek help and 176 for those who did not. ANCOVAS revealed F's of fathers of those who sought help scored significantly higher on factors I and II at the .05 level, and mothers on factors I at the .001 level, II at the .05 level, and III at the .004 level.

117

To answer this question we used one-way ANOVAs to compare the responses of the same two sets of COS as in the previous analysis to the questions "How would you describe the relationship between your parents when you were growing up?" and "How would you describe the relationship between your parents now?" Responses were on a five-point scale ranging from "Exceptionally good" (scored 1) to "Exceptionally poor" (scored 5).

The mean ratings of their parents' relationship in the past and the present was better-than-average for both groups. For the past, the means (s.d.) were 2.54 (1.150) and 2.16 (1.000), respectively, for the COS who sought professional help and those who did not. For the present, they were 2.44 (1.235) and 2.08 (1.038), respectively. One-way ANOVAs revealed that those who sought help perceived their parents to have had a poorer relationship than those who did not, both at the time of the interview (in the present) and in the past ($p < .06$ in the present, and $p < .02$ in the past). Clinicians' reports are, therefore, likely to be based on material from COS whose parents were in conflict, and not be applicable to COS from harmonious families.

Correlates of Heterogeneity in Relationship with the Parents

A troubled relationship with the parents could also lead to the child's being emotionally troubled or feeling stressed.

We used a 2 × 2 two-way (group × parent) ANOVA to compare those who sought treatment and those who did not on the following questions: "How would you describe your relation with your mother now?" and "How would you describe your relationship with your father now?" Responses were on the same five-point scale. After each question we asked the respondent if there was a time when the relationship was different. If he or she answered Yes, the interviewer asked when and in what way it was different. The responses were recorded verbatim and coded subsequently.

The mean scores of the two groups were well within the range of favorable relationships with both their mothers and their fathers: mean (s.d.) for mothers 2.071 (0.970) and 1.772 (0.782), respectively, and for fathers 2.255 (1.260) and 1.844 (0.833), respectively. Even within this limited range, the ANOVAs revealed that those COS who sought professional help reported significantly poorer relationships with their parents currently than those who did not, and that it was not different in the past with their mothers: $p < .03$ and $p < .01$, for the current relationship to mothers and fathers, respectively; $p =$ n.s. for their relationship with their mothers in the past compared with the present; and $p < .01$ for their fathers. Seventy-two percent indicated that the relationship was worse with their fathers in the past, and 18% that it was better. The change in the relationship did not predict whether the respondent sought professional help.

The clinical literature suggests that parents' silence about their experiences during the Holocaust can have negative psychological repercussions on the children (Axelrod, Schnipper, & Rau 1980; Gampel 1982; Kleinplatz 1980). Our own observations suggest that parents' incessant referral to these experiences may have similarly detrimental effects. Accordingly, we cross-tallied the reports of relative silence and the opposite with whether the COS had sought professional help. The categories used for the former variable were "Silence or Little Talk" and "Much or Endless Talk."

The cross-tallies revealed that among those COS who reported having sought professional help, 20% (out of 20) reported their mothers were completely silent or talked little about their experiences during World War II, and 33.3% (out of 21) reported this for their fathers. The equivalent percentages for much or endless talk were 37.5% and 47.0% for mothers and fathers, respectively. Parents' talking a great deal or endlessly about their experiences during World War II appears to result in more stress for their children, but a chi-square test revealed no difference between the two degrees of parental communiction and the COS seeking professional help.

The type of relationship that COS have with their parents could explain the discrepancy between our findings and those of others, but the parents' openness about their wartime experiences does not.

Discussion

We are now in a position to suggest a possible explanation for the discrepancy between the clinical and anecdotal reports of considerable psychopathology among COS and our failure to find evidence for it. In the light of the findings reported in this section, it appears likely that clinicians' observations may be accurate, but only insofar as they apply to some of those COS who come from families in which the relationship is poor between them and their parents, and between their parents. We can even specify the personality of the parents of the COS on whom the clinical and anecdotal observations are probably based. The father is likely to be distant or suspicious, or the mother is likely to be distant, suspicious, or anxious and depressed.

On the basis of our findings in the previous sections of this chapter, we might conclude that the clinical and anecdotal reports, and those studies in which COS were found to be psychologically impaired, derive from children of these families. Because the design of our study did not permit us to determine the scores on each of the personality factors that would detect significant psychopathology in the parents, we are not able to say what percentage of families is involved. Our not finding evidence for greater psychopathology in the COS group as a whole, however, suggests that the generalization from those who do seek help to those who do not is not justified.

OCCUPATIONAL AND EDUCATIONAL ACHIEVEMENT

We wished to explore whether COS have lower levels of educational and occupational achievement because of their parents' experiences. This might have arisen because of the lower postwar occupational status of the survivor parents themselves, or because the burden of the parents' impairment might have resulted in a family environment that was inimical to the development of good coping skills in the children.

Holocaust survivors faced a dual set of problems in establishing themselves in the New World. One was the difficulty facing any impoverished immigrant group forced to adapt to a new society, language, and work environment. The second was the set of burdens of the Holocaust trauma, with its documented toll on the physical and mental health of survivors (see Chapter 2, section "Long Term Effects: The Survivors," and Chapter 4, section "Psychological and Physical Status"). Evidence from the few non-clinical studies that have been done suggests that these effects may have led to slightly lower levels of occupational status and/or income for Jewish and non-Jewish survivor families (Eitinger & Strøm 1973; Chapter 4, section "Economic and Social Adaptation"). These findings are inconsistent with journalistic accounts that report economic—usually entrepreneurial—success for some survivor families (Epstein 1979; Rabinowitz 1976).

Studies of status attainment have highlighted the role of class background of the parents and social psychological factors in influencing achievement. Even controlling for social class, we know that cognitive abilities, and noncognitive personality traits such as aspirations, self confidence, and self esteem, influence an individual's achievement (Jencks et al. 1972). Canadian research has led to similar findings, including the importance of significant others, especially parents, in influencing educational and career choices (Porter, Porter, & Blishen 1982). Our studies have noted the importance of a stable and tranquil home environment for children's success in school (Rutter & Madge 1976).

What of the psychological climate in survivor households? We have already summarized the clinical reports of pressures from survivor parents for the achievement of their children, often as a compensation for the privation experienced by the parents during the war. Tied to this are reports of parental sacrifices to facilitate their children's achievements, which may be associated with subsequent guilt feelings in the children (see Chapter 3, section "The Second-Generation Study"). On the other hand, one might hypothesize that excessive parental pressure to achieve, as well as any other patterns of parental preoccupation or strained relations deriving from the Holocaust, might prove counterproductive in creating a domestic environment supportive of achievement.

Another issue of some interest is the question of whether COS may be drawn to certain types of occuptions more than to others. At gatherings of survivors and their children one routinely encounters the suggestion that COS are overrepresented in the "helping professions," such as medicine, teaching, or social work.

We might indicate at this point that the extensive literature that has focused on explaining Jewish educational and occupational achievement in relation to other groups is tangential to our interest here (Glazer 1958; Rosen 1959; Slater 1969). Our concern is with variations within our group of Jewish respondents that might be explained by the trauma experienced by their parents.

Measures

Occupational status was measured by the Blishen index, computed on the basis of 1971 census data for Canada (Blishen & McRoberts 1976). The index is derived from equations linking average income and educational levels associated with given occupations. Respondents identified their occupation and that of their parents, and these occupations were assigned the appropriate Blishen scores. Educational achievement was measured by the response to the question "What is the highest level of education you [or your father, mother] have completed?" Response categories were none, elementary/primary, secondary/high school, post high school/junior college, bachelor's, master's, doctorate, and professional degree.

Findings

Table 5.6 presents the educational attainment levels for our three groups of respondents. Note that 62% of the COS claim at least a bachelor's degree, compared with 47.4% of the COI and 55.5% of the CON. Indeed, the COS and CON distributions are similar, with the smaller COI group having lower levels of educational achievement. There is a marginally significant difference among the groups ($p < .06$), but it is clear that all three subgroups of the sample represent an educated, middle-class group.

We compared the 75 respondents who were still studying at some level and who reported on their future occupational choices. The 33 COS among them appeared to have much higher expectations than the controls, but the difference is not statistically significant.

Table 5.7 presents a distribution of Blishen occupation ranks for the three groups. There is no difference among them.

Table 5.8 presents the distributions of the Blishen rank of the respondents' fathers' first and current occupations. COS and COI fathers are far more likely to be concentraterd in the lower economic status levels. This is to be expected, given the educational differences noted earlier.

We might note that for the sample as a whole, the general process of

Table 5.6

Respondents' Education by Group (percentage at each educational level)

Rank	COS N = 242	COI N = 76	CON N = 209	Row Total N = 527
Elementary– Primary	1.7	2.6	1.4	1.7
Secondary– High School	10.7	26.3	15.8	15.0
Post High School– CEGEP	25.2	23.7	27.3	25.8
Bachelor's or Equivalent	47.1	26.3	44.0	42.9
Master's or Equivalent	9.1	14.5	7.7	9.3
Doctorate or Equivalent	5.4	5.3	3.8	4.7
Professional Degree	0.4	1.3	0.0	0.4
Other	0.4	0.0	0.0	0.2
	100.0	100.0	100.0	100.0
N	242	76	209	527

Note: Chi square is significant at the .06 level for the three groups.

Source: Weinfeld & Sigal 1985.

status attainment varies from what we have come to expect based on other studies in the Blau-Duncan (1967) tradition. We found a negligible impact of parental socioeconomic status (fathers' education and occupation) on educational and occupational achievements of the children, evident from a pattern of low and generally insignificant correlation coefficients (not reproduced here). These findings contradict those usually reported in stratification studies. It may be that for North American Jews, variance in cognitive skills, culturally related noncognitive personality traits, and aspirations that affect social mobility may be independent of parental social class.

The absence of any observable effects of the Holocaust on respondents' occupational and educational achievements was confirmed in two additional

Table 5.7
Respondents' Present Occupation by Group (percentages at each occupational level)

Rank[a]	COS	COI	CON	Row Total
	N = 198	N = 63	N = 162	N = 423
2	2.0	1.6	1.2	1.7
3	3.0	3.2	2.5	2.8
4	10.6	15.8	12.3	12.1
5	26.3	28.6	27.2	27.0
6	42.4	36.5	45.7	42.7
7	15.7	14.3	11.1	13.7
	100.0	100.0	100.0	100.0

[a]Occupational rank is for current or, if unemployed, last full time occupation ranked on Blishen's scale (Blishen & McRoberts 1976). Chi square is not significant.

Source: Weinfeld & Sigal 1985.

ways. A multiple-regression analysis in which parental status as COS or COI was a dummy variable revealed no effects, controlling for age, sex, and parental socioeconomic status.

A second confirmation was obtained by a within-group analysis. In an open-ended question, respondents had been asked whether and how their parents had been affected by World War II, and the responses were coded and classified. Among the categories that emerged were two that measured general personality traits and psychological symptoms, positive and negative (Chapter 4, section "Adult Children's Perception of Their Survivor Parents"). COS respondents were divided into two groups, those reporting that their parents had negative personality or psychological effects, and those who did not. These groups were compared for the same set of parental and respondent socioeconomic status variables (education and occupation). No differences were found on any of the measures.

There were also no differences among the three groups in the percentage who were in the helping professions (21.5%, 18.4%, and 15.8% in the COS, COI, and CON groups, respectively). Included in this group were such occupations as physician, teacher, nurse, social worker, occupational therapist, and psychologist.

Table 5.8
Fathers' Occupational History by Group (percentage at each occupational level)

Occupational Rank[a]	Occupation in Europe[b]	First Occupation in Canada[c]				Present or Last Full Time Occupation in Canada[c]			
		COS	COI	CON	Total	COS	COI	CON	Total
1	3.2	0.9	2.8	2.3	1.7	0.4	0.0	0.0	0.2
2	46.2	53.2	48.6	30.5	44.2	26.0	25.3	6.8	18.0
3	12.4	22.1	22.2	20.9	21.7	7.2	8.5	4.4	6.3
4	18.3	10.8	12.5	18.6	14.0	11.9	19.7	14.6	14.1
5	8.6	5.6	4.2	10.2	7.1	11.9	8.5	16.5	13.3
6	8.6	7.0	6.9	11.3	8.5	41.3	33.8	49.0	43.4
7	2.7	0.4	2.8	6.2	2.8	1.3	4.2	8.7	4.7
	100.0	100.0	100.0	100.0	100.0	100.0	100.0	100.0	100.0
N	186	231	72	177	480	235	71	206	512

[a]Occupational rank is for current or, if unemployed, last full time occupation ranked. Ranking is that used by the Canadian Census; higher numbers represent more prestigious occupations.
[b]For fathers of COS only.
[c]Chi square for the three groups is statistically significant at the .001 level, but is not significant between fathers of COS and COI.

Source: Weinfeld & Sigal 1985.

Discussion

Nonclinical studies of survivors have noted higher rates of mortality, morbidity, and mental stress, and clinical studies have documented episodes of parent–child tensions. Yet our findings suggest that these effects may have been compartmentalized sufficiently by the victims or by their children so as not to lead to negative outcomes for the offspring's achievement. Indeed, it seems that COS respondents have eliminated in one generation the socioeconomic deficits that characterized their parents' condition. This is even more remarkable for the COS, given the expectation of the additional psychological burdens that might affect the family environment.

One might even speculate as to whether some traits associated with survivor families might be beneficial to the achievement process. We know from Table 5.8 that 80% (186/242) of COS fathers were identified as having had a full-time occupation prior to arrival in North America. Comparing this occupational distribution with that for fathers' first and current job in North America, we note that the survivors, like many postwar immigrants to Canada, may have experienced an initial drop in occupational status on arrival, which was recouped steadily with the passage of time (Richmond 1967). They demonstrated substantial occupational mobility. Even though this group of fathers remained below CON fathers for their last or current job, they, like the COI fathers, made substantial progress in an absolute sense. One might argue that some of the qualities of perseverance, pluck, and luck that enabled COS fathers to survive the war may have continued to affect the quality of their family life, including attitudes transmitted to children. Indeed, these qualities may be typical, to some degree, of the general immigrant population. Our findings do not support clinical observations and anecdotal reports; we found no evidence that COS parents used pressure or other psychological ploys to produce greater achievement in their offspring, compensating for their lower socioeconomic status.

One area in which significant differences were found between COS respondents and both control groups was in the level of Jewish education and religiosity. COS respondents and their parents had received more Jewish schooling (more intensive types and for longer periods of time) and were more religious, as measured in frequency of synagogue attendance. COS reported 34% of their fathers with at least ten years of Jewish education and 38% with frequent (at least all major holidays and most Sabbaths) attendance at services, compared with 10% and 21% for CON parents. These same "more religious" COS, however, compared well with the CON on our measures of achievement.

At first glance, this finding appears puzzling, since we would expect to find religiosity to be negatively associated with educational and occupational achievement. This has long been the conventional wisdom of American Jewish sociology, based on the fact that Reform Jews have higher levels of socioeconomic status than do the Orthodox (Sklare 1958). Yet recent studies suggest that this gap may be declining for Jews, particularly among the "modern" Orthodox (Cohen 1983, pp. 87–92). A study of American Catholics even found that those with more Catholic education did better socioeconomically than those with less (Greeley & Rossi 1966). Thus, the relation between religiosity and economic achievement may be changing.

In this study, it is possible that religion may provide a familial anchor for survivor families that enables them to cope more effectively with the trauma of their Holocaust experience, helping create a stable home environment for the effective nurturance of children.

Alternative explanations for the unexpected achievement of the COS and COI relative to their parents are possible. A macrohistorical perspective would frame the issue differently. Much of the observed gap in parental status between COS (and COI) and CON can be attributed simply to the relative—though far from absolute—economic freedom in the New World compared with the Old.

Most of the COS and COI parents lived in the strongly anti-Semitic Eastern European countries during the prewar period, which artificially restricted the opportunities available to Jews relative to their talents and drive. These barriers were dramatically reinforced by the Holocaust itself, which for many refugees resulted in stunted or abandoned education and careers. Emigration to the comparative freedom of North America, where in the postwar years demand for labor was great and entrepreneurial effort could be rewarded, yielded opportunities. The effects of this economic freedom began to operate for COS and COI parents and were realized more fully for COS and COI themselves.

The impact of economic opportunity may have swamped any residual effects of parental trauma on the economic achievement of their children. Thus the apparent intergenerational mobility demonstrated by our COS, as by our COI, may be due more to increased opportunities in an open social structure than to microsociological, individual traits.

Other historical evidence suggests that the fact of persecution need not inevitably lead to educational or occupational failure. Pariah groups such as Jews, Parsees, and Chinese have often been victimized politically or socially while achieving high socioeconomic status. The causal nexus can run both ways: minorities may be resented and victimized because of their economic success, or minorities may be economically successful because discrimination either pushes them into a lucrative economic niche (such as the middleman minority) or prods them to harder effort (Bonacich 1973; Light 1972).

The case of Japanese Canadians interned during the 1940s also provides support for our findings. The material and psychological distress caused to those who were forcibly resettled has been well documented (Adachi 1976). Yet the children of many of these Japanese Canadians have been able to prosper despite the suffering of their parents; the 1971 census reveals that Japanese Canadians had average annual incomes well above the national average (Li 1980, p. 365).

KNOWLEDGE OF THE HOLOCAUST

This section focuses on the impact of the Holocaust on adult COS in the cognitive/attitudinal domain. This is an area of inquiry that even clinical studies, with their focus on psychological and social adjustment, have neglected. Yet, as we shall see, our study may provide insight into more general processes, such as socialization and information seeking.

In popular discourse we use phrases like "history repeats itself" to paraphrase Santayana's dictum that those who do not learn from the mistakes of history are doomed to repeat them. Such phrases imply that there are lessons of history, and that they are not usually learned. The school plays a role here, of course. The history curriculum attempts to impart historical information and interpretation. But what role does the family play as a direct or indirect educative institution? To what extent, and how, do families transmit knowledge of their experiences during events of historical consequence to the next generation?

One element in such investigation is the cognitive one. Do children of parents who have experienced such events know more about those events than those who have not? How do they gain information about those events? Do they claim that they or their parents are particularly affected by them?

The issues explored here can be situated within two research contexts. The first is the study of ethnic relations. The second is the largely sociological study of intergenerational socialization, with particular emphasis on the role of the family as an agent of socialization and of the transmission of historical knowledge.

The history of interethnic relations has been largely a history of conflict, and thus of victimization. At any given point in time, relations between two ethnic groups, or self-perceptions by members of a group, are a product of two forces: the actual conditions affecting the group or groups, and the historical (perhaps ideological) legacy affecting each group. This historical legacy is shaped by factual or symbolic cognitive elements, which are internalized. These factors explain why any attempt to understand either intergroup relations in Canada or any multiethnic society, or any ethnic group's self-identification, cannot concern itself only with the current social conditions affecting the group, but must deal with people's knowledge of their collective past.

There are relatively few studies of the determinants of general or historical knowledge. The basic findings of a comprehensive review of U.S. and Canadian sample surveys of such knowledge stress the key and independent role of education (Hyman et al. 1975). That study did not examine the link between respondents' knowledge of recent history and parental experience and parent-child interaction.

Two studies on second-generation survivors did include questions of a cognitive nature. One study of undergraduate and graduate college students asked, "Are you familiar with the trial of Adolf Eichmann? Please write all that you know about the trial and related events" (Heller 1982, p. 251). Heller found no difference between children of concentration camp survivors and children of other immigrant Jews on this measure of Holocaust knowledge. By contrast, Klein and Last (1974), in a study of U.S. Jewish high school seniors, found children of survivors more knowledgeable about the war than controls. Both studies relied on small, nonrandom samples.

We explored whether being a COS, and other related variables, may affect information seeking and knowledge about the Holocaust. This can then introduce the broader question of the attitudinal legacy of the Holocaust for COS and the role of knowledge and familial socialization therein.

Measures

Our survey of COS and controls provided several measures relating to knowledge of and curiosity about the Holocaust. Objective knowledge about the Holocaust was measured by two short quizzes in the questionnaire. The first consisted of 20 items relating to World War II (HISTORY) that respondents were asked to identify briefly in a space of two lines. Interviewers recorded the verbatim replies. Scores of 0 were given for incorrect or omitted responses, scores of 1 for partially correct answers, and 2 for clearly correct responses. Total scores had a maximum range of 0 to 40. (Coders assigned the scores after completion of the questionnaire and were instructed to grade the answers rather leniently. Thus, for the item "Heinrich Himmler" a response of "a leading Nazi" was scored as 1 and "head of the Gestapo" as 2.) The reliabilities ranged from .72 to .85.

The second quiz was concerned more directly with the destruction of European Jewry, and specifically with familiarity with the names of major concentration camps (CAMPID). Ten names of camps or other European locations were listed, and respondents were asked to identify which were concentration camps. Correct responses (either a Yes or No) were given a score of 1, with the total score ranging from 0 to 10. The correlation between these two measures was 0.68. (Both quizzes are described in Appendix B.) Subjectively perceived effect of World War II (EFFWW2) was measured by asking respondents: 1. "Would you say that WWII had any lasting effects of any kind on your parents?" 2. "Do you think that you today are affected by your parents' experience during WWII?" Response categories were either Yes or No. The term "World War II" was used rather than "Holocaust," to extend applicability to all three sample groups in comparable fashion.

Information seeking was measured from both extrafamilial and intrafamilial sources. Questions measuring information seeking from extrafamilial sources were whether respondents had participated, and if so how often, in the following activities, within the past two years: attended any lecture, seminar, conference, or commemorative event dealing with the Holocaust; read any fiction or nonfiction books about the Holocaust; had ever attended a conference or group meeting dealing with children of Holocaust survivors; had watched any or all of the "Holocaust" TV series, and the made-for-TV film *Skokie*. (The film was based on the tensions that emerged when neo-Nazis planned a march through the Chicago suburb of Skokie, which has a large population of survivors of Nazi persecution.) An additive index of information seeking other than from television was created (INFOSK) with a range of 0 to 11, and was used in subsequent analysis.

Intrafamilial information seeking refers to the nature of communication between respondents and their parents concerning the events of World War II. One question asked whether respondents felt their father or mother had told them "too much, just enough, or too little" about the historical events that affected their lives. The second question was asked only of those respondents who claimed that World War II had had a lasting effect of any kind on their parents. Those answering Yes (see below) were asked, "What were these effects and how did you know about them?" in an open-ended question format. Among the response codes that emerged were items referring to the nature of verbal communication, and these were coded into three responses: much or endless talk; steady verbal communication, quality unspecified; and silence or little talk. The interrater reliability was 0.82. These questions were asked for both parents; responses for mothers and fathers were combined into one parental measure.

We tested for differences on the above variables between the COS and the two control groups.

Perceived Effects of World War II

We have already noted that COS differed dramatically from the controls in their perceptions of the effects of World War II on their parents, and of any effects on themselves of their parents' experiences during World War II. Thus, whether or not objective effects exist, and whatever their configuration, it seems clear that children of survivors believe strongly that they, and of course their parents, have had lasting effects stemming from the experiences of World War II.

Obviously, such responses tell us far more about the perceptions of respondents than about any actual effects of the Holocaust on their parents or themselves. Respondents may be unaware of effects, and even if they are aware, may choose to deny them.

Table 5.9
Knowledge of World War II Events, Prominent People, and
Concentration Camps

A. Overall World War II History Quiz (HISTORY)

Score	COS	COI	CON	All Groups
0-6	22.4%	27.7%	39.8%	30.0%
7-14	32.9	31.5	34.5	33.3
15-40	44.7	40.8	25.7	36.7
	100.0	100.0	100.0	100.0
N	242	76	209	527

B. Identification of Concentration Camps (CAMPID)

Score	COS	COI	CON	All Groups
0-3	16.9%	31.5%	35.9%	26.6%
4-6	37.6	38.2	39.7	38.6
7-10	45.5	30.3	24.4	34.8
	100.0	100.0	100.0	100.0
N	242	76	209	527

Note: Chi square is significant at the .01 level in A and B for the three groups and at the .01 level for the COS-COI comparison in B, but not significant for this comparison in A.

Source: Weinfeld & Sigal 1986a.

Knowledge About World War II

As seen in Table 5.9, COS were more informed about the details of World War II and the Holocaust than were the CON. While statistically significant ($p < .01$), the substantive differences were modest, less than one standard deviation. The mean scores were 14.02, 12.39, and 9.89 in the general history quiz and 5.95, 5.05, and 4.58 in the concentration camp quiz for the COS, COI, and CON, respectively.

The history quiz was perhaps more difficult than we had intended. Eight percent of the entire sample scored zero. In other words, these 42 people could not even minimally identify any of the test items. Only 23 respondents, 4.4% of the sample, scored 30 or above; the highest individual score was 37. Our pretest results had been slightly higher. The two most difficult questions were "Arthur Morse," author of *While Six Million Died* (97.3%

incorrect or blank), and "Munich 1938" (93.2%). The easiest item was "Eva Braun," with 69.6% giving a fully correct response. Our overall assessment is that the level of historical knowledge in our total sample of a relatively educated group of Jewish young adults must be considered low in absolute terms and certainly lower than we had expected.

On the concentration camp quiz a more even distribution was found, with 5.9% (30 resondents) scoring zero and 5.1% (27 respondents) scoring a perfect ten points. "Dachau" was the most correctly identified of the camps, by 86.7% of the 527 respondents.

Information Seeking. Table 5.10 presents the data concerning extrafamilial information seeking in some detail. We see that COS are more likely to attend lectures, read books, and attend meetings on Holocaust-related matters, but the difference between them and the critical comparison groups, the COI, is not statistically significant. What is intriguing is the sizable minority of respondents who are not themselves children of survivors, yet who are curious about the Holocaust. Over 11 percent of the respondents from both control groups together claim to have read at least four books relating to the Holocaust in the previous two years.

Montreal, in the years prior to the survey, had been the scene of several conferences dealing with COS. In addition, several groups of COS had been formed in the city and had been meeting on a regular or semiregular basis. We inquired about participation in such conferences and group meetings, which are common in other North American cities (see Table 5.10). The vast majority of COS and controls had attended no such gatherings. The reader will also note that substantial minorities from both control groups attended events devoted to children of the Holocaust. These findings suggest that Holocaust-related issues have an appeal that extends beyond the descendants of those who survived.

Some confirmation of this observation can be discovered from the data on the likelihood of having watched the two television shows dealing with the Holocaust. The TV series "Holocaust" was watched in its entirety by 55% of all the respondents, in part by 31%, and not at all by only 14%. The made-for-TV movie *Skokie* was watched in its entirety by 40%, in part by 12%, and not at all by 48%. There were no significant differences at all among our three groups for either TV program. This finding may not be surprising for "Holocaust," given the publicity and the high Nielsen ratings the show received. The film *Skokie* received far less publicity, and thus it was assumed that a greater effort might be required of persons to find out about and watch the film. But here, too, COS were no different in their viewing pattern.

The responses to the open-ended questions were coded into four major categories; the interrater reliabilities ranged from .73 to .83:

1. Personal compulsion or conviction based on principle ("The world should always remember these events"; "People should know what happened").

Table 5.10
Information–Seeking Behavior

	COS	COI	CON	All Groups
1. Lectures (past two years) number				
0	60.3%	72.0%	72.1%	66.7%
1	20.7	18.7	18.3	19.4
2	7.2	4.0	3.8	5.4
3+	11.8	5.3	5.8	8.5
	100.0	100.0	100.0	100.0
2. Books (past two years)				
0	41.8%	58.7%	55.6%	49.7%
1	14.6	13.3	13.1	13.1
2	14.6	6.7	12.9	12.9
3	9.6	6.7	9.2	9.2
4+	19.4	14.6	9.2	15.1
	100.0	100.0	100.0	100.0
3. Meetings				
0	85.0%	90.8%	89.4%	87.6%
1	8.3	3.9	8.2	7.6
2+	6.7	5.3	2.4	4.8
	100.0	100.0	100.0	100.0
N	240	76	208	524

Note: Chi squares for the three groups are significant at the .08 level and .05 level for Lectures and Books, respectively, and not significant for meetings. They are not significant for any of the COS–COI comparisons.

Source: Weinfeld & Sigal 1986a.

2. Personal conviction or compulsion based on personal, family, or Jewish experience ("I wanted to understand what my parents [relatives] went through").

3. Detached interests of an artistic, cultural, or aesthetic nature ("How would Hollywood treat this topic?" "Promised to be a quality production").

4. Circumstance ("Happened to be on TV when I began watching").

For each group of respondents, the major reasons for watching "Holocaust" were, first, detached artistic interest and, second, familial Jewish experience. Yet, there were meaningful differences in the relative weight given to each. Among COS, these two reasons were, respectively, cited by 48% and 43% of respondents, compared with 50% and 36% for COI and 60% and 25% for CON. Thus, the familial or Jewish connection was relatively more prevalent among COS ($p < .001$).

Those respondents who watched none or a part of the series were asked why they did not watch more of it. Again responses were coded into four general categories:

1. Refusal to watch on the basis of principle ("Hollywood trivializes everything").

2. Negative emotional affect ("Can't stand watching the suffering, get too depressed").

3. Not interested in the show ("Boring, slow").

4. Circumstance (no TV, exams conflicted, "Didn't know it was on").

Interestingly, there were no differences among the groups in the reasons for not watching. The major reason given by all three groups was circumstance. The factor of negative emotional affect was cited by roughly 30% of the respondents, with no differences across the groups. This finding is of interest, given the references in the clinical literature to difficulties (nightmares, negative symptomatology) experienced by some COS, stemming from the horror of their parents' wartime experience.

Communication with Parents. The COS were more likely than other groups to indicate that their parents had told them too little about their experiences during the war. This is puzzling, given that these respondents were those most informed about World War II, and were most likely to indicate that their parents and they themselves had been affected by that event. One possible interpretation is that in fact COS were told very little about their parents' pasts, compared with the controls. This would correspond to the clinical portrait of the silent, withdrawn survivor who does not talk about wartime and/or prewar experiences. Thus, the greater knowledge of COS

Table 5.11
Mean Scores on Information Seeking (INFOSK) and Knowledge of
Aspects of World War II History (CAMPID and HISTORY) Controlled
for Perceived Effect on Parental Experiences during World War II

Dependent Variable		COS Effect		COI Effect		CON Effect	
		1 No	2 Yes	3 No	4 Yes	5 No	6 Yes
A.	INFOSK	1.69	2.70	1.72 *	1.57	1.60	2.51
	N	(35)	(197)	(46)	(28)	(170)	(35)
B.	CAMPID	4.42	6.22	5.06 *	5.03	4.41	5.43
	N	(36)	(206)	(47)	(29)	(174)	(35)
C.	HISTORY	11.64	14.44	11.83	13.31	8.88	14.94
	N	(36)	(206)	(47)	(29)	(174)	(35)

Note: *t*-tests for differences of mean scores between and within groups are significant at the
.05 level for the following columns: 1 and 6, 2 and 5, 5 and 6, and 3 and 4C (World
War II history), with the exception of those designated by *, which are not statistically
significant.
Source: Weinfeld & Sigal 1986a.

would presumably be gained through books, school, or other sources.
Another, perhaps more plausible explanation, would be that the response
of "too little" should be interpreted relative to the greater knowledge (and
curiosity) of COS concerning their parents' pasts, compared to other
groups. Thus, it is possible that survivors told their children as much as—
or more than—other parents about their encounters with history, but that
for their children this was not enough and they would have preferred still
more.

Our second measure of the extent of communication with parents regarding effects of World War II was defined only for respondents who
claimed their parents had been affected, that is, primarily COS. Of the total
of 242 COS, 91 (37.6%) claimed that their mothers and 95 (39.3%) claimed
that their fathers had used verbal communication from which the children
based their inference of lasting effects. This verbal communication, reported
by approximately 38% of the respondents, consists essentially of stories
and anecdotes about wartime experiences. Only 14% of both control groups
together report similar parental communiction.

Table 5.11 summarizes the amount of information seeking and knowledge of the selected aspects of World War II history at controlled levels of the perceived effect of World War II on the parents.

For both COS and CON, those indicating they were affected by their parents' wartime experiences scored higher on the three outcome measures than did those claiming no such effects (columns 1 and 2, 5 and 6 of Table 5.11). For COI, this was the case only for the history variable (columns 3 and 4). Not surprisingly, COS who claimed these effects were far more curious and knowledgeable than CON who did not (columns 2 and 5 of Table 5.11). But being a child of a survivor was by no means a necessary condition for our respondents to display high degree of information seeking and knowledge. This is seen in columns 1 and 6 of Table 5.11. Native-born respondents who, somehow, came to perceive themselves as affected by the war scored high on these measures while unaffected COS scored lower.

Other findings based on correlational and regression analyses of the data (not presented) deserve brief comment. A pattern of sex differences was striking. For all respondents, despite the fact that women were more likely to indicate they had attended lectures and meetings, or read books on the Holocaust, men were far more informed, even controlling for their greater amounts of Judaic or secular education. This may be due to socialization patterns of men, in which exposure to war films or television programs about World War II, and reading about battles or military figures, may have indirectly provided them with more information about the war. Also noteworthy and expected was the positive association of level of secular education with level of knowledge, with other factors controlled.

Discussion

At the affective level we did find some evidence for an impact of the Nazi persecution on the second generation. The responses to our open-ended question suggested that the COS have a greater identification with the Jewish people and closer family ties, confirming Heller's (1982) findings.

The vast majority of the respondents in all our groups, on the other hand, had little or no knowledge of events relating to World War II. The pattern by sex for this variable is of some interest. Like Heller, we found that men were more likely to have a greater knowledge of these events. This may simply reflect men's greater interest in aggressive activities.

Our respondents' general lack of knowledge about events relating to the war suggests that three of the major agents of socialization—the family, the school, and the media—have failed to convey historical facts needed to avoid the errors of the past.

SOCIOPOLITICAL ATTITUDES

We now shift our attention to the relationship between a historical event experienced by one generation and the political attitudes and predispositions manifested by the adult children of that generation, born after the event. As we have noted, research on survivors of the Holocaust and their offspring is generally situated in the context of psychological and social adjustment, and has been overwhelmingly clinical, carried out by psychiatrists, psychologists, psychoanalysts, or social workers, with unrepresentative and/ or self-selected samples. Cognitive, intellectual, or normative consequences, particularly those with political ramifications, have not been studied for representative samples of survivor offspring. Research on the determinants of political values or behaviors of adults has emphasized both the role of the family as an agent of intergenerational transmission, and that of generational effects (zeitgeist) of the events experienced by the maturing generation. Discussions of the parental role in socialization do not usually refer to the parents' experience of major historical events, but to factors such as parental social class or political party preference. It is perhaps assumed that historical events either experienced by the parents directly or that occurred during their lifetimes would be in some way internalized, and their impact transmitted.

One of the first arguments for the role of the family in political socialization was that of Hyman (1959), supported subsequently by Acock and Bengston (1978), Bengston (1975), and Thomas (1971). The influence of familial socialization on a variety of dimensions was first examined by Cohen (1961) and Kohn (1969). The trend of more recent research has been to modify the view of the dominant role of the family (Beck 1977; Connell 1972; Jennings & Niemi 1968; Niemi, Ross, & Alexander 1978; Thomas 1974).

Political socialization entails a process of social learning, through which individuals acquire their values, standards, and views on public affairs (McClosky & Brill 1983, p. 28). Whether a person or group is likely to learn a certain set of political values or predispositions depends on exposure to those values, their comprehension, and their internalization (McClosky & Brill 1983, p. 29). Historical events may affect subsequent generations, either cognitively or noncognitively, being transmitted through the family or some other institutions that engage in teaching.

Every historical event has a universal message, and this is certainly true of the Holocaust. Yet it is interesting to determine whether children of those directly victimized by the Holocaust—the survivors—differ in political predispositions from other young Jews. This would be expected from the research on the family and political socialization, and the studies of survivor families.

Are the political attitudes of children colored by the historical events experienced by their parents? What are the effects of the parents' experience of the Nazi persecution on their children in this area? When we speak of the effects of the Holocaust, we mean effects as mediated through families of survivors as well as cognitive or moral impacts related to knowledge of the events. We would assume that those more affected by the Holocaust would be more opposed to fundamental tenets of Nazism, and thus more committed to principles of democracy and civil liberties, and more tolerant of minorities. Finally, we might presume that the COS, more than the others, might have a sense of indignation at the injustices suffered by their parents. As a result we would hypothesize that one effect on the COS would be greater sensitivity to injustices committed by the state against minorities and against Jews, and an advocacy by them of militant action to oppose those injustices, including militant defense of the state of Israel.

These hypotheses are intuitive and logical, and can be derived from the well-known avoidance learning paradigm of psychology. They are not based on previous empirical socialization studies, which have not addressed this issue. Our hypothesis is that former victims might have more compassion for other victims, and that victims (or descendants of victims) might undertake actions that would prevent a repetition of such episodes of victimization.

Such a hypothesis would apply to the Jewish case. There is a substantial literature on the issue of traditional Jewish political liberalism that relies on this assumption (Fuchs 1958). Certainly, Jewish religious sources link the commandment of compassion for all weak minorities to previous cases of Jewish victimization; note, for example, the biblical injunction to the Jews to be kind to strangers since they had once been strangers in Egypt. Jewish civil rights agencies (such as the Anti-Defamation League or the Canadian Jewish Congress) regularly justify their strong defense of civil rights for non-Jewish minorities with the argument that safeguarding the rights of all minorities enhances the democratic quality of the society, and thus safeguards the rights of Jews as well (Cohen 1983; Hertzberg 1979). And finally, the slogan "Never Again," and the publicized historical research and retrospective debates about the ineffectiveness of North American Jewry in defense of their European brethren during and before the war might suggest a commitment to greater militancy in the future (Abella & Troper 1983; Bauer 1976; Feingold 1970).

On the question of tolerance for minorities, and concern for their civil liberties, an alternative hypothesis is conceivable. Those more affected by the Holocaust and the isolation of the Jews in the face of the impending disaster might turn inward and become less concerned for the civil liberties of other groups. Such sentiments indeed exist among segments of the survivor groups. Yet this is not the position articulated by the major Jewish community organizations in North America, where concern for the civil rights of all minorities has featured prominently on their political agenda.

Dependent Variables

Six variables were studied as measures of sociopolitical attitudes:

1. Propensity for militant political action in opposition to anti-Semitic policies (MILJEW). This scale is based on the measure of the degree of political action, if any, respondents might take in opposition to both a hypothetical government restriction against the number of Jews in the civil service, and a government decision to stop the immigration of Jews to Canada. The Guttman-type scale ranged from signing a petition to armed resistance.

2. Support for Israel (ISRDEF). A measure of the degree of personal action that the respondent would take, and the governmental action the respondent would support for Canada, if Israel were invaded by enemy troops. For individual action, the options ranged from doing nothing to going to Israel to participate in the resistance; for Canadian action, the options ranged from neutrality to having Canada declare war and send troops to support Israel.

3. Commitment to civil liberties (CIVLIB). This is a modified verson of the Stouffer (1955) scale measuring whether individuals would allow a specific extremist or deviant person to speak, teach at a university, or have his or her book in the public library.

4. Propensity for militant political action in opposition to racist governmental policies directed at nonwhites (MILNONW). This scale is identical to MILJEW, except that "nonwhites" is substituted for "Jews" as the object of restrictive measures.

5. Racial tolerance (BLACKS). A measure of how respondents would feel if "a black family," and then "many black families," were to move onto their street, with response options varying from "very pleased" to "very displeased."

6. Attitudes on immigration and admission of refugees (IMMIG). Two questions, one asking whether Canada should permit more, fewer, or the same number of immigrants, and one whether Canada took in too many, too few, or the right number of Indo-Chinese refugees, were used to construct an index of pro-immigration and pro-refugee sentiment.

The measures MILJEW and ISRDEF are of a more particular, Jewish nature, while CIVLIB, MILNONW, BLACKS, and IMMIG are of a more universal nature. The first two reflect a commitment to vigorous Jewish self-defense. The last four measure the responses as to whether the impact of the Holocaust on respondents includes greater general commitment to civil liberties, to minority rights, and to tolerance, including their aggressive defense.

Explanatory Variables

Holocaust-Related Variables. The following served as independent variables:

1. A biological descent variable for being a child of at least one survivor of the Holocaust (COS) was coded as a dummy variable.

2. A set of cognitive-attitudinal variables including EFWW2, HISTORY, CAM-PID, and INFOSK, defined above.

In addition, respondents were asked an open-ended question designed to elicit their views directly as to whether the Holocaust is primarily an event of significance for Jews or for all humankind. Responses were coded into three categories: those seeing it as primarily a Jewish tragedy; those seeing it primarily as a general human tragedy; and those who answered both equally (HOLOVIEW). These categories were coded ordinally from 1 to 3, with 3 being the universal category. The reliability was 0.85.

Control Variables. The following served as control variables:

1. Sex of respondent (dummy variable) (SEX).

2. Highest level of secular education completed (EDUC), measured by level: none, elementary/primary, secondary/high school, post-high school/CEGEP, bachelor's, master's, doctorate.

3. Extent of formal Jewish education (JEDUC), measured in years of attendance at a Jewish school.

Findings

Table 5.12 shows the intercorrelations of all variables.

Particularistic Variables (MILJEW, ISRDEF). As shown in Table 5.13, we did find some significant differences among the three groups in terms of propensity to take militant action against governmental anti-Semitism (MILJEW) ($p < .05$) or in defense of Israel against invasion (ISRDEF) ($p < .05$). Certainly columns 1 and 8 suggest that children of survivors affected by their parents' experiences are likely to defend Jewish interests more vigorously than unaffected CON. The regression equation in Table 5.14 reveals a small but statistically significant effect of being a COS on ISRDEF. Yet, on balance, it would seem that being COS or even perceiving oneself as affected by parental wartime experiences (EFFWW2), neither of which has statistically significant Betas, is less important than the cognitive variables, all of which have significant Betas. We note from Table 5.14 that information seeking (INFOSK) and knowledge of World War II (HISTORY) have in four of four cases significant ($p < .01$), if modest, Betas. These findings reveal that claiming to be affected by the parents' experiences during World War II does not in itself determine the sociopolitical attitudes of the children. These attitudes are shaped insofar as they are mediated by information seeking about and knowledge of the events of World War II. Thus, those respondents who are more curious about the Holocaust, and know more about World War II (though not about concentration camps per se), are more militant in defense of Jewish interests.

All the cognitive Holocaust-related variables together—specifically

Table 5.12
Pearson Correlation Coefficients for Education, Religiosity, and Cognitive Variables

	INFOSK	SEX	COS	COI	EFFWW2	JEDUC	EDUC	HIST	CAMPID	RELIG	HOLO-VIEW	LIB	MIL-NONW	MILJEW	BLACKS	IMMIG	ISRDEF
INFOSK		-0.08	0.17*	0.19*	0.20*	0.10	0.36*	0.40*	0.20*	0.20*	-0.15	0.08	0.20*	0.23*	0.11	0.27*	0.21*
SEX			0.02	0.07	0.23*	0.30*	0.42	0.15*	-0.02	0.22*	-0.03	0.09	0.17**	0.07	0.10	0.10	0.12
COS				-0.38*	0.62*	0.20*	0.09	0.20*	0.23*	0.12	-0.07	0.02	0.04	-0.14	0.04	0.10	0.13
COI					-0.11	-0.03	-0.06	0.01	-0.03	-0.06	-0.01	0.01	-0.03	-0.10	0.01	0.00	-0.01
EFFWW2						0.13*	0.10	0.26*	0.27*	0.05	-0.03	0.03	0.11	0.15*	0.02	0.15	0.07
JEDUC							0.27*	0.29*	0.24*	0.46*	0.15	0.02	0.05	0.21*	-0.09	0.04	0.18
EDUC								0.38*	0.22*	0.07*	-0.03	0.27*	0.12	0.20	0.02	0.17*	0.12
HISTORY									0.68*	0.09	-0.04	0.34*	0.28*	0.28*	0.18*	0.39*	0.23*
CAMPID										0.17*	-0.12	0.17*	0.15*	0.21*	0.07	0.32*	0.19*
RELIG											-0.18*	-0.14	-0.06	0.08	-0.21*	0.00	0.27*
HOLOVIEW												0.01	0.09	-0.08	0.16*	0.06	-0.11
CIVLIB													0.20*	0.17*	0.13	0.20*	0.06
MILNONW														0.49*	0.28*	0.34*	0.19*
MILJEW															0.04	0.25*	0.40*
BLACKS																0.35*	-0.09
IMMIG																	0.15*

Note: N's for all correlations range between 496 and 527, except for those involving IMMIG, which range from 227 to 350.
*significant at the .01 level.
Source: Weinfeld & Sigal 1986b.

Table 5.13
Mean Scores of Sociopolitical Attitudes for Sample Groups and
Subgroups Controlled for Perceived Effect of Parental Experiences during
World War II

	Children of Survivors			Immigrant Controls			Native Controls		
	EFFWW2		ALL COS	EFFWW2		ALL COI	EFFWW2		ALL CON
Column Number	1	2	3	4	5	6	7	8	9
Dependent Variables	Yes	No		Yes	No		Yes	No	
A. CIVLIB	8.63	7.89	8.52	8.14	8.98	8.65	9.57	8.49	8.67
N	206	36		29	47		35	174	
B. MILNONW	6.16	6.06	6.15	6.34	5.12	5.59	8.06	5.41	5.86
N	206	36		29	47		35	174	
C. BLACKS	5.49	5.28	5.42	5.41	5.47	5.45	5.83	5.47	5.54
N	194	36		27	47		35	165	
D. IMMIG	4.64	4.42	4.61	4.63	4.41	4.49	4.79	4.18	4.30
N	150	24		19	34		24	99	

Table 5.13 (continued)

	Children of Survivors			Immigrant Controls			Native Controls		
	EFFWW2		ALL COS	EFFWW2		ALL COI	EFFWW2		ALL CON
Column Number	1	2	3	4	5	6	7	8	9
	Yes	No		Yes	No		Yes	No	
Dependent Variables									
E. MILJEW	11.51	10.58	11.38	10.03	9.63	9.79	11.69	10.21	10.46
N	206	36		29	47		35	174	
F. ISRDEF	5.50	5.75	5.53	5.28	5.28	5.27	5.09	5.10	5.10
N	206	36		29	47		35	174	

Note: EFFWW2 = respondent reports being affected by parents' experience during World War II. t-tests revealed the following difference between the means at the .05 level: B7-B8; D1-D8; D3-D9; D7-D8; E1-E6; E3-E9; E7-E8; F3-F9; F1-F8. B1-B8 is significant at the .10 level.

Source: Weinfeld & Sigal 1986b.

Table 5.14
Standardized Betas for Regression Equations

Dependent Variables	Respondent Group						Holocaust Cognitive Variables						Percentage Total R^2 Explained by	
	SEX	JEDUC	EDUC	RELIG	COI	COS	INFOSK	HIST	CAMPID	HOLO-VIEW	EFFWW2	R^2	Group (COS)	Holocaust Cognitive Variables
CIVLIB	.05	-.03	.51*	-.16*	-.02	-.06	.02	.32*	-.04	-.01	.02	18.1*	0.1	6.1*
MILNONW	-.02	.01	.02	-.09	-.05	-.07	.15*	.29*	-.10	.10*	.07	12.3*	0.2	9.5*
BLACKS	.02	-.04	-.04	-.19*	-.04	-.07	.14*	.22*	-.06	.13*	.01	12.0*	0.1	7.1*
IMMIG	-.02	-.08	.05	-.02	.02	.00	.16*	.29*	.07	.09*	.04	19.2*	1.1	15.1*
											(.69)			
MILJEW	.08	.10*	.08	-.02*	-.09*	-.01	.14*	.12*	.00	-.03	.07	13.5*	1.3	4.7*
											(.53)			
ISRDEF	.08	-.03	.03	.23*	.04	.12*	.12*	.13*	-.01	-.04	-.08	13.8*	1.0	3.8*
											(-.22)			

*F is significant at .01 level.

Source: Weinfeld & Sigal 1986b.

INFOSK and HISTORY—contribute significantly to explaining 4.7% and 3.8% of the variance in MILJEW and ISRDEF, respectively.

Universal Variables (CIVLIB, MILNONW, BLACKS, IMMIG). Before reviewing the evidence on the determinants of the generalized support for free speech and noncensorship, we might note the interesting variation in the attitudes toward the subcategories of the Stouffer scale. As seen in Table 5.15, it is clear that all respondents, regardless of origin group, vary in their general tolerance for the five target groups. Homosexuals and Communists are granted the right of free speech by large majorities (approximately 94%). Advocates of military (and presumably right-wing) dictatorship would be tolerated by a much smaller majority, approximately 60%. The largest drop occurs as we move more explicitly toward target groups such as racists and, finally, Nazis, where only one-third and one-quarter of the respondents, respectively, would grant such freedoms. This variation supports the arguments made by Sullivan, Pierson, and Marcus (1979) concerning the importance of measuring political tolerance specifically for groups or opinions with which the respondent is likely to disagree. For this reason, revised Stouffer measures, including ours, generally include target groups of both the right and the left.

Table 5.15 also presents comparisons with a national U.S. sample in 1982. The Montreal Jewish sample (younger, urban, more highly educated, and of course all Jewish) was more tolerant toward Communists and homosexuals, but less tolerant toward racists and, one presumes, toward Nazis, though this was not measured by NORC.

The effect of the Holocaust as transmitted through familial experience is ambiguous, as seen in Table 5.13. Only among the CON are those who claim to have been affected by their parents' experiences during World War II significantly ($p < .01$), though only slightly, more politically tolerant than those who claim they were not affected. The regression analysis reveals that, among Holocaust-related variables, historical knowledge (controlled for educational level and sex) is strongly associated with greater tolerance, and helps explain most of the 6.1% of the variance in the set of Holocaust variables.

The variables MILJEW and MILNONW are mirror images of each other, and it is interesting to compare the two. The means of these two variables differ substantially. They are 10.8 for MILJEW and 6.0 for MILNONW for the entire sample. This reflects the sample's much greater propensity toward militancy in Jewish self-defense than in defense of nonwhites. (The standard deviations are similar, 4.0 for MILJEW and 4.6 for MILNONW.)

From Table 5.14 we note that the cognitive Holocaust-related variables explain 9.5% of the 12.3% variance in the equation. INFOSK and HISTORY are again the dominant variables associated with such militance; having a universalist orientation is significantly if not substantially related to militant defense of victimized nonwhites.

Table 5.15
Percentage (number) of Respondents Answering "Yes" to Stouffer
Question "If _____ Wanted to Make a Speech in Your Community,
Should They Be Allowed to Speak or Not?"

	Children of Survivors	Immigrant Controls	Native Controls	Full Sample	NORC[a] 1982
1. Persons who believe blacks are genetically inferior (racist)	37.5	43.1	36.3	37.0(492)	60.9
2. Persons who admit they are Communists	81.8	73.6	81.7	80.6(500)	56.6
3. Persons who advocate doing away with elections and letting the military run the country (dictator)	59.5	54.5	64.4	60.6(495)	56.0
4. Persons who admit they are homosexual	92.4	93.2	96.0	94.0(505)	67.7
5. Persons who admit they are Nazis	24.6	37.3	28.3	27.9(505)	--

[a]1982 US national sample (NORC, 1982, 82–87)

Source: Weinfeld & Sigal 1986b.

Racial tolerance, as measured in attitudes to blacks on the respondent's street, is affected by the Holocaust experience not through familial transmission directly, but through the cognitive measures as seen in Table 5.14. Information seeking, historical knowledge, and perceiving the Holocaust in universal terms are significantly associated, and help explain 7.2% of the 12% variance. For this measure, as for CIVLIB, we might note that more religious respondents are more likely to be less politically and racially tolerant.

Cognitive-attitudinal Holocaust-related variables here are particularly dominant in explaining 15.1% of the total 19.2% explained variance. In particular, INFOSK and HISTORY are independently associated with liberal immigration views; so, too, although not attaining statistical significance, are knowledge of concentration camps and having a universalistic orientation to the Holocaust. The mean differences in Table 5.13 suggest that familial Holocaust effects are significant. The regression results suggest they operate largely through the cognitive variables.

Discussion

The findings raise the possibility that the Holocaust has, in a variety of ways, helped shape the political attitudes of the young adult Jews in our sample. For one thing, it may have affected the broad contours of the trditional Jewish liberalism and support for civil liberties, so that our full sample was far more tolerant of left-wing or homosexual groups than of Nazis or racists. This finding is not surprising. The controversy affecting Jewish American Civil Liberties Union members who opposed their organization's support for the right of Nazis to march in Skokie, Illinois, reflected a similar predisposition. In Canada, the well-publicized trial of Ernst Zundel, a publisher of Holocaust-denial literature, may have confirmed for many Jews the urgency of taking strong measures against the dissemination of hate literature.

As seen from Table 5.13, COS affected by parental experiences differed modestly ($p < .05$) from CON who were unaffected in three of the six measures (IMMIG, MILJEW, ISRDEF) and in anticipated directions, but they do not differ significantly from the COI. As seen from Table 5.12, being a COS and being affected by World War II were associated with information seeking and knowledge. Yet from the regression analyses in Table 5.14, it seems that an independent effect of the Holocaust may lie in the cognitive domain, such that those who tended to be more knowledgeable and seek more information, regardless of parental status, were also likely to be affected in hypothesized directions. Not surprisingly, respondents whose interpretation of the Holocaust was more universalistic also were modestly yet significantly likely to score high on the universal dependent measures, in three of the four cases.

We found earlier that COS who were affected by the Holocaust sought more information and knew more about World War II. Yet clearly, being a COS is neither necessary nor sufficient for respondents to demonstrate an effect of the Holocaust. After the introduction of many controls, information seeking and knowledge of events of World War II (themselves correlated at 0.36) make the only substantial contributions to the explained variance of the political attitudes.

U.S. national surveys have found relationships between higher levels of education and greater tolerance or political liberalism (Nunn, Crockett, & Williams 1978; McClosky & Brill 1983). Presumably, the better educated are also better read and more informed. However, some researchers have questioned whether higher education per se leads to more favorable intergroup attitudes (Jackman & Muha 1984). It is possible that different types of educational experiences (within comparable levels) may have different attitudinal outcomes, and that educational attainment and actual historical knowledge, which we found to be correlated positively (0.38), may not be equivalent in their consequences.

Our findings on the importance of knowledge and information seeking complement what is known about the greater support for civil liberties by social science or liberal arts graduates (Selvin & Hagstrom 1960), if we assume that knowledge about World War II and reading books and going to lectures are the kinds of traits associated with such an educational experience. Our data do not directly indicate the source of respondents' knowledge of World War II, though it is more likely to be books or other media than college courses. The percentage of our sample who would have studied such material explicitly in college-level courses is low, though many might have been introduced to it at a superficial level in Jewish school.

Yet it is still not clear why this relationship of historical knowledge and tolerance should occur. Beck (1977, p. 129), summarizing the studies on education and political socialization, reveals that studies of the effects of civics courses in high school have shown them to be neither comprehensive nor overwhelming, but negligible. Perhaps knowledge of World War II or the Holocaust differs from knowledge of the content of a civics curriculum. Moreover, there is some evidence that greater interest in current events is associated with higher measures of tolerance, as found by Stouffer (1955) and in the 1973 replication of his work by Nunn, Crockett, and Williams (1978, pp. 163–164). Other national surveys have yielded similar findings (McClosky & Brill 1983, p. 372). These studies measured interest in current rather than historical events. However, we might assume that these interests—usually satisfied through books or other information media—might be correlated, reflecting a common factor of intellectual curiosity.

The respondents in our study who claimed they were affected by their parents' experience during World War II were asked open-ended questions designed for them to specify and elaborate on the nature of these effects. Interestingly, political attitudes were most infrequently cited; far more prevalent were effects involving familial relations, psychological adjustment and coping styles, or reinforcement of Jewish identification.

The qualitative data, based on verbatim transcripts, support our findings about Holocaust effects on the particularistic outcome measures MILJEW and ISRDEF, the propensity for militant action in defense of Jews and of Israel, respectively. There were many respondents who clearly declared, often as part of their Jewish commitment, a militant vigilance to the possibilities of recurrent anti-Semitism as well as strong pro-Israel inclinations. However, there were very few respondents who volunteered a general tolerance for minorities or dissenters as a perceived effect of their parents' experience of World War II. Perhaps one might not expect generalization to others from one's personal experiences as a perceived response.

In our analysis, respondents' political attitudes are the dependent variables, to be explained by the Holocaust-related variables. While parental status during the war and EFFWW2, being affected by the parents' wartime experiences, can be considered as causally prior, what of the other Holocaust-related explanatory variables (information seeking and knowledge)? It is possible, for example, that respondents highly committed to civil liberties and defense of minority rights and Jewish interests might, as a consequence, take an interest in World War II and seek out information. In our view, this causal specification is less likely, since the information-seeking questions reflect activities of the recent past, and factual knowledge is usually gained cumulatively, while the political attitudes elicited derived from the time of interview.

It is also possible that the relation observed between the cognitive measures and tolerance found in this study can be explained by an underlying personality variable—a general curiosity, openness, and independence, possibly correlative with both knowledge and information seeking—as well as tolerance as measured here. (This would account for low Betas found for the independent effects of parental status during World War II.) We might also note the negligible independent effect of CAMPID (the quiz based on names of concentration camps) on the dependent variables. Specific knowledge of concentrtion camp names was not the type of knowledge independently associated with the outcome measures. The HISTORY measure is broader. This suggests that the relevant knowledge here is more generally wide-ranging than that which pertains directly to the Holocaust itself.

Further studies along this line might explore further the issue of causal direction as well as the hypothesis of an underlying explanatory personality trait, independent of parental status during World War II.

These limitations and questions of interpretation ought not to detract from our central conclusion. The data analyzed here do alert us to the possible relationship of the Holocaust to contemporary political attitudes of Jewish COS and controls. COS are more likely to claim to be affected by their parent's experiences during World War II, to be more knowledgeable about those events, and to have attitudes affected in hypothesized directions. Yet biological descent alone may be a sufficient but not necessary condition for second-generation effects. Those who are more informed and more curious are more likely to tolerate divergent and distasteful views, accept blacks as neighbors, accept more immigrants as refugees to Canada, militantly oppose the infringement of the rights of both non-whites and Jews, and advocate stronger measures in support of Israel in the face of an invasion, regardless of their parents' whereabouts during World War II.

6

The Third Generation

Investigators have documented psychological repercussions of nonnormative events such as the loss of a spouse through death or divorce two generations later (Frommer & O'Shea 1973; Levy 1943; Sigal, Meislova, Beltempo, & Silver 1988). In these studies, the second generation was exposed to the event as well. As a result, it is impossible to determine the degree to which the effects on the third generation, the grandchildren, are due to the experience of the first generation, the second generation, or both. Our clinic and community samples permit us to identify the contribution of each, since, with few exceptions, all our second- and third-generation subjects did not experience the events that affected the first generation.

CLINIC SAMPLE

The clinic study of the third generation was based on questionnaires completed by the parents and the school for all referrals to a children's psychiatric outpatient department over a period of ten years. We had two index groups of grandchildren of survivors (GCOS): Index 1 were children who had at least one grandparent who was a survivor. Index 2, in addition to meeting the criterion for Index 1, also had at least one parent who was a survivor. The two comparison groups were parallel to the comparison groups for the study of the second generation: The GCOI had one grandparent who immigrated to Canada prior to World War II, and all four grandparents of GCON were native born. Further inclusion and exclusion criteria are given in Chapter 3.

Findings

Some of the results, culled from the checklists of character, mood, and behavior problems, are shown in Table 6.1.

For purposes of statistical analysis, in order to remove ambiguity from the rating scale and to ensure resaonable cell sizes, ratings of "sometimes," "often," and "very often" were grouped, to indicate the presence of a symptom at the time of referral, and ratings of "never" and "used to" were grouped to indicate the absence of a symptom. We then used the chi-square statistic to compare GCON, GCOI, and Index 1 groups. We did not include Index 2 in our statistical analysis because of the small sample size, 11 subjects.

Only three comparisons were statistically significant. First, on the check-list item "Fear of ordinary situations," 32.1%, 38.4%, and 66.0% of the parents in the GCON, GCOI, and Index 1 groups, respectively, responded affirmatively (sometimes, often, very often; $p < .05$ for the three groups). The difference between Index 1 and the other two groups is also significant ($p < .02$). Second, 13.8%, 16.2%, and 1.8%, respectively, of the parents in the GCON, GCOI, and Index 1 groups reported that their child was one or more grades behind at school ($p < .05$). Third, the COS in this sample were more likely to identify family problems as the root of their children's difficulties than were the comparison groups; among the possible causes for the child's difficulty, 37.9%, 6.33%, and 6.67% of the parents in the Index 1, GCON, and GCOI groups, respectively, checked "Part of a family problem" ($p < .02$). This finding is particularly striking in view of the fact that the same proportion (about 50%) of each of the three main groups was school referred as was self referred.

Although the small sample size of the Index 2 group precluded statistical analysis, the data indicate that these parents also more frequently perceived the problem with their children as part of a family problem. The data also suggest that the Index 2 are as frequently fearful of ordinary situations as the Index 1 group. In addition, the data indicate that these children are sad and have had eating problems more frequently than the others. Finally, they more frequently have serious difficulties in their school performance (see Table 6.1). School-related problems were found in 8 of the 11 Index 2 families. In one of these only the mother was a survivor, in four only the father was, and in the remaining three both the mother and the father were survivors. Thus, the mother was a survivor in four of these families, and the father in seven of them.

We considered the possibility of attention deficit disorders in these children. Examination of the psychological test data available on them and their diagnoses, however, failed to confirm this speculation. Similarly, we were able to rule out perinatal problems as a cause by examining the data on birth histories.

Table 6.1
Problem Areas in Index 2 Children Reported by Parents or School

	GCON	GCOI	Index 1	Index 2
	N = 30	N = 28	N = 58	N = 11
Fear of ordinary situations				
Often and very often	10.7%	19.2%	33.9%	40.0%
Eating problems				
Never	60.7	5.0	31.6	63.6
Sad				
Often and very often	23.4	30.0	21.3	<u>57.2</u>
Unusually active				
Often and very often	8.4	13.7	23.6	37.5
Attention span problems				
Often and very often	20.0	26.6	26.0	<u>55.5</u>
Problems completing homework				
Often and very often	36.9	30.0	48.4	<u>66.6</u>
Poor motivation to learn				
Often and very often	37.5	27.3	40.5	<u>75.0</u>
School learning difficulties				
Often and very often	33.3	34.5	28.3	63.6
School work at age level	57.7	69.0	70.9	<u>30.0</u>
Special class	3.8	0	7.3	<u>20.0</u>
Explanation of problem				
Part of family problem	6.7	6.3	37.9	28.6

Note: GCON=grandchildren of native-born grandparents and parents; GCOI=grandchildren whose parents were native born and with at least one grandparent who immigrated to Canada before World War II but was raised in a European country later occupied by Nazis; Index 1=grandchildren whose parents were native born and with at least one grandparent who was a survivor of the Nazi persecution; Index 2=grandchildren with at least one parent and one grandparent who were survivors of the Nazi persecution, and all others native born.

Underlining is for emphasis only—to highlight areas of possible difference.
Source: Sigal, DiNicola, & Buonvino 1988.

Discussion

Contrary to our clinical impressions, GCOS did not differ from the control groups when the nature of the referral symptoms was used as the dependent variable. The only three differences we did find could have been due to chance alone, since we performed more than 50 statistical tests.

On the basis of these data, we concluded that while there may be individual exceptions, as a group the GCOS are not distinguishable from other clinic children with respect to their mood, personality, or behavioral items included in this study.

Inspection of the relative size of the groups, however, added a disquieting note. The data that are available on the relative sizes of our index and control groups in the community suggest that the GCOS are grossly overrepresented in our clinic sample: The first of the community surveys we reported, that of the survivors, conducted in 1978, established that 20% of Jewish household heads in Montreal were survivors, and that survivors had fewer children per family than the comparison group. Furthermore, analysis of data from the second community study we reported, that of the COS, revealed that the COS had the same number of children per family (1.4) as CON. (A comparison with COI was not justifiable because the COI were older than the others in the study.) Based on the conservative assumption that the 58 GCOI and GCON represent the same proportion of the clinic population (80%) as their grandparents represent in the general population, there should only be about 15 GCOS in the clinic population. In fact, there were 69—over 300% more.

At least two methodological issues should be addressed before one may conclude tht the third generation is overrepresented in the clinic population.

First, it may be that the second generation tends to identify behavior as problematic, or has a greater tendency to seek professional help than parents in the comparison groups. Data from the second community survey, however, suggest that this is unlikely. The second generation tends to seek the help of mental health professionals less often, and to stay in treatment for briefer periods, than comparison groups.

Second, it may be that because of its historical ties to the Jewish community, survivors' children tend to turn to the hospital where the data were gathered for help, whereas others turn to other clinics. Unfortunately, the records of the other major hospital in the community to which this population turns for treatment do not permit verification of this hypothesis. Until this potentially confounding factor is investigated, the available data suggest that GCOS may be psychologically vulnerable, and that their vulnerability manifests itself not in the uniqueness of their presenting complaints, but in the frequency of their occurrence.

It should be noted that the similarity of symptomatology does not establish similarity of etiology, nor does it necessarily indicate the appropriateness of similar treatment plans. For other than the most behaviorally oriented clinician, a proper assessment should include an exploration of the fantasies and affects underlying past and current parent-child interactions over three generations. Others have provided much clinical evidence for the impact of grandparents' experiences during the Nazi persecution on the thoughts and fantasies of the parents (Bergmann & Jucovy 1982). Our clinicians provided us with some examples of effects on the children, the GCOS. For example, one child denied being Jewish and wanted to become a Nazi. Another had a terror of Nazis. Yet another, whose mother was shot while carrying food in Nazi-occupied Europe, developed primary anorexia.

An intriguing finding calling for further exploration is the clear presence of school-performance-related difficulties among the Index 2 group. To establish whether this finding is due to some bias in our sample or some chance event, one would require a larger sample and a comparison group of children of parents who were survivors and of grandparents who were native-born. The children of Jewish ex-prisoners of war (POWs) in the Pacific theater during World War II or during the Korean war who had been referred to child psychiatry clinics could be one such comparison group. Ex-POWs in these groups (but not those in the World War II European POW camps) have been shown to suffer long-term physical and psychological difficulties similar to those of survivors of the Nazi persecution, particularly Jewish and non-Jewish civilian and military survivors of the Nazi concentration camps (Beebe 1975; Eitinger 1980; Eitinger & Strøm 1973; Nefzger 1970; Kral, Pazder, & Wigdor 1967).

As they stand, the Index 2 data do suggest at least three possible hypotheses.

The first hypothesis is that there is a cumulative psychological effect of having grandparents and parents who were exposed to extreme, and possibly excessive, prolonged stress. Such a cumulative effect might be found, for example, in families in which the grandparents' presence in the home of their children and grandchildren creates the same separation-individuation difficulties for the grandchildren as clinicians have reported for the COS (Barocas & Barocas 1973, 1979; Freyberg 1980). According to this hypothesis, the parents, because they are still overinvolved with their parents, are unable to intervene effectively between them and their children. As a result, the grandchildren suffer the same developmental problems as the parents. At least one community study (Podietz et al. 1984) offers support for separation-individuation problems between COS and their parents (that is, for a second-generation effect), but the results of our study and one other (Ofman 1981) do not. We were, however, unable to find any support for this three-generation hypothesis when we examined the clinical reports in the charts. Because family interviews in our clinics rarely include the grand-parents, unless they are living with their children, the clinicians may not have explored this possibility.

The second hypothesis follows from evidence we found in support of an early clinical observation on effects on the second generation (Rakoff, Sigal, & Epstein 1966): that children of survivors tend to have more school prob-lems than others. If substantiated, this observatation would suggest that the fact that a grandparent was also a survivor may be irrelevant. In a subsequent study, we failed to find evidence to support this early observation (Sigal & Rakoff 1971), but sampling procedure in that study was less adequate than the current one, and the parents were older at the time of their wartime experiences.

In the great majority of families in the Index 2 group, it was the father who was a survivor. We therefore examined the clinicians' observations on the fathers' role in their families, and found two possible sources of their negative impact. The most immediate one was that the fathers were ex-tremely well organized in their work, but were either disorganized or totally uninvolved in the family, much to the distress of the mothers. A more remote potential source was that almost half of the paternal grandfathers and almost as many of the paternal grandmothers were killed by the Nazis. It is possible, therefore, that the combined effect of the absence of a role model and the distorted socializing experiences of the war years prevented the fathers from creating a family environment for the mothers and the children that would facilitate the structuring of an internal milieu in the child conducive to the child's benefiting from the educational process. These are clearly speculations. They are offered here in order to suggest areas that merit exploration by clinicians who work with these families.

A further consistency between our data and the earlier observations is noteworthy. Sigal (1972) had previously observed hypermotility in children of families in which one parent was preoccupied (physically present but psychologically absent). In the present study, parents of both GCOS groups reported their children to be "unusually active for their age" more frequently than the parents of the control groups. Although the difference fell short of statistical significance, the consistency with observations in other contexts (Cork 1969; Sigal 1982; Sigal, Silver, Rakoff, & Ellin 1973; Weissman, Paykel, & Klerman 1972) suggests that when clinicians observe such be-havior in a child, they should probe for the possibility that a parent is depressed or otherwise absorbed.

Assuming our data are valid, can we generalize from them to the whole community of GCOS? We have already noted the failure of a well-designed community study of COS to confirm widely accepted clinical findings. Similar community-based data are required to determine the relevance of the present study for the broader community. Our community study pro-vided such data. They are presented below.

COMMUNITY SAMPLE

We asked all respondents in our community sample of young adults to rate their oldest child, if she/he was at least four years old, on each item of a 50-item checklist of children's behavior and mood. Most of the adjectives were taken from the list constructed by Peterson (1961), which was later developed as the Behavior Problem Checklist (Peterson & Quay 1967). Nouns in the list were changed to adjectives. Thus, "shyness" was changed to "shy," "destructiveness" to "destructive," and so on. Items shown to tap positive coping were added to the list (Sigal, Chagoya, Villeneuve, & Mayerovitch 1971). On the scale for each item, respondents were asked to indicate if their child was "Not at all like that," "Somewhat like that," or "Exactly like that."

Varimax orthogonal factor analysis revealed six factors that accounted for 81% of the variance. For purposes of this study, whenever possible we selected only those items which had a loading of .50 or greater. When this would have resulted in too few items, we accepted items with loadings of .40 or higher.

Table 6.2 shows the items in each factor and their respective loadings. Based on the items loading highest in the factors, we labeled them Conduct Problems, Strangeness, Hypersensitivity, Low Self-Esteem, Flag, and Good Coping.

Method

To eliminate any possible confounding (mitigating) effect of having a parent or parents of mixed backgrounds, for this analysis we selected only those families in which both parents were COS, COI, or CON. This yielded 70 GCOS, 14 GCOI, and 48 GCON. Because of the small size of the GCOI sample, we had to omit it from this analysis. We used one-way ANOVAs to compare the two groups on each of the six factors.

In addition, to complement our work on the stability of survivors' coping style, we constructed groups of grandchildren of survivors who were in hiding and of those who were in the partisans during World War II. Because of limited sample size, we had to be content to select families in which at least one parent was a child of a survivor who had been in hiding or in the partisans. We then compared the grandchildren of these groups with each other, using one-way ANOVAs.

Findings

The mean scores of the GCOS and GCON on each of the factors are shown in Table 6.3 (unit weight for each item was used for this study). The one-way ANOVAs revealed that GCOS had significantly lower scores

Table 6.2
Factor Loadings and Cronbach Alphas for Child Behavior Items: Community Sample

Variable	Factor					
	1	2	3	4	5	6
Conduct problems						
Argues a lot	.73	-.03	-.06	.28	.04	.17
Disobedient, hard to discipline						
and control	.61	.17	.07	.19	.19	.17
Irritable, hot-tempered, easily						
aroused to anger	.59	.18	.24	.10	.20	.17
Stubborn	.59	.12	.11	.04	.05	.13
Peaceful, easygoing	-.55	.01	.00	.00	.06	.57
Negativistic, tends to do the						
opposite of what is requested	.55	.28	.11	.38	.09	.08
Restless, unable to sit still,						
hyperactive	.51	.03	.32	-.17	.20	-.05
Has temper tantrums	.51	-.02	-.27	.06	.06	.04
Boisterous, rowdy	.51	.04	.12	-.05	-.16	-.05
Strangeness						
Clumsy, awkward, has poor muscular						
coordination	.02	.72	.01	.10	.16	.17
Aloof, socially reserved, keeps						
his distance from people	.19	.67	-.01	.12	.22	.22
Odd, bizarre, peculiar, strange	.04	.61	.01	.04	.20	.07
Uncooperative in group situations	.22	.56	.12	-.03	.10	-.16
Hypersensitivity						
Hypersensitive, feelings easily						
hurt	.28	.02	.60	-.07	-.09	-.03
Tense, unable to relax	.34	.12	.49	.10	.23	.06
Self-conscious; easily embarrassed	.01	-.05	.44	.20	-.00	.06
Anxious, fearful	.08	.16	.41	.06	.04	.06

Table 6.2 (continued)

	Factor					
Variable	1	2	3	4	5	6
Low self-esteem						
Lacks self-confidence	.06	.21	.37	<u>.65</u>	.23	.31
Easily flustered and confused	.09	.23	.02	<u>.57</u>	.13	.03
Feels inferior	.19	.29	.38	<u>.52</u>	.09	.27
Lies	.38	-.10	-.16	<u>.51</u>	.09	.11
Cannot concentrate	.41	.12	.12	<u>.50</u>	.26	.11
Flag						
Speaks incoherently, does not make sense when he/she talks	.12	.26	-.15	.05	<u>.80</u>	.02
Defecates (makes) in his pants	.10	.05	.05	.13	<u>.70</u>	-.06
Uses profane language, swears, curses	.03	.39	-.10	.14	<u>.59</u>	.23
Good coping						
Warm, affectionate	-.13	-.07	-.06	-.07	-.18	<u>.66</u>
Happy, in good mood	-.20	-.20	-.12	-.09	-.02	<u>.61</u>
Friendly	-.13	-.13	-.06	-.09	-.06	<u>.61</u>
Self-confident	.06	-.15	-.30	-.28	-.17	<u>.55</u>
Peaceful, easygoing	-.55	.01	.00	.00	.06	<u>.57</u>
Alpha	.85	.74	.57	.62	.73	.77

Note: Underlined loadings indicate the items used to define the factor for purposes of comparing index and comparison groups.

Source: Sigal, DiNicola, & Buonvino 1988.

than the GCON ($p < .05$) on the factor we labeled Low Self-Esteem and the one containing the Flag items (items indicative of possible severe psychopathology requiring further exploration). They also scored marginally lower ($p < .10$) on the factor labeled Strangeness. The COS scored higher than the CON ($p < .05$) on the factor labeled Good Coping.

None of the differences between the grandchildren of survivors who were in the partisans and those who had been in hiding was statistically significant.

Table 6.3
Means and Standard Deviations for Factor Scores of Personality Variables for GCOS and GCON: Community Sample

Factor	Group	Mean	S.D.	F	P
1 Conduct problems	GCOS	3.67	3.33	2.56	.11
	GCON	4.77	4.12		
2 Strangeness	GCOS	0.23	0.54	3.45	.07
	GCON	0.65	1.19		
3 Hypersensitivity	GCOS	0.31	0.97	0.52	.47
	GCON	0.69	1.21		
4 Low self-esteem	GCOS	2.46	1.46	4.74	.03
	GCON	2.67	1.67		
5 Flag	GCOS	1.17	1.39	6.59	.01
	GCON	1.77	1.57		
6 Good coping	GCOS	7.44	1.77	6.81	.01
	GCON	6.50	2.14		

Note: Means and standard deviations are based on unit weight assigned to variable groups as in Table 6.2. GCOS had at least one grandparent who was a survivor of the Nazi persecution of Jews. All four grandparents of GCON were born in the U.S.A. or Canada. All parents were born in U.S.A. or Canada. N = 70 for GCOS and 48 for GCON.

Discussion

On three of the six factors the evidence suggests that, if anything, the GCOS are functioning *better* than the GCON. The scores on the remaining three factors are in the same direction. The test proposed by Rosenthal and Rubin (1979) did not reveal heterogeneity among the probabilities. We could, therefore, calculate the probability of this array of findings using the methods proposed by Fisher (1954, pp. 99–100) and by Stouffer et al. (cited in Mosteller & Bush 1954). According to both methods, the two groups differed at a highly significant level ($p < .001$). This means that the overall results are convincingly in favor of the GCOS functioning much better than the GCON. In the absence of comparable data from the GCOI, we cannot be sure whether the advantage of the GCOS is an immigration-related experience or a survivor-related experience. The evidence appears quite clear, however, that in this community sample the GCOS are not impaired in their psychosocial functioning.

A further suggestion that the GCOS may be faring better than the comparison groups is derived from the responses we obtained when we asked our respondents to specify how others have reacted to their oldest child in the past 12 months, if there were any reactions. An apparent difference emerged in the area of intelligence or general cognitive abilities, not in the area of personality. About twice as many COS reported favorable comment by others on the child's intelligence or cognitive abilities (23.5% of the 51 COS who replied vs. 10.3% of the 29 and 14.7% of the 34 COI and CON who replied to this question). However, the difference is not statistically significant.

We are confronted with the same discrepancy between clinic and community data as we were for the COS.

How are we to explain the finding of a marked overrepresentation of GCOS in our clinic sample? We earlier discussed the problem of potential sampling bias in the clinic sample. If we assume that sampling bias is unlikely to have resulted in an overrepresentation of the magnitude we found, we should explore other possibilities. One of these is that COS are more sensitive to a child's need for professional help. Unfortunately, we did not have any information that would determine if this is so. As a result we do not have a direct way of addressing the question.

The fact that more of the parents or the school reported that the child's problem was part of a family problem provides us with an indirect way of answering the question. We examined the information we obtained on the respondents' relationship to their spouses and vice versa, their relationship to their parents, and their parents' relationship to each other. In so doing, we could also search for possible explanations for our discovery of psychologically healthier functioning of the GCOS in our community sample.

To assess the marital relationship, we used the same questions that we used for this purpose when we compared marital relationships of the three groups of respondents earlier (Chapter 5, "Relationship with Spouse or Parent"). This time, however, we used only those who completed the behavior checklist for their oldest child (provided the child was four years of age or older). To assess relationships in the families of origin, we examined the responses of the same group to the questions "How would you describe your parents' relationship with each other when you were growing up?" "How would you describe your parents' relationship now?" "How would you describe your relationship to your mother (father) now?" Answers were on a five-point scale ranging from "Exceptionally good" to "Exceptionally bad" for all of these questions. We also asked if respondents' relationships to their mothers (fathers) had been different at any time in the past, and coded the responses to this open-ended question by developmental stage and type of difference.

The COS's responses did not differ significantly from those of both comparison groups on any of these variables.

The overrepresentation of GCOS in the clinic might also be traceable to differences in child-rearing practices. In our interviews we asked the respondents to rate themselves on the same dimensions of parental behavior they had rated their parents: strictness vs. permissiveness, involvement vs. detachment, and warmth vs. coldness. We also asked them to rate whether they thought their children would prefer more or less of each of these qualities. Finally, we asked them if there were any areas in which they were concerned about themselves as parents. We found no differences among the COS, COI, and CON on any of these items.

Our data not only have failed to explain the overrepresentation of GCOS in our clinic sample, they also have failed to reveal why the GCOS in our community sample show less psychopathology and a better level of social adaptation. While sampling bias may explain the first finding, it is unlikely to be the explanation for the second. Response bias may explain the second finding. COS may tend to deny problematic behavior and view their children more favorably than the comparison groups. Alternatively, the COI and CON may exaggerate problems and minimize the healthy functioning of their children. That is, the difference may not be a real one, but may reflect distorted perceptions by either set of respondents. We have no evidence to support either possibility. Evidence we have from the responses to other parts of the questionnaire, however, that are consistent with what one might expect on an a priori basis, suggest that these possibilities are unlikely. For example, COS reported more negative psychological consequences of World War II for their parents, and had more knowledge of people and events relating to World War II.

On the basis of clinical observations, we advance the speculation that the reason for the superior psychological functioning of the GCOS has something to do with the nature of their parents' and grandparents' psychological investment in them. They represent hope for the rebirth and regeneration of families that were truncated by the Nazi persecution.

7

Summary and Conclusions

In this chapter we shall first summarize our findings. Then we shall discuss some methodological issues that may affect their interpretation. Finally, we shall discuss their general implications.

SURVIVORS

Throughout this study we have used the term "survivors" to refer to persons who were subjected to the Nazi persecution, regardless of whether they were in ghettos, in hiding, in labor or concentration camps, or in the partisans.

Psychological Well-being

Consistent with the findings of others, we found evidence for psychological and physical impairment among survivors some three and a half decades after the end of World War II. We also found evidence to suggest that they did not have access to common means of coping with stress. Not all survivors were psychologically impaired. Fully 64% of the male survivors and 35% of the female survivors did not give evidence of psychiatric impairment according to the cutoff criterion we used for our rating scale, Langner's 22-item list. This heterogeneity of consequences of survival was amplified by our principal components analysis of the adjectives used by adult children of survivors to describe their parents' personalities; we were able to define four types: schizoid, paranoid, depressive/masochistic, and

Type A/normal aggressive. Furthermore, we found some evidence suggestive of the persistence, to the present day, of coping styles used in World War II.

The survivors appear to be functioning well in socioeconomic terms despite their psychological and physical handicaps; we found little evidence for serious impairment in the work place or for nonparticipation in communal activities. Reports from their children did not reveal any evidence of excessive disruptions or deviance in their relationships with their spouses or with their children.

Social Adaptation

We found that our sample of survivors seemed reasonably well adjusted both sociopolitically and economically in Montreal. This social adaptation is made more remarkable given the fact that our sample was found to be more highly stressed, as measured by their scores on the 22-item scale. Indirect confirmation of these findings for the survivors can be inferred from the findings in our study of survivors' adult children (COS) . The fact that an unbiased sample of the children seemed to do well on measures of psychological functioning and economic performance also attests to the parenting achievements of survivors.

The survivors were found to be somewhat more segregated socially within Montreal's Jewish community, and they tended to marry other survivors. But they were comparatively satisfied with conditions in Quebec, and were no more predisposed to consider emigration than were controls. This was so despite the upsurge of militant nationalism that was (incorrectly) perceived by many minority groups, including the Jews, as a direct threat to them. That the Holocaust was found to have had a modest yet statistically significant negative effect on survivors' socioeconomic achievement would seem to be a normal outcome of disrupted educational or career opportunities.

The report by COS of some positive long-term effects of persecution on their parents was unexpected, although a few clinicians had reported them. These were a more positive attitude to family, and heightened ethnic identification.

ADULT COS

Psychological Well-being

Contrary to the majority of clinical and anecdotal reports, we did not find much evidence that the COS have greater difficulty in communicating with their parents or separating from them than do others. Nor did we find much evidence that they had greater difficulty with the control of aggression or allied problems of anxiety, depression, phobias, low self-esteem, or psychosomatic complaints than our comparison groups. Furthermore, they seemed to have neither more nor fewer problems in academic or occupational achievement and their degree of satisfaction with these, or in their relationships with their siblings, their spouses, or their children.

The only difficulties with their parents that COS reported were in the area of parental discipline. Male COS wanted their mothers to be less strict and less involved with them, and female COS wanted their fathers to be less strict with them. There were only two suggestions that the COS had difficulties in the control of aggression. The first was a tendency for more female COS to score above a somewhat arbitrarily determined cutting point for passive-aggressive behavior. The second was the possibility that the COS had a higher suicide rate, but our data were not good enough to permit a firm conclusion on the matter. None of our numerous other attempts to verify the clinical and anecdotal reports of impaired functioning succeeded.

The information we obtained from an open-ended question concerning intergenerational effects of the parents' experiences during World War II yielded an unexpected result. Some respondents reported positive effects for themselves, as some had done for their parents. The COS reported significantly more such effects than the comparison groups; the effects were primarily in the area of Jewish identification, followed closely by general mental health. Thus the discrepancy between our findings and the clinical findings was widened.

In a search for an explanation of this discrepancy we first compared children of concentration camp survivors (CCOS) with our two comparison groups for problems in the control of aggression and allied difficulties. The majority of clinical and anecdotal reports are based on this subgroup of survivors' children, and the control of aggression is among the most problematic areas reported. We failed to find any differences in this area of aggression and allied difficulties between the CCOS and our comparison groups. We did, however, note that the conclusion of one study that was similar in design, in which a difference was found, was based on the results of projective tests, in contrast with our questionnaire method.

Having failed to find an explanation for the discrepancy between the two sets of findings in our first attempt, we turned to an examination of the differences between those COS who sought professional help for emotional problems and those who did not. Two findings provided us with clues as to where we might look for these differences. The first was that we had established that there was a heterogeneity of coping styles and personalities among survivors. The second was derived from our study of a clinical population of grandchildren of survivors. There we found that the school suggested that the child's problem was part of a family problem more frequently for grandchildren of survivors than for grandchildren in our comparison groups. We therefore examined the relationship between family variables and whether or not the COS sought professional help for emotional problems.

Here we finally found a possible explanation for the discrepancy. We were able to identify the profile of parental personality, wartime experience, and family interaction that probably defines the particular subgroups from which reporters and clinicians have attempted to generalize to the entire population. Their observations are limited, not necessarily incorrect.

Sociopolitical Attitudes

We also set out to discover if the Holocaust had any cognitive and attitudinal effects on the second generation. COS seemed to be more knowledgeable about concentration camps but, within a context of minimal information seeking generally, were not likely to read more books or attend more lectures relevant to the Holocaust than were our comparison groups.

The relative importance of knowledge of the Holocaust over biological status as a child of survivors also emerged when we examined social and political attitudes. We found that those who were more informed or more often sought information about the Holocaust were also more liberal and compassionate, and favored militant self-defense, if necessary, whether or not they were children of survivors. The explanation of this finding is open to question. It may lie in the exposure to the educational, familial, or social settings in which these people found themselves, or in an underlying set of intellectual and personality traits, or an interaction between these social and personal variables. Our study was not designed to select among these possibilities.

GRANDCHILDREN OF SURVIVORS

We did not find a unique set of referral problems among grandchildren of survivors in our psychiatric outpatient clinic. We did, however, note a 300% overrepresentation of them compared with what might be expected on the basis of their representation in the general community relative to the comparison groups. Furthermore, the referring problem was seen as part of a family problem by at least one referring body more frequently for grandchildren of survivors. A small subgroup, children who had at least one parent and one grandparent who was a survivor, had school achievement problems unrelated to intelligence. Almost all of these were boys, and it was the father who was the survivor parent in the majority of cases.

Grandchildren of survivors in the community at large, by contrast, were found to be psychologically healthier and to give less evidence of psychopathology than comparison groups. This may be an effect due to having had a grandparent who was an immigrant, and not an intergenerational effect of psychosocial trauma; we did not have a sufficiently large sample to rule out this possibility. Clearly, this question calls for further research.

CAVEATS

Given the objective of arriving at valid generalizations concerning the personality and social attitudes of survivors and their children, we feel that the studies reported here represent significant improvements on earlier efforts. The sampling procedures employed in the study of survivors, the study of children of survivors, and the nonclinic study of grandchildren of survivors all avoided the biases of self-selected, clinical samples. Similarly, the use of one or two control groups allowed for a more refined examination of the specific impact of the Holocaust experience by removing the confounding features of Jewish origin or the immigrant experience in general. We also were able to control for the possible mitigating effects of a parent who was not exposed to the traumatic events or who was not an immigrant; in the majority of our studies of the psychological and familial effects, we used families in which both parents were exposed to the potentially traumatizing events of the Holocaust or were both immigrants.

In these respects our studies differ from, and improve on, practically all previous studies of survivors and the second generation. Our controlled studies of possible third-generation effects stand alone.

Moreover, the questionnaire instruments we used generally allowed us to explore a greater range of areas compared with earlier studies. This is particularly true for the studies of the second generation, where we were able to combine batteries of psychological measures with sociological variables. The questions on knowledge, information seeking and sociopolitical attitudes in particular constitute new departures in research on second-generation effects of the Holocaust.

Similarly, our open-ended questions, from which we recorded and catalogued the self-perceptions of COS of the effects of the Holocaust (positive and negative) on their parents and on themselves, afforded a unique set of data.

Finally, the setting for our studies, Montreal in the late 1970s and early 1980s, was well chosen to highlight effects of the Holocaust, if these persisted. This was a result of the reawakening of French nationalism in Quebec, and the attendant insecurities about the political and economic future of the province. In some quarters, the uncertainties facing Jews in conditions of instability and rising nationalism echoed the conditions of life in Weimar Germany. This should have provoked more manifestations of fear or insecurity. That very few were in fact observed among survivors suggests that in other, more tranquil political environments, a similar pattern of findings would be found.

Yet we are aware that our data set and method, inevitably, have limitations. One area of selectivity lies in the fact of our investigations of long-term effects. Clearly, those most traumatized by the Holocaust are under-represented among our respondents or their parents. Our subjects are by definition those who not only survived the Holocaust but also were able to live long after the event, produce functioning offspring, and respond to our questionnaire. Our sampling design also ignored the institutionalized population in both surveys, and we also excluded from our COS study those respondents whose parents were divorced when the respondents were young. Finally, our COS were in young adulthood, when morbidity is low. Survivors and their children are a hardy group. But this problem is unavoidable, given the questions at issue: in order to study the long-term consequences of any major trauma, one needs to sample those individuals who were able to survive the trauma.

A second methodological problem is statistical. Our analyses revealed a pattern of no significant difference for survivors or their chldren. But, of course, the findings for no significant effects cannot be established with confidence, compared with statistically significant findings. One cannot prove the null hypothesis. Other questions or other measurement techniques, for example, might have revealed differences where ours failed. On the other hand, a consistent pattern of findings of minimal or no effects in anticipated or hypothesized directions is certainly worthy of note, given the many approaches we took to test clinicians' generalizations.

As noted elsewhere, it is also possible that the heterogeneous nature of our survivor category—anyone who lived for any length of time under Nazi occupation—may have masked more pronounced effects on subcategories, such as concentration camp survivors. We have tried to address some of these concerns in selected analyses. More generally, social scientific analysis consists, in essence, of comparisons using groups that are both homogeneous (relative to other groups) and heterogeneous: racial, sexual, or occupational groups come to mind. We feel that the variance in life experience in our group of Jewish survivors is no greater than that found in most other groups, and does not impede valuable comparisons with our controls; clinical and historical work has suggested that some survivors who hid or were hidden, or fought in armies or with guerrillas, suffered from the daily insecurity and fears of discovery, betrayal, capture, or death in combat, with often equally harmful long-term consequences compared with survivors of labor camps or concentration camps.

Finally, it is possible that the nature of long-term effects of the Holocaust is so subtle, or so deeply embedded in the subconscious (or even the unconscious), that direct objective questions might not elicit them. Questions that are retrospective, or rely on self-reported perceptions, also may vary in the accuracy of the responses yielded. Other approaches, such as the projective tests, may evoke latent vulnerabilities, as could stronger social stimuli. For example, in a three-year follow-up study of Israeli soldiers who became dysfunctional in combat during the 1982 Lebanese campaign, Solomon, Kotler, and Mikulincer (1988) found that those whose parents were Holocaust survivors had a different pattern of posttraumatic stress disorders than did others, and their dysfunction lasted longer. No differences were apparent between them prior to exposure to this extreme stress. Unfortunately, those investigators did not report the numbers in each group in the parent population, so it is impossible to determine if the COS were more vulnerable to the stress of combat.

The questions raised here illustrate the research dictum that there is no perfect design that leaves all methodological questions resolved. We hope that future studies wil bear more directly on these outstanding points.

IMPLICATIONS

Our studies have raised more general thematic issues.

It may be useful to undertake detailed comparative studies of survivors in other communities, and those in Israel. Was there some process of postwar self-selection that differentiated survivors coming to Montreal from those going elsewhere in North America, and the North Americans from the Israelis? A meta-analysis of existing research could also attempt to identify the impact of differential societal settings on possible outcomes. Survivors in Israel belong to a majority group, while those elsewhere are part of a minority group. Both groups would experience stresses in their environment, from overt national aggression in Israel to subtle or not so subtle anti-Semitic manifestations in other communities. But in Israel, the occasion of armed conflict could lend legitimacy to the externalization of aggression, whereas in other countries the thought of an open expression of aggression to the would-be persecutor could give rise to anxiety and avoidance.

Our findings suggest that differences between the COS and the other respondents may manifest themselves primarily in cognitive areas rather than in the areas of affect, anxiety, or defense. We recognize that the two sets of manifestations may be intimately linked; conflict, anxiety, or defense may determine the direction taken by cognitive inquiry or political orientation. In the absence of any convincing evidence for excessive family enmeshment or alienation, it appears more likely that this inquiry or orientation is based on the children's positive identification with the parents' interest and participation in Holocaust-related activities. The suggestion that there may be some positive cognitive consequences for the second generation is consistent with findings by others (Russell, Plotkin, & Heapy 1985).

In brief, we may conclude that the negative psychological consequences of prolonged victimization, be it for ethnic, racial, economic, or other reasons, need not be transmitted to a large proportion of the members of subsequent generations. Indeed, psychological impairments may be compartmentalized, coexisting with normal activity and even possible benefits.

If evidence for such negative effects cannot be found in the prolonged, extreme, life-threatening conditions such as those to which survivors were subjected, they are unlikely to be found in less extreme conditions.

Quarantelli (1985) has postulated two contrasting research approaches in the study of the consequences of major disasters. The first, called the individual trauma approach, assumes that disasters are always highly stressful, traumatic life events. Survivors inevitably face a difficult process of coping with the aftereffects of the events, trying to overcome inevitable negative psychological consequences.

The second approach is called the social sponge approach. This view holds that disasters will have differential effects across the board, some of which may even be positive. Negative effects are often seen as of short duration. Following in this metaphor, survivors of traumatic events are enveloped, spongelike, within community structures that will play a role in reintegration and subsequent adjustment.

Some of the divergences in research findings are reflected in the different research traditions of mental health practitioners and social scientists (Quarantrelli 1985, pp. 199–200). The former are trained more to find and treat individual dysfunction; the latter, to analyze social interactions and the link between individuals and the social environment. The former might focus on impairment; the latter (social sponge adherents), on adaptation and well-being.

Our findings for the survivors are consistent with both approaches, but tend to favor the individual trauma model. Consistent with the individual trauma model, we found evidence for long-lasting negative effects of trauma among survivors. But, consistent with the social sponge model, we also found that they have adapted well socioeconomically despite their personal problems. The findings for the second generation, on the other hand, favor the social sponge model. While the COS did report some negative effects of their parents' experiences on them, on the vast majority of our measures they could not be differentiated from our comparison groups. Our sense is that this horrible trauma, like many searing human experiences, has had heterogeneous effects on survivors, with consequences that have not irrevocably debilitated substantial numbers of survivors over the long term, or spilled over into subsequent generations. That stress can be managed and trauma overcome in no way suggests, in a sociobiologically vulgar Darwinism, that survivors are better off for their travails. They were not and are not. But neither survivors nor their offspring need remain stigmatized by questions of their adequate functioning or psychosocial disability. Substantial numbers of survivors and the majority of their children do not feel emotionally troubled, and have been able to integrate themselves and establish meaningful lives, as individuals and as part of both the Jewish and the general communities.

Our study has also raised the question of how, if at all, historical events establish a legacy for succeeding generations. History is passed on through formal institutions, like school and the media, and is filtered through the socialization process in families. Yet we can legitimately ask whether the socialization process works as comprehensively as is often assumed. To what extent do parents transmit consequences of their historic experience—whether the Holocaust, the Vietnam war, or the Depression—to their offspring? The passage of time may dilute historical messages in favor of the immediacy of new generational experience.

We must, then, ask whether the nonfamilial agencies are adequately performing their socialization function for those who have no familial or communal link with the major event. It is unlikely that our finding of an association between degree of secular education and knowledge of World War II and the Holocaust reflects the curricular content of secondary and post-secondary schools. Glickman and Bardikoff (1982) reviewed 43 English-language history and social studies textbooks used in Canadian high schools, and found them woefully inadequate, making a meager contribution at best to a student's knowledge or understanding of the Holocaust. At the university level, it is unlikely that the more educated of our sample had greater exposure to courses dealing specifically with the Jewish dimension of World War II or the Holocaust.

Certainly, in the study of minorities, there is no tradition of investigating the issue of knowledge of ethnically salient historical events, for either the general population or for members of the specific group. This is surprising, because historical memory is, in a very basic sense, central to both ethnic group identity and the evolving patterns of intergroup relations. Indeed, almost every minority group has its own collective self-image and relationship to other groups affected by more or less recent major historical events. A very partial listing would include events such as the massacres of 1915 for Armenians; the Holocaust for Jews; the internment for Japanese Americans and Canadians; and the famine of 1932–1933 for Ukrainians.

As indicated earlier, we felt the levels of Holocaust knowledge in our sample to be low, for all groups. We suspect strongly that replicated studies for other ethnic minorities might find their respective groups comparably low. Indeed, it is a common complaint of North American academics that most students seem ignorant of basic facts even of recent world history.

It is appropriate to ask whether knowledge of the facts about major historical events is in any way intrinsically important. Strong feelings about one's ethnic identity or a related event may exist without the bookish kind of knowledge measured in this study. Indeed, many of the respondents who scored low in their knowledge of such facts nevertheless affirmed the importance they attached to the Holocaust as a meaningful event for themselves, for Jews, and for all humanity.

Yet knowledge of this kind is important for at least two reasons. One is, as we have seen, that such knowledge may well play a role in the process of shaping sociopolitical attitudes on important public issues.

Second, the climate of race relations may well be affected by perceptions or reinterpretations of historical events. As firm a grounding in facts as possible may help counter those forms of historical revisionism which distort the truth and undermine intergroup harmony. The historicity of the Holocaust itself has not been immune from the onslaught of a coordinated revisionist movement, which has been the subject of two Canadian court proceedings. As a result, at its annual meeting in May 1985, the Canadian Historical Association adopted the following resolution:

The membership of the Canadian Historical Association feels compelled to inform the Canadian public about its view of literature which denies that the Holocaust occurred. The extensive coverage given this literature has raised the issue of the Holocaust itself as an item of public debate. As historians, we feel obliged by our professional integrity to state our response unequivocally. Though scholars may debate detail and nuance, there can be no question about the fundamental fact that the Nazis carried out a program of systematic murder of millions of Jews and other people. We believe that historians must publicly assert their certain knowledge that the Holocaust took place and that this is a matter of historical record.

A final question is whether the issues of long-term, intergenerational effects and our findings are in any way unique to the Jewish experience, to the process of ethnic victimization generally, or even to all forms of victimization. Comparative studies involving other, similarly victimized groups, whose victimization is both recent or experienced by earlier generations, might shed light on the generalizability of these findings. Japanese survivors of the North American internment (and offspring), as well as survivors of Hiroshima, are one such group. Indo-Chinese refugees (the boat people) are another. Very little systematic research has been undertaken on long-term and intergenerational effects of other forms of trauma. Follow-up studies of survivors of rape, of other crimes, or of natural disasters are often of three months' duration or a few years at most (Figley 1985). The study of intergenerational consequences—specifically where the offspring did not experience the event—remains an underdeveloped field. We suspect that other studies in this field will yield more evidence for human resilience in the face of social catastrophe.

Appendix A: Coding for Effects of World War II on Respondents' Parents

POSSIBLE RESPONSES FOR EACH CATEGORY:

0   No (R didn't state) .

1   Yes, mother—positive

2   Yes, mother—negative

3   Yes, father—positive

4   Yes, father—negative

5   Yes, both parents—positive

6   Yes, both parents—negative

7   Mixed effect (include here any combination of the above or any responses for which the effect is not clear)

8   R didn't know if effect positive or negative

9   No answer/Not applicable

CATEGORIES

1. Physical Health   includes general or specific comments about physical health (such as parents' death resulting from poor physical health as a consequence of the Holocaust; chronic ailment)

2. Familial Death

Includes any reference to death of family members during the war

3. General Mental Health

Code here general statements about mental health or function, such as cognitive skills/personality or character traits/affect (for example, character traits such as pessimistic, heightened perceptive or cognitive abilities, better memory, learned to sense danger, clearer sense of reality; or affects such as very moody, no sense of humor, cries a lot)

Never overcame death of parent or moody because lost family coded here (as well as above) because refers to affect

Specific phobia coded in following category, general avoidance of risk here

Note: Anything that refers to a specific relationship or person is not coded here—for instance, "My father was always angry with us" is coded under attitudes to family, whereas "My father is an angry man" is coded here

4. Specific Psychological Symptoms

Phobias, nightmares, depression, specific food-related nonnormative habits (such as "Mom never wanted to waste food"), won't or can't watch TV show or read book on Holocaust, guilt feelings. (This would be coded only in negative categories)

5. Familial Attitudes

Family relationship and attitudes to family and children. Positive—value education, very involved with family. Negative—bugged child about school, parents were always quarreling, were overprotective of children, were excessively involved with family, have nothing to do with any family members

6. Hostility to Other Groups

Negative attitudes to groups or products of groups. Hate, prejudice (for instances prejudice toward Germans, hatred of anything German, won't buy German products, distrust of non-Jews)

7. Life Course Change

Change in life course, career, marriage, education. Negative—would have been a lawyer but education interrupted. Positive—war opened up new opportunities in career or education; father left Poland and went to France, and therefore got to me my mother

8. Adaptation to Canada   Problems of adjusting to a new society or lack of problems adjusting. Negative—nostalgia for the old country, for life before the war. Positive—had a better life after the war and felt more secure here

9. Religiosity   Increase (positive) or decrease (negative) in Jewish religious attitude or behavior

10. Israel   Increased commitment to Israel, involvement with Zionist organizations (positive)

11. Jewish Identification   Awareness (includes perceived anti-Semitism and guardedness against non-Jews—for instance, Jews must stick together or must marry a Jew). This is coded as an increase

12. Other, Unspecified   Other effects of World War II on R's parents

Note: With the omission of categories 1 and 8, the same list of categories applies to effects of World War II on respondents themselves.

Appendix B: Coding for Sociopolitical Variables— First Generation Study

I. PERCEIVED ANTI-SEMITISM

Responses to the following two questions were combined into an additive ordinal index of perceived anti-Semitism:

A. Do you feel there is prejudice against Jews in Quebec?
   Yes, a great deal; Yes, some; Yes, a bit; No, none.

B. Anti-Semitism is a problem in this city.
   Strongly agree; Agree somewhat; Don't know; Disagree somewhat; Strongly disagree.

The average interitem correlation was .47; the alpha reliability coefficient, .64. This index of perceived anti-Semitism ranges from a low of 2 to a high of 9, with a mean of 5.78 and a standard deviation of 1.90. Scores between 2 and 6 were recoded as low, those between 7 and 9, as high.

II. SATISFACTION (ECONOMIC AND POLITICAL)

An ordinal index of satisfaction was formed by combining responses to the following questions.

A. Generally speaking, would you say that in Quebec society at present things are going . . .
   Very well; Rather well; Not well; Poorly.

B. How would you rate the state of Quebec economy? It is . . .
   Very good; Rather good; Poor; Very poor.

C. Generally speaking, how do you judge the present provincial government of Quebec? Are you...
Very satisfied; Rather satisfied; Not too satisfied; Not at all satisfied.

D. How do you feel about Bill 101, the French-language law adopted last summer by the Quebec government? Are you...
Strongly in favor; In favor; Against; Strongly against.

The average interitem correlation of these three variables was .327; the alpha reliability coefficient, .71. The values were recoded into a six-point ordinal index with a mean of 3.8 and a standard deviation of 1.49. High scores indicate high levels of satisfaction. Ranks 1–3 were recoded as low; ranks 4–6, as high.

III. INDEX OF SEGREGATION

Responses to the three questions below were combined to form an ordinal, additive index.

A. Being Jewish affects my choice of a place to live.
Strongly disagree; Disagree somewhat; Don't know; Agree somewhat; Agree strongly.

B. Among my friends...
None are Jewish; Few are Jewish; Some are Jewish; Most are Jewish; All are Jewish.

C. Among people in my neighborhood...
None are Jewish; Few are Jewish; Some are Jewish; Most are Jewish; All are Jewish.

The interitem correlation of the three variables was .18; the alpha reliability coefficient, .40. The index ranged in value from a low score of 3 to a high of 15, with high scores indicating high segregation. The mean was 11.09, and the standard deviation was 2.43. Values of 3–9 were recoded as low, 10–12 as medium, and 13–15 as high.

While the correlation and reliability coefficients are relatively low, these three variables did factor out together on a common factor with loadings of .43, 36, and .71, respectively, in a varimax rotated factor analysis performed on the data.

IV. PROBABILITY OF EMIGRATION FROM QUEBEC

Responses to the following questions were combined to form an ordinal index:

1. (Rate) the chances of your moving out of Quebec in the next five years (if referendum strongly supports Quebec independence from Canada). Are you...
Definitely leaving; Proably leaving; Proably not leaving; Definitely not leaving.

2. (Rate) the chances of your moving out of Quebec in the next five years (if a referendum strongly rejects Quebec independence from Canada).

Ratings were on the same four-point scale. Responses were combined to form an ordinal index of the propensity to emigrate. The correlation of the two variables was .61; the alpha reliability coefficient, .76. The index had a low of 2 and a high of 8, with a mean of 4.60 and a standard deviation of 1.59. The index was recoded with values 2,3 = low; 4,5 = medium; and 6–8 = high.

V. RELIGIOSITY

An ordinal, additive index of religiosity was computed from responses to the following:

1. Apart from weddings or bar mitzvahs, how often do you attend synagogue religious services?
   Never; Primarily on the High Holidays; Primarily on the major holidays; On major holidays and some Sabbaths; All Sabbaths and holidays; Daily.
2. It is all right for Jews to marry non-Jews.
   Strongly agree; Agree somewhat; Don't know; Disagree somewhat; Strongly disagree.
3. How well do you read Hebrew?
   Very well; Fairly well; With some difficulty; With great difficulty; Not at all.
4. How many of the following rituals do you observe?
   Take part in a Passover seder; Keep kosher at home; Light Sabbath candles; Fast on Yom Kippur; Refrain from eating bread on Passover; Light Chanukah candles.

The interitem correlation was .42; the alpha reliability coefficient, .74. The index of religiosity ranged from a low of 4 to a high of 22, with a mean of 14.2 and a standard deviation of 4.4. The index was recoded with values of 4–11 = low, 12–16 = medium, and 17–22 = high.

Appendix C: Questions Used to Assess Knowledge of World War II

HISTORY

Here are the names of some events, terms, or people associated with World War II. Though people nowadays may have forgotten some of these, I'd like you to tell me what you know about them.

Kristallnacht; Panzer; Wehrmacht; Luftwaffe; Josef Mengele; Munich 1938; Nuremberg 1945–1946; Judenrat; Zyklon B; Kapos; Julius Streicher; Arthur Morse; Eva Braun; Hannah Senesh; Mordecai Anielewicz; Ezra Pound; Dresden; Rommel; Heinrich Himmler.

CAMP ID

I will read you a list of places in Central and Eastern Europe. Please identify which of these had concentration camps:
Bremen; Buchenwald; Lodz; Treblinka; Breslau; Cologne; Dachau; Babi Yar; Theresienstadt; Maathausen.

References

Abella, I., & Troper, H. (1983). *None is too many*. Toronto: Lester, Orpen, & Dennys.

Acock, A. C., & Bengston, V. L. (1978). On the relative influence of mothers and fathers: A covariance analysis of political and religious socialization. *Journal of Marriage and the Family, 40*, 513–530.

Adachi, K. (1976). *The enemy that never was*. Toronto: McLelland & Stewart.

Aleksandrowicz, D. R. (1973). Children of concentration camp survivors. In E. J. Anthony & C. Koupernik (Eds.), *The child in his family: Vol. 2. The impact of disease and death* (pp. 385–392). New York: Wiley.

Antonovsky, A., Maoz, B., Dowty, N., & Wijsenbeek, H. (1971). Twenty-five years later: A limited study of the sequelae of the concentration camp. *Social Psychiatry, 6*, 186–193.

Archibald, H. C., & Tuddenham, R. D. (1965). Persistent stress reaction after combat. *Archives of General Psychiatry, 12*, 475–481.

Askevold, F. (1980). The war sailor syndrome. *Danish Medical Bulletin, 27*, 220–223.

Axelrod, S., Schnipper, O. L., & Rau, J. H. (1980). Hospitalized offspring of Holocaust survivors. *Bulletin of the Menninger Clinic, 44*, 1–14.

Barocas, H. A., & Barocas, C. B. (1973). Manifestations of concentration camp effects on the second generation. *American Journal of Psychiatry, 130*, 820–821.

———. (1979). Wounds of the fathers: The next generation of Holocaust victims. *International Review of Psychoanalysis, 4*, 331–343.

Bauer, Y. (1976). *From diplomacy to resistence: A history of Jewish Palestine 1939–1945*. Philadelphia: Jewish Publication Society.

Beck, P. A. (1977). The role of agents in political socialization. In S. A. Renshon (Ed.), *The handbook of political socialization* (pp. 115–141). New York: The Free Press.

Becker, W. C. (1964). Consequences of different kinds of parental discipline. In M. L. Hoffman & L. W. Hoffman (Eds.), *Review of child development research: Vol. 1* (pp. 169–208). New York: Russell Sage Foundation.

Beebe, G. H. (1975). Follow-up studies of World War II and Korean War prisoners. II. Morbidity, disability and maladjustments. *American Journal of Epidemiology, 101,* 400–422.

Bengston, V. L. (1975). Generation and family effects in value socialization. *American Sociological Review, 40,* 358–371.

Bercuson, D., & Wertheimer, D. (1985). *A trust betrayed: The Keegstra affair.* Toronto: Doubleday.

Bergmann, M. S., & Jucovy, M. E. (Eds.). (1982). *Generations of the Holocaust.* New York: Basic Books.

Bergmann, M. V. (1982). Recurent problems in the treatment of survivors and their children. In M. S. Bergmann & M. E. Jucovy (Eds.), *Generations of the Holocaust* (pp. 248–286). New York: Basic Books.

Blau, P. M., & Duncan, O. D. (1967). *The American occupational structure.* New York: John Wiley & Sons.

Blishen, B. (1967). A socioeconomic index for occupations in Canada. *Canadian Review of Sociology and Anthropology, 4,* 41–53.

Blishen, B. R., & McRoberts, H. A. (1976). A revised socio-economic index for occupations in Canada. *Canadian Review of Sociology and Anthropology, 13,* 71–79.

Bonacich, E. (1973). A theory of middlemen minorities. *American Sociological Review, 38,* 583–594.

Bowen, H. R. (1977). *Investment in learning: The individual and social value of American higher education.* San Francisco: Jossey-Bass.

Breton, R. (1964). Institutional completeness of ethnic communities and the personal relations of immigrants. *American Journal of Sociology, 70,* 193–205.

Chodoff, P. (1963). Late effects of the concentration camp syndrome. *Archives of General Psychiatry, 8,* 323–333.

Cohen, S. M. (1983). *American modernity and Jewish identity.* New York: Tavistock.

Cohen, Y. A. (1961). *Social structure and personality.* New York: Holt, Rinehart & Winston.

Connell, R. W. (1972). Political socialization in the American family: The evidence re-examined. *Public Opinion Quarterly, 36,* 323–333.

Cork, B. (1969). *The forgotten children.* Toronto: Alcohol Research Foundation Books.

Coser, L. (1956). *The functions of social conflict.* New York: The Free Press.

Danieli, Y. (1980a). Countertransference in the treatment and the study of Nazi Holocaust survivors and their children. *Victimology, 5,* 355–387.

————. (1980b). *Matching intervention to different adaptational styles of families of survivors.* Paper presented at the meeting of the American Psychological Association, Montreal, August.

————. (1981). Differing adaptational styles in families of survivors of the Nazi holocaust: Some implications for treatment. *Children Today, 10,* 6–10.

————. (1982). Families of survivors of the Nazi Holocaust: Some short- and long-term effects. In C. D. Spielberger, I. G. Sarason, & N. A. Milgram (Eds.),

Stress and anxiety: Vol. 8 (pp. 405–421). New York: McGraw-Hill/Hemisphere.

———. (1984). Psychotherapists' participation in the conspiracy of silence about the Holocaust. *Psychoanalytic Psychology, 1,* 23–42.

Davidson, S. (1980). The clinical effects of massive psychic trauma in families of Holocaust survivors. *Journal of Marital and Family Therapy, 6,* 11–21.

Dawidowicz, L. (1976). *The war against the Jews, 1933–1945.* New York: Baytown.

De Graaf, T. (1975). Pathological patterns of identifiction in families of survivors of the Holocaust. *Israel Annals of Psychiatry and Allied Disciplines, 13,* 335–362.

Des Prés, T. (1977). *The survivor: An anatomy of life in the death camps.* New York: Pocket Books.

Dohrenwend, B. P., Shrout, P. E., Egri, G., & Mendelsohn, F. S. (1980). Nonspecific psychological distress and other dimensions of psychopathology. *Archives of General Psychiatry, 37,* 1229–1236.

Eaton, W. W., Sigal, J. J., & Weinfeld, M. (1982). Impairment in Holocaust survivors after 33 years: Data from an unbiased community sample. *American Journal of Psychiatry, 139 (6),* 773–777.

Eitinger, L. (1961). Pathology of the concentration camp syndrome: Preliminary report. *Archives of General Psychiatry, 5,* 371–379.

———. (1964). *Concentration camp survivors in Norway and Israel.* London: Allen & Unwin.

———. (1980). The concentration camp syndrome and its late sequelae. In J. E. Dimsdale (Ed.), *Survivors, victims and perpetrators.* New York: Hemisphere.

Eitinger, L., & Krell, R. (1985). *The psychological and medical effects of concentration camps and related persecutions on survivors of the Holocaust.* Vancouver: University of British Columbia Press.

Eitinger, L., & Strøm, A. (1973). *Mortality and morbidity after excessive stress: A follow-up investigation of Norwegian concentration camp survivors.* New York: Humanities Press.

———. (1981). New investigations on the mortality and morbidity of Norwegian ex-concentration camp prisoners. *Israel Journal of Psychiatry and Related Sciences, 18,* 173–196.

Engelsmann, F., Murphy, H. B. M., Prince, R., Leduc, M., & Demers, H. (1972). Variations in responses to a symptom check list by age, sex, income, residence, and ethnicity. *Social Psychiatry, 7,* 150–156.

Epstein, H. (1979). *Children of the Holocaust: Conversations with sons and daughters of survivors.* New York: Putnam.

Feingold, H. L. (1970). *The politics of recue.* New York: Holocaust Library.

Figley, C. R. (Ed.) (1985). *Trauma and its wake: The study and treatment of postraumatic stress disorders.* New York: Brunner/Mazel.

Fisher, R. A. (1954). *Statistical methods for research workers* (12th ed.). New York: Hafner.

Fleiss, J. L., Gurland, B. J., & Cooper, J. E. (1971). Some contributions to measurement of psychopathology. *British Journal of Psychiatry, 119,* 647–656.

Flor, H., & Turk, D. C. (1985). Chronic illness in an adult family member: Pain as a prototype. In D. C. Turk & R. D. Kerns (Eds.), *Health, illness, and families: A life-span perspective.* New York: Wiley.

Fogelman, E., & Savran, B. (1979). Therapeutic groups for children of survivors. *International Journal of Group Psychotherapy, 29,* 211–235.

Fogelman, E., & Savaran, B. (1980). Brief group therapy with offspring of Holocaust survivors: Leaders' reactions. *American Journal of Orthopsychiatry, 50,* 96–107.

Freyberg, J. T. (1980). Difficulties in separation-individuation as experienced by offspring of Nazi holocaust survivors. *American Journal of Orthopsychiatry, 50,* 87–95.

Frommer, E. A., & O'Shea, G. (1973). The importance of childhood experience in relation to problems of marriage and family-building. *British Journal of Psychiatry, 123,* 157–160.

Fuchs, L. (1958). Sources of Jewish individualism and liberalism. In M. Sklare (Ed.), *The Jews.* New York: The Free Press.

Gampel, Y. (1982). A daughter of silence. In M. S. Bergmann and M. E. Jucovy (Eds.), *Generations of the Holocaust* (pp. 120–136). New York: Basic Books.

Gay, M., & Shulman, S. (1978). Comparison of children of Holocaust survivors with children of the general population in Israel. *Mental Health and Society, 5,* 252–256.

Gilbert, M. (1987). *The Holocaust.* London: Collins/Fontana.

Glazer, N. (1958). The American Jew and the attainment of middle class rank: Some trends and explanations. In M. Sklare (Eds.), *The Jews.* New York: The Free Press.

Glickman, Y., & Bardikoff, A. (1982). *The treatment of the Holocaust in Canadian history and social science textbooks.* Toronto: League for Human Rights of B'nai Brith.

Goldstein, S. (1974). American Jewry, 1970: A demographic profile. In M. Sklare (Ed.), *The Jew in American society* (pp. 93–162) New York: Behsman House.

Grauer, H., Mueller, D., & Zelnicker, R. (1984). A fifteen-year psychogeriatric patient follow-up study. *Canadian Journal of Psychiatry, 29,* 412–416.

Greeley, A. M., & Rossi, P. (1966). *The education of Catholic Americans.* Chicago: Aldine.

Gurland, B. J., Yorkstone, M. J., Stone, A. R., Frank, J. D., & Fleiss, J. L. (1972). The structured and scaled interview to assess maladjustment (SSIAM): I. Description, rationale and development. *Archives of General Psychiatry, 27,* 259–263.

Heller, D. (1982). Themes of culture and ancestry among children of concentration camp survivors. *Psychiatry, 45,* 247–261.

Helweg-Larsen, P., Hoffmeyer, H., Kieler, J., Thaysen, E. H., Thaysen, J. H., Thygesen, P., & Wulff, M. H. (1952). Famine and disease in German concentration camps. Complications and sequels. *Acta Psychiatrica et Neurological Scandinavica, 34* (Suppl. 83).

Hermann, K., & Thygesen, P. (1954). KZ-syndromet. *Ugeskr-Laeger, 116,* 825–836. Cited in P. Thygesen (1980), The concentration camp syndrome. *Danish Medical Bulletin, 27,* 224–228.

Hertzberg, A. (1979). *Being Jewish in America.* New York: Schocken.

Herzog, J. (1982). World beyond metaphor: Thoughts on the transmission of trauma. In M. S. Bergmann & M. E. Jucovy (Eds.), *Generations of the Holocaust* (pp. 103–109). New York: Basic Books.

Himmelfarb, H. S., Loar, M. D., & Mott, S. H. (1983). Sampling by ethnic surnames: The case of American Jews. *Public Opinion Quarterly, 47,* 247–260.

Hoppe, K. N. (1971). The aftermath of the Nazi persecution reflected in recent psychiatric literature. In H. Krystal & W. G. Niederland (Eds.), *Psychic traumatization: Aftereffects on individuals and communities* (pp. 169–204). Boston: Little, Brown.

Hunter, E. J. (1986). Families of prisoners of war held in Vietnam: A seven-year study. *Evaluation and Program Planning, 9,* 243–251.

Hyman, H. H. (1959). *Political socialization.* Glencoe, Il.: The Free Press.

Hyman, H. H., Wright, C. R., & Reed, J. S. (1975). *The enduring effects of education.* Chicago: University of Chicago Press.

Jackman, M. R., & Muha, M. J. (1984). Education and inter-group attitudes: Moral enlightenment, superficial democratic commitment or ideological refinement? *American Sociological Review, 49,* 751–769.

Jencks, C., Smith, M., Acland, H., Bane, M. J., Cohen, D., Gintis, H., Heyns, B., & Nickelson, S. (1972). *Inequality: A reassessment of the effect of family and schooling in America.* New York: Basic Books.

Jennings, M. K., & Nienmi, R. G. (1968). The transmission of political values from parent to child. *American Political Science Review, 42,* 169–184.

Kage, J. (1962). *With faith and thanksgiving.* Montreal: Eagle Publishing.

Kantrowitz, N. (1973). *Ethnic and racial segregation in the New York metropolis.* New York: Praeger.

Karr, S. D. (1973). *Second-generation effects of the Nazi Holocaust.* Unpublished doctoral dissertation, California School of Professional Psychology, San Francisco.

Kav-Venaki, S., Nadler, A., & Gershoni, H. (1985). Sharing the Holocaust experience: Communication behaviors and their consequences in families of ex-partisans and ex-prisoners of concentration camps. *Family Process, 24,* 273–280.

Keehn, R. J. (1980). Follow-up studies of World War II and Korean conflict prisoners. III. Mortality to January 1, 1976. *American Journal of Epidemiology, 111,* 194–202.

Kessel, S. (1972). *Hanged at Auschwitz.* (Melville Wallace and Delight Wallace, Trans.). New York: Stein & Day. Cited in Terrence Des Prés, *The Survivor.* New York: Pocket Books, 1977.

Kestenberg, J. (1972). Psychoanalytic contributions to the problem of survivors from Nazi persecution. *Israel Annals of Psychiatry and Related Disciplines, 10,* 311–325.

———. (1982). Survivors' parents and their children. In M. S. Bergmann and M. E. Jucovy (Eds.), *Generations of the Holocaust* (pp. 83–102). New York: Basic Books.

Khan, K. (1981). *Psychosocial sequelae to prolonged psychological stress and trauma.* Paper presented to the International Congress of Psychosomatic Medicine, Montreal, September.

Klein, H. (1971). Families of Holocaust survivors in the Kibbutz: Psychological studies. In H. Krystal & W. G. Niederland (Eds.), *Psychic traumatization: Aftereffects in individuals and communities* (pp. 69–72). Boston: Little, Brown.

———. (1973). Children of the Holocaust: Mourning and bereavement. In E. S.

Anthony & C. Koupernik (Eds.), *The child in his family: Vol. 2. The impact of disease and death* (pp. 393–410). New York: Wiley.

Klein, H., & Last, U. (1974). Cognitive and emotional aspects of the attitudes of American and Israeli Jewish youth towards the victims of the Holocaust. *Israel Annals of Psychiatry and Related Disciplines, 12,* 111–131.

Klein, H., Zellermayer, J., & Shanan, J. (1963). Former concentration camp inmates on a psychiatric ward. *Archives of General Psychiatry, 8,* 334.

Kleinplatz, M. M. (1980). *The effects of cultural and individual supports on personality variables among children of Holocaust survivors in Israel.* Unpublished doctoral dissertation, University of Windsor (Canada).

Kohn, M. L. (1969). *Class and conformity.* Homewood, Il: Dorsey.

Kral, V. A., Pazder, L. H., & Wigdor, B. T. (1967). Long-term effects of a prolonged stress experience. *Canadian Psychiatric Association Journal, 12,* 175–181.

Krystal, H. (1971). Trauma: Considerations of its intensity and chronicity. In H. Krystal & W. Niederland (Eds.), *Psychic traumatization: Aftereffects in individuals and communities* (pp. 11–28). Boston: Little, Brown.

Krystal, H., & Niederland, W. G. (1968). Clinical observations on the survivor syndrome. In H. Krystal (Ed.), *Massive psychic trauma* (pp. 327–348). New York: International Universities Press.

Langner, T. S. (1962). A twenty-two item screening score of psychiatric symptoms indicating impairment. *Journal of Health and Human Behavior, 3,* 269–276.

Langner, T. S., & Michael, S. T. (1963). *Life stress and mental health.* New York: Macmillan.

Last, V., & Klein, H. (1981). Impact de l'holocauste: Transmission aux enfants du vécu des parents [Impact of the Holocaust: Transmission of parents' experience to the children]. *Evolution Psychiatrique, 41,* 375–388.

Lazarus, R. S. (1976). *Patterns of adjustment* (3rd ed.). New York: McGraw-Hill.

Leon, G., Butcher, J. M., Kleinman, M., Goldberg, A., & Almagor, M. (1981). Survivors of the Holocaust and their children. *Journal of Personality and Social Psychology, 41,* 303–316.

Levav, I., & Abramson, J. H. (1984). Emotional distress among concentration camp survivors—a community study in Jerusalem. *Psychological Medicine, 14,* 215–218.

Levine, H. B. (1982). Toward a psychoanalytic understanding of children of survivors of the Holocaust. *Psychoanalytic Quarterly, 51,* 70–92.

Levine, R. A., & Campbell, D. T. (1972). *Ethnocentrism: Theories of conflict, ethnic attitudes and group behavior.* New York: Wiley.

Levy, D. (1943). *Maternal overprotection.* New York: Columbia University Press.

Li, P. (1980). Income, achievement and adaptive capacity: An empirical comparison of Chinese and Japanese in Canada. In V. K. Ujimoto & G. Hirabayashi (Eds.), *Visible minorities and multiculturalism: Asians in Canada* (pp. 363–378). Toronto: Butterworth.

Light, I. (1972). *Ethnic enterprise in America.* Berkeley: University of California Press.

Light, R. L. (1971). Measures of response agreement for qualitative data: Some generalizations and alternatives. *Psychological Bulletin, 76,* 365–377.

Loevinger, J., & Wessler, R. (1970). *Measuring ego development: Vol. 1. Construction and use of the sentence completion test.* San Francisco: Jossey-Bass.

McClosky, H. H., & Brill, A. (1983). *Dimensions of tolerance.* New York: Russell Sage.

McCubbin, H., & Dahl, B. (1976). Prolonged separation in the military: A longitudinal study. In H. McCubbin, B. Dahl, E. J. Hunter (Eds.), *Families in the military system* (pp. 112–145). Beverly Hills, CA: Sage.

Mahler, M., Pine, F., & Bergman, A. (1975). *The psychological birth of the human infant. Symbiosis and individuation.* New York: Basic Books.

Matussek, P. (1975). *Internment in concentration camps and its consequences.* Heidelberg: Springer-Verlag.

Meile, R. L. (1972). The twenty-two item index of psychiatric disorder: Psychological or organic symptoms? *Social Science and Medicine, 6,* 643–648.

Minuchin, S. (1974). *Families and family therapy.* Cambridge, MA: Harvard University Press.

Mosteller, F. M., & Bush, R. R. (1954). Selected quantitative techniques. In G. Lindsay (Ed.), *Handbook of social psychology: Vol. 1. Theory and method.* Reading, MA: Addison-Wesley.

Muller, D. J. (1971). Discussion of Shader, R. I., Ebert, M. H., Harmatz, J. S. Langner's psychiatric impairment scale: A short screening device. *Journal of Psychiatry, 128,* 601.

Nadler, A., Kav Venaki, S., & Gleitman, B. (1985). Transgenerational effects of the Holocaust: Externalization of aggression in second-generation Holocaust survivors. *Journal of Consulting and Clinical Psychology, 53,* 365–369.

Nathan, T. S., Eitinger, L., & Winnik, H. Z. (1964). A psychiatric study of survivors of the Nazi Holocaust. *Israel Annals of Psychiatry, 2,* 47–80.

Nefzger, M. D. (1970). Follow-up studies of World War II and Korean war prisoners. I. Study plan and mortality findings. *American Journal of Epidemiology, 91,* 123–138.

Neugebauer, R., Dohrenwend, B. P., & Dohrenwend, B. S. (1980). Formulation of hypotheses about the true prevalence of functional psychiatric disorders among adults in the United States. In B. P. Dohrenwend, B. S. Dohrenwend, M. S. Gould, B. Link, R. Neugebauer, & R. Wunsch-Hitzig (Eds.) *Mental illness in the United States: Epidemiological estimates* (pp. 45–94). New York: Praeger.

Nezu, A. M., & Carnevale, G. J. (1987). Interpersonal problem solving and coping reactions of Vietnam veterans with post-traumatic stress disorder. *Journal of Abnormal Psychology, 96,* 155–157.

Nice, D. S. (1978). *Children of returned prisoners of war: Are there really second generational effects?* (Naval Health Technical Report 78-17). Washington, DC: Department of the Navy.

Niederland, W. G. (1968). The problem of the survivor. In H. Krystal (Ed.), *Massive psychic trauma* (pp. 8–22). New York: International Universities Press.

Niemi, R., Ross, R. D., & Alexander, J. (1978). The similarity of political values of parents and college-age youths. *Public Opinion Quarterly, 42,* 503–520.

Nixon, J., and Pearn, J. (1977). Emotional sequelae of parents and sibs following the drowning or near-drowning of a child. *Australian and New Zealand Journal of Psychiatry, 11,* 165–168.

NORC (National Opinion Research Cernter). (1982). *General social survey, 1972–*

82: Cumulative codebook. J. A. Davis (Principal investigator). Chicago: NORC.

Nunn, C. Z., Crockett, H. J. J., & Williams, J. A. (1978). *Tolerance for nonconformity.* San Francisco: Jossey-Bass.

Ofman, J. (1981). Separation-individuation in children of Nazi Holocaust survivors and its relationship to perceived parental overvaluation (Doctoral dissertation, California School of Professional Psychology). *Dissertation Abstracts International, 42/08-B* (1982), 3434.

Oliner, M. M. (1982). Recurrent problems in the treatment of survivors and their children. In M. S. Bergmann & M. E. Jucovy (Eds.), *Generations of the Holocaust* (pp. 270–286). New York: Basic Books.

Ornstein, A. (1985). Knowing and not knowing the Holocaust. *Psychoanalytic Inquiry, 5,* 99–130.

————. (1986). The Holocaust: Reconstruction and establishment of psychic continuity. In A. Rothstein (Ed.), *The reconstruction of trauma: Its significance in clinical work* (pp. 171–190). (Workshop series of the American Psychoanalytic Association, Monograph II). Washington, DC: American Psychoanalytic Association.

Peterson, D. R. (1961). Behavior problems of middle childhood. *Journal of Consulting Psychology, 25,* 205–209.

Peterson, D. R., & Quay, H. C. (1967). *Behavior problem checklist.* Champaign: Children's Research Center, University of Illinois.

Pilcz, M. (1975). Understanding the survivor family: An acknowledgement of the positive dimensions of the Holocaust legacy. In L. Y. Steinitz & D. M. Szonyi (Eds.), *Living after the Holocaust: Reflections by children of survivors in America* (rev. 2nd ed., pp. 157–167). New York: Bloch.

Piper, W. E., Debbanne, E. G., Bienvenu, J. P., & Garant, J. (1984). A comparative study of four forms of psychotherapy. *Journal of Consulting and Clinical Psychology, 52,* 268–279.

Podietz, L., Zwerling, I., Ficher, I., Belmont, H., Eisenstein, I., Shapiro, M., & Levick, M. (1984). Engagement in families of Holocaust survivors. *Journal of Marital and Family Therapy, 10,* 43–51.

Poppel, S. M. (1977). *Zionism in Germany, 1897–1933: The shaping of a Jewish identity.* Philadelphia: Jewish Publication Society of America.

Porter, J., Porter, M., & Blishen, B. R. (1982). *Stations and callings: Making it through the school system.* Toronto: Methuen.

Quarantelli, E. L. (1985). An assesment of conflicting views of mental health: The consequences of traumatic events. In C. R. Figley (Ed.), *Trauma and its wake* (pp. 173–218). New York: Brunner/Mazel.

Quinton, D., Rutter, M., & Liddle, C. (1984). Institutional rearing, parental difficulties and marital support. *Psychological Medicine, 14,* 107–124.

Rabinowitz, D. (1976). *New Lives.* New York: Knopf.

Rakoff, V. (1966). A long-term effect of the concentration camp experience. *Viewpoints, 1,* 17–22.

Rakoff, V., Sigal, J. J., & Epstein, N. B. (1966). Children and families of concentration camp survivors. *Canada's Mental Health, 14,* 24–26.

Rich, M. S. (1982). *Children of Holocaust survivors: A concurrent validity study of a survivor typology*. Doctoral dissertation, California School of Professional Psychology, Berkeley.

Richmond. A. (1967). *Post-war immigrants in Canada*. Toronto: University of Toronto Press.

————. (1972). *Ethnic residential segregation in Toronto*. Toronto: Institute for Behavioral Research, York University.

Rosen, B. (1959). Race, ethnicity, and the achievement syndrome. *American Sociological Review, 24,* 47–60.

Rosenheck, R., & Nathan, P. (1985). Secondary traumatization in children of Vietnam veterans. *Hospital and Community Psychiatry, 36,* 538–539.

Rosenthal, R., & Rubin, D. B. (1979). Comparing significance levels of independent studies. *Psychological Bulletin, 86,* 1165–1168.

Russell, A. (1980). Late effects—influence on children of concentration camp survivors. In J. E. Dimsdale (Ed.), *Survivors, victims, and perpetrators* (pp. 175–204). New York: Hemisphere.

Russell, A., Plotkin, D., & Heapy, N. (1985). Adaptive abilities in nonclinical second-generation Holocaust survivors and controls: A comparison. *American Journal of Psychotherapy, 39,* 564–579.

Rutter, M., & Madge, N. (1976). *Cycles of disadvantage*. London: Heinemann.

Rutter, M. L., Quinton, E., & Yule, B. A. (1976). *Family pathology and disorder in children*. New York: Wiley.

Seiler, L. H. (1973). The 22-item scale used in field studies of mental illness: A question of method, a question of substance, and a question of theory. *Journal of Health and Social Behavior, 14,* 252–264.

Selvin, H. C., & Hagstrom, W. O. (1960). Determinants of support for civil liberties. *British Journal of Sociology, 11,* 51–73.

Shader, R. I., Ebert, M. H., & Harmatz, J. S. (1971). Langner's psychiatric impairment scale: A short screening device. *American Journal of Psychiatry, 128,* 596–601.

Sherif, M., & Sherif, C. W. (1953). *Groups in harmony and tension: An integration of studies of intergroup relations*. New York: Harper & Bros.

Shuval, J. T. (1957). Some persistent effects of trauma: Five years after the Nazi concentration camps. *Social Problems, 5,* 230–243.

Sigal, J. J. (1971). Second-generation effects of massive psychic trauma. In H. Krystal and W. G. Niederland (Eds.), *Psychic traumatization: Aftereffects in individuals and communities* (pp. 55–66). Boston: Little, Brown.

————. (1972). *Familial consequences of parental preoccupation*. Paper presented at the meeting of the American Psychiatric Asociation, Dallas, May.

————. (1973). Hypotheses and methodology in the study of families of Holocaust survivors. In E. J. Anthony and C. Koupernik (Eds.), *The child in his family: Vol. 2. The impact of disease and death* (pp. 411–415). New York: Wiley.

————. (1976). Effects of parental exposure to prolonged stress on the mental health of the spouse and children. *Canadian Psychiatric Association Journal, 21,* 169–172.

————. (1982). Enduring disturbances in children following acute illness in early childhood. In E. J. Anthony & C. Koupernik (Eds.), *The child in his family: Vol. 3. Children at psychiatric risk* (pp. 55–65). New York: Wiley.

————. (1986). The nature of evidence for intergenerational effects of the Holocaust. *Simon Weisenthal Center Annual*, vol. 3. White Plains, N.Y.: Kraus International Publications.

Sigal, J. J., Chagoya, L., Villeneuve, C., & Mayerovitch, J. (1971). Later psychological consequences of near-fatal illness (nephrosis) in early childhood: Some preliminary findings. *Laval Medical, 42,* 103–108.

Sigal, J. J., DiNicola, V., & Buonvino, M. (1988). Grandchildren of survivors: Can negative effects of prolonged stress be observed two generations later? *Canadian Journal of Psychiatry, 33,* 207–212.

Sigal, J. J., Meislova, J., Beltempo, J., & Silver, D. (1988). Some determinants of individual differences in the behaviour of children of parentally deprived parents. *Canadian Journal of Psychiatry, 33,* 51–56.

Sigal, J. J., & Rakoff, V. (1971). Concentration camp survival: A pilot study of the effects on the second generation. *Canadian Psychiatric Association Journal, 16,* 393–397.

Sigal, J. J., Silver, D., Rakoff, V., & Ellin, B. (1973). Some second generation effects of survival of the Nazi persecution. *American Journal of Orthopsychiatry, 43,* 320–327.

Sigal, J. J., & Weinfeld, M. (1985a). Stability of coping style 33 years after prolonged exposure to extreme stress. *Acta Psychiatrica Scandinavica, 71,* 554–566.

Sigal, J. J., & Weinfeld, M. (1985b). Control of aggression in adult children of survivors of the Nazi persecution. *Journal of Abnormal Psychology, 94,* 556–564.

Sigal, J. J., & Weinfeld, M. (1977). Mutual involvement and alienation in families of Holocaust survivors. *Psychiatry, 50,* 280–288.

Simmel, G. (1955). *Conflict.* Glencoe, IL: The Free Press.

Sklare, M. (Ed.). (1958). *The Jews.* New York: The Free Press.

————. (1971). *America's Jews.* New York: Random House.

Slater, M. K. (1969). My son the doctor: Aspects of mobility among American Jews. *American Sociological Review, 34,* 359–373.

Solkoff, N. (1981). Children of survivors of the Nazi Holocaust: A critical review of the literature. *American Journal of Orthopsychiatry, 51,* 29–42.

Solomon, Z., Kother, M., & Mikulincer, M. (1988). Combat-related post-traumatic stress disorders among second generation Holocaust survivors: Preliminary findings. *American Journal of Psychiatry, 145,* 865–868.

Statistics Canada. (1983a). *Demographic characteristics for the metropolitan area of Montreal* (Catalogue 95–918). Ottawa: Queen's Printer.

————. (1983b). *Causes of death* (Catalogue 84–203). Ottawa: Queens Printer.

Stouffer, S. (1955). *Communism, conformity, and civil liberties.* New York: Doubleday.

Stretch, R. H. (1985). Posttraumatic stress disorder among U.S. army reserve Vietnam and Vietnam-era veterans. *Journal of Consulting and Clinical Psychology, 53,* 935–936.

Sullivan, J. L., Pierson, J. E., & Marcus, G. E. (1979). An alternative conceptualization of political tolerance: Illusory increases 1950s–1970s. *American Political Science Review, 73,* 781–794.

Thomas, C. W., & Hyman, J. M. (1977). Perceptions of crime, fear of victimization, and public perceptions of police performance. *Journal of Police Science and Administration, 5,* 305–317.

Thomas, L. E. (1971). Political attitude congruence between politically active parents and college-aged children. *Journal of Marriage and the Family, 33,* 375–386.

——. (1974). Generational discontinuity in beliefs: An exploration of the generation gap. *Journal of Social Issues, 30,* 1–22.

Thygesen, P. (1980). The concentration camp syndrome. *Danish Medical Bulletin, 27,* 224–228.

Torczyner, J. (1976). *Census tabulations of the Jewish population of Montreal, 1971.* Montreal: McGill School of Social Work. (Mimeo).

Trossman, B. (1968). Adolescent children of concentration camp survivors. *Canadian Psychiatric Association Journal, 13,* 121–123.

Waelder, R. (1936). The principle of multiple function: Observations on overdetermination. *Psychoanalytic Quarterly, 5,* 45–62.

Wallis, W. A. (1942). Confounding probabilities from independent significance tests. *Econometrica, 10,* 229–248.

Weinfeld, M. (1977). La question Juive au Québec. *Midstream, 23,* 20–29.

Weinfeld, M., & Sigal, J. J. (1986a). Knowledge of the Holocaust among adult children of survivors. *Canadian Ethnic Studies, 18,* 66–78.

Weinfeld, M., & Sigal, J. J. (1986b). Effects of the Holocaust on selected sociopolitical attitudes of adult children of survivors and controls. *Canadian Review of Sociology and Anthropology, 3,* 365–382.

Weinfeld, M., & Sigal, J. J. (In press). Educational and occupational achievement of adult children of Holocaust survivors. In *Proceedings of the World Congress of Jewish Studies, 1985.* Jerusalem: Demographic Section, Institute of Contemporary Jewry.

Weinfeld, M., Sigal, J. J., & Eaton, W. W. (1981). Long-term effects of the Holocaust on selected social attitudes and behaviors of survivors: A cautionary note. *Social Forces, 60,* 1–19.

Weiss, E., O'Connell, A. N., & Siiter, R. (1986). Comparison of second-generation Holocaust survivors, immigrants, and non immigrants on measures of mental health. *Journal of Personality and Social Psychology, 50,* 828–831.

Weissman, M. M., Paykel, E., & Klerman, S. L. (1972). The depressed woman as a mother. *Social Psychiatry, 7,* 98–108.

Wijscnbcek, H. (1979). *Is there a hiding syndrome?* Paper presented at the Israel-Netherlands Symposium on the Impact of Persecution, Jerusalem, May.

Winnicott, D. W. (1953). Transitional objects and transitional phenomena. *International Journal of Psychoanalysis, 34,* 89–97.

Wirth, L. (1928). *The ghetto.* Chicago: University of Chicago Press.

Zlotogorski, Z. (1983). Offspring of concentration camp survivors: The relationship of perception of family cohesion and adaptability to levels of ego functioning. *Comprehensive Psychiatry, 24,* 345–354.

Index

About the Authors

JOHN J. SIGAL is presently research director, Department of Psychiatry, Sir Mortimer B. Davis–Jewish General Hospital; professor (part-time), Department of Psychiatry, McGill University, Montreal; and a faculty member and supervisor of child analysis of the Canadian Psychoanalytic Institute (Quebec E. Branch). He received his undergraduate degrees from the University of Alberta, and his Ph.D. in psychology from the Université de Montréal. He then spent a year working in the laboratories of Hans Eysenck at the Maudsley Hospital, London, on a postdoctoral fellowship from the National Research Council of Canada. This was followed by three years at the Hampstead Child Therapy Clinic in London, where he worked with Anna Freud and Dorothy Burlingham. During the four years in London he also completed his training as a psychoanalyst with the British Psycho-Analytical Institute. Since his return to Montreal in 1960, he has been involved in various teaching, research, and administrative roles in the Departments of Psychiatry of the Jewish General Hospital and at McGill University, in the areas of individual and family therapy. His research interests have centered on the empirical evaluation of his and others' clinical observations and hypotheses, primarily in the area of the familial consequences of parental preoccupation. These interests have led to publications that bridge the fields of psychiatry, psychology, pediatrics, epidemiology, and sociology. With Vivian Rakoff, he pioneered the empirical study of intergenerational effects of the Holocaust.

MORTON WEINFELD is associate professor and chairman of the Department of Sociology, McGill University. He received his undergraduate education at McGill University, and his graduate education at Harvard University, where he received the Ed.M. and the Ph.D. in education and sociology. He then joined the Sociology Department at McGill University.

Professor Weinfeld has specialized in the area of ethnic and race relations, with emphasis on the study of North American Jewry. For almost ten years he has studied survivors of the Holocaust and their families with John Sigal, using two surveys of Montreal Jews as a data base. He also has published on Jewish out-marriage, Jewish educational systems, comparative studies of Jewish identity in Canada and the United States, and Jewish economic behavior.

Professor Weinfeld was senior editor of the *Canadian Jewish Mosaic* (1981), a collection of social scientific essays about the Jewish community of Canada. He coauthored (with Harold Troper) *Old Wounds: Jews, Ukrainians and the Hunt for Nazi War Criminals in Canada,* a case study of ethnicity and public policy in a multicultural society.

In addition, Professor Weinfeld has coedited an introductory textbook for Canadian sociology students, *Introduction to Sociology* (1987); has published policy studies of affirmative action in Canada, and in Quebec in particular; and has written government reports on the social costs of discrimination, and on immigration and Canada's population future.